Achieving Competencies in Public Service

Achieving Competencies in Public Service
The Professional Edge
Second Edition

James S. Bowman
Jonathan P. West
Marcia A. Beck

Routledge
Taylor & Francis Group

LONDON AND NEW YORK

Dedication

For Lyla—*JSB*
For Colleen—*JPW*
For Jackie—*MAB*

First published 2010 by M.E. Sharpe

Published 2015 by Routledge
2 Park Square, Milton Park, Abingdon, Oxon OX14 4RN
711 Third Avenue, New York, NY 10017, USA

Routledge is an imprint of the Taylor & Francis Group, an informa business

Library of Congress Cataloging-in-Publication Data

Bowman, James S., 1945–
  Achieving competencies in public service : the professional edge / by James S. Bowman, Jonathan P. West, and Marcia A. Beck—2nd ed.
      p. cm.
Previous edition cataloged under title.
Rev. ed. of: The professional edge. Armonk, N.Y. : M.E. Sharpe, © 2004.
Includes bibliographical references and index.
ISBN 978-0-7656-2347-8 (cloth : alk. paper) — ISBN 978-0-7656-2348-5 (pbk. : alk. paper)
  1. Public administration. 2. Civil service positions. 3. Public officers. 4. Nonprofit organizations—Employees. 5. Executives. 6. Human services personnel. 7. Service industries workers. 8. Professional employees. 9. Vocational qualifications. I. West, Jonathan P. (Jonathan Page), 1941– II. Beck, Marcia A. III. Professional edge. IV. Title.

JF1351.B63 2009
352.3—dc22   2009006869

ISBN 13: 9780765623485 (pbk)
ISBN 13: 9780765623478 (hbk)

Contents

Preface

The new context and character of public service—shifting values, eroding human capital, aggressive entrepreneurship, exploding information technology, developing performance management, emerging multisector careers, spreading contracting reforms, a diminishing managerial corps, shocking internal economic and external security threats—requires enhanced professional technical, ethical, and leadership competencies. Indeed, each of these competencies is needed in all three arenas of public service: government agencies, nonprofit organizations, and private vendors. Professionalism emphasizes both technical skills (to do "things right") and ethical skills (to do "right things"). Together, they are key to defining leadership. The resulting responsibility—the professional edge—is clear: It is simply unthinkable not to do one's best to improve the quality of democracy.

This book examines components of public service professionalism—excellence in technique, ethics, and leadership for the new century. The possession of only some but not all of these elements is insufficient. For instance, the business, nonprofit, and governmental debacles during the last twenty-five years—the Savings and Loan scandal of the 1980s, the widespread wrongdoing of the Enron Era, the subprime mortgage/credit crisis—reveal that talented professionals sacrificed the independent judgment they claimed to possess. In contrast, authentic professionals integrate the technocratic, ethical, and leadership dimensions of their craft, as was dramatically demonstrated by the emergency teams after the attacks on the World Trade Center and the Pentagon on September 11, 2001. Public service today must be led by consummate professionals steeped in both technical and ethical competencies. The pursuit of quality—made all the more difficult, but more necessary, in turbulent times—requires the robust practice of public service.

Chapter 1, "Public Service Today: Complex, Contradictory, Competitive," briefly reviews the transition from the "old" public service (government-centered functions characterized by lifelong careers and cumbersome bureaucracy) to the "new" public service (multisectored activities featuring short-term jobs and dynamic networklike structures). How postmodern trends create a heightened need for professional proficiencies is then explored.

The next three chapters scrutinize what it means to be a true public servant—that is, someone with subject matter background and moral imagination who is prepared to lead. Chapter 2, "The Technical Professional: Developing Expertise," probes the faculties needed and links these with strategic planning, program management, and resource stewardship in financial, human resource, and information management. Chapter 3, "The Ethical Professional: Cultivating Scruples," investigates values, professional moral development, public vs. private morality, decision-making tools, and organizational integrity. Chapter 4, "The Consummate Professional: Creating Leadership," focuses on assessment and goal setting, the use of "hard" and "soft" skills, personal styles, political skills, evaluation, and how specialized knowledge and ethical bearing are integral to true professionalism. Realistic contemporary scenarios and skill-building exercises appear in each of these chapters.

Chapter 5, "The Future of Public Service: Cases and Commentary for the New Millennium," explores professional challenges to come in the years ahead. Both mundane and dramatic cases illustrate how government, business, and nonprofit officials—as managers of the state—must master professional competencies. Finally, the Epilogue discusses how technical, ethical, and leadership competencies could have been used to avert the three crises discussed in Chapters 4 and 5. This overview of competencies and crises develops the lessons learned and presents overarching conclusions on the crucial role of public service in contemporary society.

This revised and expanded edition contains approximately 50 percent more material than the first edition. Among the many new features are:

- A magnified analysis of professional competencies and competency modeling
- An updated look at the commonalities among the Savings and Loan fiasco, the Enron Era, and current financial crises
- An augmented assessment of the significance of public service and the role of government in American life
- A discussion of issues such as strategic planning, sustainability, broadbanding, benchmarking, mentoring, and E-Government
- The similarities and differences between public and private ethics
- The charting of ethical skills, knowledge, abilities, and performance standards
- An articulation of challenges to corruption
- An exploration of skills and traits in the "leadership cycle"
- The cultivation of negotiation leadership competencies
- An expanded examination of cybersecurity and cyberwarfare issues
- A searing analysis of the war on terror and the use of torture

Table P.1

Matrix of Coverage

Matrix of Coverage	1. Public Service Today	2. Technical Professional	3. Ethical Professional	4. Consummate Professional	5. Future of Public Service
Old public service	X				
New public service	X			X	
Competencies	X	X	X	X	X
Technical skills	X	X			X
Governance	X				X
Organizational theory/ dynamics	X	X	X		X
Resource management	X	X			X
Program/project management	X	X			
Program evaluation	X	X		X	
Human resource management		X			
Performance management	X				
IT skills and e-government	X	X			
Administrative law and values		X	X	X	X
Government regulation/ deregulation	X				X
Mentoring		X			
Politics and professionalism	X	X	X		X
Networking/outsourcing	X				X
Public-private partnerships	X			X	
"Hard/soft" management skills	X	X		X	
Ethical theories			X		
Moral reasoning	X		X		
Ethical decision making	X		X	X	X
Private versus public morality			X		
Codes of ethics			X	X	
Organizational ethics			X		
Leadership skills/traits	X	X		X	X
Leadership styles				X	
Cybersecurity					X
Political/negotiation skills				X	
Social change/cultural competency	X	X		X	
Strategic planning case		X			
Savings and Loan case				X	X
Enron case			X		X
Subprime Mortgage Loan case					X

The use of this companion volume with introductory textbooks is enhanced by the matrix shown in Table P.1, which links the topics here with those commonly found in texts in the field.

The classic definition—and vow—of a professional is leadership in technical competency and ethical character. "Our lives," Martin Luther King once observed, "begin to end the day that we become silent about things that matter." The ability to contemplate, enhance, and act upon these faculties is the essence of professional life. Those dedicated to excellence, and who use the text to cultivate their capacity for critical judgment—the *sine qua non* of a professional—will get the most out of this book.

Acknowledgments

The authors are pleased to acknowledge Professors Randy Paul Battaglio, N. Joseph Cayer, Jerrell D. Coggburn, Stephen Condrey, Doug Goodman, Carole Jurkiewicz, and Bob Smith, whose thoughtful comments on the first edition were important in the preparation of this work. Adrian Buckland and Martha Medina should also be recognized for their research and technical assistance. Any errors are the responsibility of the authors.

Achieving Competencies in Public Service

Chapter 1

Public Service Today
Complex, Contradictory, Competitive

There is no higher religion than human service.
To work for the common good is the greatest creed.
—Woodrow Wilson

Joshua Bennett was excited to start work as a management analyst in his south-eastern state government office's human resources department immediately upon graduation with a Masters of Public Administration degree. During his six-month probationary period, he was given varied assignments of increasing difficulty. While he had to struggle with some of them, he gained confidence. At the end of the probation period he received a good performance evaluation. Joshua is now ending his first full year of employment. He likes his job, but he is concerned that he lacks the skills to successfully complete the complex assignments he is now receiving as the state adapts to E-Government. At the time of his hiring he was promised job-related training and resources that would equip him with the information technology skills necessary to meet performance expectations. Such hardware, software, and technical training was not provided. Joshua's inability to satisfactorily complete recent assignments has resulted in job stress and frustration.

Maria Rodriguez has worked for twenty years as a clinical psychologist in a nonprofit hospital on the West Coast. She derives substantial satisfaction from her work and feels that she is making a difference in the lives of her patients. Her accomplishments have been recognized with awards, promotions, and certificates of appreciation. Two years ago the chief of staff appointed her to the hospital's ethics committee and last month she was made chair of the committee. The thorny problems brought to this committee, often involving new medical technologies and changing managerial philosophies or fiscal policies, have occupied an increasing amount of Maria's time and attention. She is perplexed by one case in particular. The case involves a conflict between protecting the privacy of patient records and meeting the reimbursement requirements of third-party payers. Maria is concerned that the hospital's administrative and fiscal requirements are compromising patient care, with specific ethical implications for particular patients and legal issues for the hospital. Maria is uncertain how to proceed.

Regina Blackstone is a research specialist in a large corporation located in a midwestern state. She has training as a researcher and over the years has produced several reports that have contributed to her growing reputation as a knowledgeable expert on technical issues. As a staff person she has operated mainly in a support or advisory role, often in relative isolation from others. Recently, her firm bid for and received a government contract to deliver a city service. Regina's boss asked her to lead this effort. She quickly accepted the position, flattered to be tapped for this responsibility. A few weeks later, however, Regina is apprehensive about her ability to spearhead the new initiative. She fears that she may personify the Peter Principle, previously having reached her highest level of competence and now promoted to a level at which she will prove incompetent. Neither her academic training in data analysis nor her corporate research background provided the leadership skills she must master in order to excel in service to the public. She is reluctant to relinquish her new job, but is nervous and unsure about what to do next.

Joshua, Maria, and Regina are all dedicated professionals who face unique performance challenges. These challenges result, in part, from a shift from the old public service to a new public service that requires a different set of professional competencies. Joshua works for state government, Maria performs a public service in the nonprofit arena, and Regina's new assignment with her private contracting firm requires bridge building with the public sector. All three feel poorly prepared for their current assignments: Joshua lacks the technical skills required to complete routine tasks necessitated by recent developments in information technology; Maria needs help resolving dilemmas linked to changes in the legal and ethical environment; and Regina has a skills deficit that may compromise her ability to lead a private-public partnership.

The situations confronting these three individuals illustrate the thesis of this chapter: Increasingly dynamic internal and external environments create the need for professional managers who possess technical, ethical, and leadership competencies to meet the complex governance challenges of the twenty-first century. This chapter explains the importance of the term *competencies,* summarizes the changing context of public service, contrasts the old and new characteristics of its operation, and clarifies its contemporary role. It then analyzes three competencies—technical, ethical, and leadership—that can provide employees with the "professional edge." Here the focus is on why these skills are so important in today's turbulent environment. Subsequent chapters show how these competencies may be achieved.

Competencies and Competency Modeling

The concept of "competencies" has been in use since the 1970s, when D.C. McClelland (1973) developed the idea that particular sets of skills and/or personal qualities would be better indicators of job performance than standard intelligence tests. This idea was first tested in the U.S. State Department. Since then there has been an explosion of interest in the concept, as analysts and employers set out to determine which competencies are applicable to specific positions. Dozens of companies now offer "competency modeling," whereby they work with employers to develop sets of competencies as a guide for hiring and training employees in order to give organizations a competitive edge in performance and productivity.

The term *competency* is used in a variety of ways in the literature. Some understand it to mean specific skills—abilities to perform concrete tasks that result in specific outcomes—that an individual has already learned or can attain. Others add personal traits—individual attributes that are either inherent or deeply ingrained, such as personality characteristics—to the skill set. This distinction is similar to that between "hard" and "soft" management skills: hard skills involve the ability to reach organizational *goals* that involve technical, financial, or other systems-related outcomes; soft skills involve *processes* of interpersonal interaction that motivate and compel employees to perform their jobs well. The difference has implications for how employers can make the best decisions as to which applicants or employees should be assigned to which tasks.

If competency is understood to be limited to specific skills, then current employees with the necessary background can be trained to perform the skill. If, however, competency includes personal traits, then only individuals with those specific traits will be suited for specific tasks or positions; if current employees do not have the desired personal qualities—such as motivation, self-confidence, or the ability to foster interpersonal communication—employers will have to seek new applicants for the position. This results in the "train versus hire," or what one study calls the "growing versus buying," dilemma (Ingraham and Getha-Taylor 2004). Of course, people can be trained to develop or alter individual traits (to have more motivation, to be more self-confident, to learn communication techniques), but employers may decide that it is easier to hire an individual who appears to exhibit these traits "naturally" rather than attempt to train employees to change their personal attributes.

In recent years, analysts have examined components of competencies that may affect how employers assess their use in recruiting, training, or evaluating employees. Studies have examined gender differences in the perception of competencies (Daley and Naff 1998), generational characteristics of certain competency attributes (Jurkiewicz and Brown 1998), and those competencies necessary for cross-organizational collaboration (Getha-Taylor 2008), mediation efforts (Mareschal 1998), and leadership transitions (Lynn 2001). Research suggests that sets of competencies used to define certain jobs must evolve over time, with dated competencies phased out, so that they correspond to the changing nature of the task at hand (Nelson 2004). Competency studies and recommendations also differ as to the projected level of job performance a set of competencies is designed to attain. Some target competencies to achieve adequate job performance, some strive for excellence in the outcomes of competency modeling, and some look for "differentiating competencies" that distinguish adequate from superior performance (Getha-Taylor 2008, 105). Underlying the differences in usage and approach is the fact that most employers in all sectors of the contemporary American workforce use a specific set of competencies to define each position in order to improve overall job performance and organizational productivity.

The U.S. government is no exception: every government agency has developed a set of competencies to guide hiring, training, and employee evaluation efforts. Although each position involves a distinct set of skills, and perhaps individual traits, this book argues that an overarching set of competencies is applicable to all public servants: technical expertise, ethical behavior, and leadership characteristics. The target of applying these competencies is excellence: public servants who strive for excellence in these competencies will gain the professional edge necessary to excel in their jobs and produce the most "public value"—or work in the interest of the common good. The term *competency* as used here includes both skills and individual traits and involves the use of both "hard" and "soft" management skills. Although it is true that most individuals can be trained to perform specific technical tasks, in the realms of ethical behavior and leadership qualities, individual traits appear to make a difference in a person's ability to excel.

Focusing on public managers, Virtanen (2000) distinguishes five competence areas: task competence, professional competence in subject area and administration, political competence, and ethical competence. He identifies permanent value competencies as "commitments." In his framework, each competency is technical, instrumental, and value-based. In task competence the key criterion is performance; in value competence it is motivation, and in instrumental competence it is abilities. Professional competence requires both substantive field and specific task mastery, value competence emphasizes control of the policy object, and instrumental competence highlights knowhow of the policy object. Administration competence centers on the execution of policy handed down by elected officials, value competence relates more to control of policy, and instrumental competence requires being adept at cooperation. The focus of political competence is values and power, for value competence it is on ideology and the interests of public managers, and for instrumental competence it centers on the possession of power. Finally, Virtanen identifies ethical competence as conforming to moral values, value competence as morality, and instrumental competence as ethical reasoning and argumentation. For the purposes of this book, Virtanen's five competencies can be reduced to three: technical (all-encompassing "will do" and "can do" task competence), ethical ("right action" and moral reasoning), and leadership (professional subject matter and task mastery, as well as administration and political skills).

In addition to mastering competencies, a strong commitment to public service can provide an individual with the motivation and the ability to develop and refine personal attributes that can furnish them and their organizations with an important advantage. Individuals can learn to behave ethically and to promote ethical behavior in others, for example, in the context of a strong organizational code of conduct supported by a culture of ethics. People can also learn to manage and lead in various capacities by developing the negotiation and political skills necessary to solve complex and controversial problems in public life. A strong and unwavering commitment to serve the commonweal and uphold professional standards can go a long way toward attaining not only the skills but also the attributes necessary for excellence in public service (Perry, Brudney, Coursey, and Littlepage 2008). After examining the context and nature of a changing U.S. public service, this book analyzes the three overarching competencies—technical, ethical, and leadership—by identifying skills and traits within each and providing examples of how they can be used to attain a public service professional edge.

The Changing Context of Public Service

Public service has been greatly affected by the rapidly changing context within which it is organized and executed. Changes affect the (1) technical, (2) internal, (3) external, and (4) managerial environments that encompass the organization and delivery of public services.

In the technical realm, information technology (IT), new media, and cybersecurity concerns all affect the way public servants work. The explosion of IT capabilities alone, as Joshua and Maria's experiences illustrate, raises new, and sometimes confounding, technical and ethical dilemmas. The rapid expansion of blogs and Internet discussion groups allows disaffected employees to publicly air their gripes about organizational and managerial changes that affect their rights and salaries. The ability of "hostile" cyberattacks or "friendly fire" computer glitches to delay or shut down government operations, such as a computer problem that forced the delay of air traffic across the United States for several hours in August 2008, has made cybersecurity a key concern of all those working in public service (Chapter 5).

Changes in the internal environment of public service—increased sector mobility, privatization, first-order devolution of decision making from federal to state and local governments, and second-order devolution from government to nonprofit and private organizations—require rethinking who provides public services and how those services are most effectively delivered. Regina's task of directing her private firm's contract with a local government to provide a city service, for example, is one facing managers in many private and nonprofit organizations in the United States as well as abroad.

The external environment that surrounds public service also profoundly affects professionals and the way they operate. Domestically, the political atmosphere, the role of the media, and demographic shifts can all have an impact on how public service professionals perform their jobs. If political loyalty instead of merit is used as the yardstick by which public servants are hired and promoted, for example, the provision of public services could be negatively affected, as some claimed was the case in Federal Emergency Management Agency's response to Hurricane Katrina in 2005. In a charged and polarized political atmosphere, professional public servants may find it difficult to carry out technical tasks or provide legally mandated services unencumbered by politically motivated criticism and obstructionism. This is especially the case if a politically polarized media purposely inflates political controversies in order to sell papers or increase viewership. More concrete domestic changes, such as demographic shifts, also significantly affect public service. The need to offer services in the Spanish language or orient health care provisions to an ever-aging population, for example, are both examples of how changing demographics compel public services to rethink their responsibilities.

Changes in the foreign external environment are also profound. The rise of supranational organizations (e.g., the World Trade Organization; multinational environmental groups), the impact of globalization on management and service provision, and the debate about whether or not American obligations under international treaties should impact domestic law will increasingly alter the way public service is organized and implemented in the United States.

All of these changes will have profound effects on the managerial environment that encompasses public service. Managers, for instance, must contend with the decentralization of decision making, which will inevitably require more specific negotiation skills (Chapter 4). They also have to deal with the complexities of cross-sectoral service provisions, which demand new ways of ensuring accountability for contractual obligations and responsibility for decision making. Managers must have a broader range of knowledge in human resource management (e.g., to understand "at-will employment") and personnel management (e.g., to understand how to "broadband" pay scales) as well as a thorough understanding of the legal controversies surrounding those technical issues (Chapter 2). Changing demographics mean that public service administrators and their organizations must have a well-developed "cultural competency" that enables them to interact effectively with various demographic groups (Chapter 4).

Clearly, the workplace of today's public service professional is in constant flux, causing apprehension and uncertainty but also providing opportunities and challenges. Leicht and Fennell (2001) identify six key characteristics of today's workplace: (1) flatter organizational hierarchies, (2) more temporary workers, (3) wide use of subcontracting and outsourcing, (4) massive downsizing of permanent workers, (5) a post-union bargaining environment, and (6) virtual organizations. Public servants, whether they work in the government or for the government in the nonprofit or business sectors, understand that these changes affect the way they work. The emergence of virtual and flatter organizations is made easier as employers like Joshua's move to E-Government. Regina's new responsibilities in supervising and overseeing her firm's delivery of a city service are indicative of the movement to both subcontract, and, eventually, in many places, downsize permanent employees and increase temporary government workers. These moves are easier to accomplish in a more flexible, postunion bargaining environment, but, as will become evident, they also cause some consternation among long-time civil servants.

The Changing Nature of Public Service: From Old to New

Significant changes are also occurring in the way public service is conceived. Previous research emphasizes, to a greater or lesser extent, government-centered work (e.g., Mosher 1982; Volcker 2003). As the boundaries among government, private, and nonprofit sectors become increasingly blurred, however, public service takes on a broader meaning. Public service no longer refers exclusively to tasks performed by government; it now involves work with nonprofit organizations and private firms. Thus, multisectored service providers, mobility or sector switching among employers, and the commitment of individuals to make a difference all animate the tectonic shift occurring in public service (Light 1999, 2008).

Building on this characterization (Sherwood 2000), public service is "the people establishment" that delivers services to citizens, promotes the collective interest, and accepts the resulting responsibilities. Individuals who advance the public welfare and uphold the public trust are part of the public service. They may work in city, county, state, or federal government, in the nonprofit sector, or for a business contractor. Indeed, contemporary public service professionals represent different sectors of the economy and are as likely as not to be salaried employees of nonprofit organizations or commercial enterprises. This heterogeneous public service is composed of people with different stakes in, and divergent expectations of, public service. Professionalism in public service, however, may be defined as the application of specialized knowledge to help solve complex social problems (Exhibit 1.1).

The craft of public service, like the practice of medicine, involves much more than technical skills. Consummate professionals must also apply decision-making skills marked by good judgment and discretion; their decisions must be both technically and morally sound. Public service magnifies these considerations in two ways. First, many problems are not simply technical and straightforward (e.g., how to build a highway); some present divisive political conundrums with only imperfect solutions that will not satisfy everyone (e.g., where to build a highway). The challenge to public officials is to make complex political problems more manageable. Second, whichever decisions are made tend to be viewed as "moral and absolute," since they symbolize the authoritative allocation of resources and values in a society. Decisions regarding public services are a public responsibility, whether the service is delivered by a government agency, nonprofit organization, or private enterprise. It is exactly the public acceptance of responsibility that provides professionals with the edge that distinguishes them from others and thereby furnishes the "right stuff." This is the key to the identity and legitimacy of public service.

The consummate professional, then, utilizes a triangle of complementary competencies—technical expertise (the "how"), ethical integrity (the "why"), and leadership (the "what") in his/her field. Conscious that their activities have significance beyond the immediate situation, professionals avoid a simple bottom-line mentality; rather than society serving the economy, it is the economy that serves society. The standard is not *caveat emptor* ("let the buyer beware"), but *credat emptor* ("let the buyer trust"). Software programmers aim to develop hackerproof code, teachers strive to educate students, program analysts seek to improve services, and health care providers struggle to improve patients' lives. Success is gauged by how decisions improve the performance of the profession and define its impact on society. When the technical, ethical, and leadership points of the Competencies Triangle (see Figure 1.1) work in harmony, they produce excellent performance and help practitioners realize the ideals of their profession.

While the locus and composition of public service have changed, the primary purpose continues to be the improvement of civic well-being. This improvement may take many forms. As Robert and Janet Denhardt (2001, 19)

Exhibit 1.1

Models of Professionalism

The definition of *professionalism* has been subject to both controversy and occupational variations. Two models—trait-based and decision-based—help explain some overarching characteristics of professional occupations:

Trait-Based

- A specialized competence
- Autonomy in exercising this competence
- Commitment to a career in this competence
- A service orientation
- Connection to a professional association
- A code of conduct that encourages the proper use of competence

Decision-Based

- Confrontation of complex tasks
- Focus on the esoteric nature of the decision-making process
- Capacity to resolve problems
- A code of conduct to guide the decision-making process

The trait-based model focuses on a set of ideals that are commonly used to characterize a profession; it establishes broad criteria for the organization and operation of the profession as a whole. The decision-based model, in contrast, emphasizes the capacity of an organization to address and resolve complex problems. Each of these frameworks embodies the classic definition of professional leaders, as well as the vow they make when assuming their position: to pursue excellence in both technical competence and moral character (Bowman 1998). The Organization for Economic Cooperation and Development (OECD) provides an excellent example of how "technical competence and moral character" can be combined to produce professional standards. OECD uses the description in the Statistical Data and Metadata Exchange (SDMX, a dictionary of common vocabulary developed by several international organizations) of "Professionalism and Ethical Standards" to illustrate how technical skills should be combined with ethical precepts:

(continued)

Exhibit 1.1 *(continued)*

Definition of Professionalism

- The standard, skill, and ability suitable for producing statistics of good quality.

Context

- Statistics are produced on an impartial basis.
- The choices of sources and statistical techniques as well as decisions about dissemination are informed solely by statistical considerations.
- The recruitment and promotion of staff are based on relevant aptitude.
- The statistical entity is entitled to comment on erroneous interpretation and misuse of statistics.
- Guidelines for staff behavior exist and procedures are used to make these guidelines known to staff.
- Other practices provide assurances of the independence, integrity, and accountability of the statistical agency.

Source: Adapted from Organization of Economic Cooperation and Development (2006).

have said of public servants, "Service to the public—helping people in trouble, making the world safer and cleaner, helping children to learn and prosper, literally going where others would not go—is our job and our calling." They observe that, "This ability to be selfless, to be open to the needs and values and wants of others, is a part of each public servant" (Denhardt and Denhardt 2001, 19). Specific examples include the heroic, selfless emergency workers in the aftermath of the terrorist attacks of September 11, 2001. Less dramatic, but critically important, is the work of safety inspectors, educators, scientists, researchers, intelligence gatherers, social workers, regulators, dam builders, court personnel, transportation employees, corrections officers, social service providers, and numerous others.

This list provides a mere sampling of public service workers. Public service is hard to define, but easy to recognize, much like U.S. Supreme Court Justice Potter Stewart's famous response when asked to clarify the meaning of obscenity: "I know it when I see it." As with the Oldsmobile of another era, "your father's public service" is not that of this generation. The following two sections briefly look backward and then forward to compare key differences between the old and the new public service.

The Old Public Service

Traditional public service was a product of industrial-era government; it was composed of government workers who carried out functions in centralized, hierarchical bureaucracies according to routine standard operating procedures. Their discretion was limited by their position in the vertical chain of command and they were accountable to their superiors.

Elected officials set public policy, defined the public interest, and monitored program management. Authority flowed from top to bottom, services were provided directly to citizens, control or regulation was government-centered, staff roles were clear, and skills were specialized. Civil service protection was granted to permanent employees whose pay and benefits came directly from government. President Bill Clinton proclaimed in the mid-1990s that "the era of big government is over."

This statement remains accurate in terms of decentralizing the bureaucratic monolith that used to characterize the civil service and decreasing the percentage of the American workforce employed directly by the federal government. The public workforce in 2007 was made up of about 17.6 million employees, down from 18.4 million in 1990. Both the reduction in military activities after the Cold War and the Clinton-Gore "reinventing government" campaign resulted in a decrease of about 500,000 civil servants at the federal level. When analyzed in different terms, however, the pre-9/11 mantra, "the era of big government is over" is clearly over.

Paul C. Light, writing for the Brookings Institution, for example, refers to a "thickening" of the federal bureaucracy, and the addition of "height" and "width" to bureaucratic departments as a result of the Bush administration's introduction of career management and political appointee positions in top layers of the government bureaucracy (Light 2004, 2008). He also argues that, despite the decrease in the number of those directly employed by the U.S. government, it has had a "largely hidden workforce" since 1990, resulting from the significant increase in federal contracts and grants. As a result, "government is now growing, almost entirely in off-budget jobs that are invisible to the American public in federal budget and headcount documents" (Light 2003). Clearly, the reach of the U.S. government is growing even as the number of federal civil servants declines, as the public sector continues to provide extensive services using government by "reinvention, network, and market" (Kamarck 2007).

Local governments, meanwhile, continue to grow as they directly hire more employees, create single-purpose entities to provide special services such as water and sewage, and increase the number of contracting and networking arrangements. Public service contracting is most often used in services such as waste collection, building maintenance, bill collecting, data processing, health and medical services, and street cleaning and repair (Andrisani, Hakim, and Leeds 2000). Many government contracts for such services are negotiated with nonprofit organizations, whose share of total U.S. paid employment was 9.5 percent in 2001, up from 7.3 percent in 1977; many other services are contracted out to the private sector. So while the sources of government service provision have changed, the level of government involvement has not.

Some view the move to outsource services as an opportunity, but to others it is a threat. It is an opportunity to those who want government to operate more like a business that promises to be cost-effective and quality conscious. It is a threat to those public employees who doubt that government can be run like a business and fear job losses and service deterioration. Because government workers are much more likely to be unionized than their private sector counterparts (38 percent vs. 9 percent), labor opposition to restructuring along corporate lines is not surprising. The post-union bargaining environment noted by Leicht and Fennell (2001) is clearly more descriptive of the private sector workplace than the public arena.

While government-run public service continues to directly provide some goods and services by civil servants, and will do so for the foreseeable future, this is changing rapidly. U.S. Comptroller General David Walker believes that, "The government is on a 'burning platform' and the status-quo way of doing business is unacceptable" (quoted in Keene 2003, 15). This perception that the old ways are no longer up to the new tasks has prompted new actors using new instruments of civic action to emerge to meet citizen needs. This necessitates a rethinking of government's role, composition, and management agenda (Exhibit 1.2), as well as a more realistic definition of the new public service.

The future portends a smaller role for government, an enlarged nonprofit sector, and an increase in public-private partnerships through contractual relationships with businesses and nonprofits.

The New Public Service

The new public service has a different set of defining characteristics more suitable to a postindustrial, service-based economy (Denhardt and Denhardt 2007). Today vertical hierarchy is giving way to horizontal networks, "flattened" bureaucracies, and shared leadership structures. The public interest is

Exhibit 1.2

Changing Composition of the Old Public Service

Impending retirements and restless workers portend drastic changes in the federal government workforce. It is estimated that more than 60 percent of federal workers are eligible to retire between now and 2016 and that a similar percentage of career Senior Executive Service (SES) members plan to leave by 2013. While the U.S. Office of Personnel Management doubts that actual retirements or departures will reach these proportions, such projections raise concerns about loss of institutional memory and knowledge about how to get things done. Some agencies will be especially hard hit: 70 percent of SES members in the Department of Veterans Affairs plan to leave the federal government by 2013. Other departments are taking steps to retain the knowledge of senior employees. For example, the Forest Service is calling back selected retired employees as mentors and both the Department of Veterans Affairs and NASA are using videotapes of senior employees and managers to share the lessons they learned in public service with newcomers. Notwithstanding these initiatives, several federal agencies lack a formal succession-planning program to replace seasoned senior executives.

A government-wide survey conducted by the U.S. Office of Personnel Management found that more than one-third of the 100,000 federal workers surveyed are considering leaving their jobs. Slightly fewer than half of the 34.6 percent contemplating departure indicate that they plan to retire within three years. While it is unclear whether these workers would seek federal employment elsewhere or plan to leave federal service altogether, findings suggest employees are not "connected" to their jobs. Pay, benefits, and job significance are not the main problem; in fact, satisfaction levels are reasonably high: 68 percent are satisfied with their jobs, 64 percent are satisfied with their pay and their retirement benefits, and nine out of ten feel their work is important. What is lacking are intangible incentives that motivate superior performance. Fewer than half of those surveyed indicate satisfaction with recognition for a job well done, less than a third believe award programs provide meaningful incentives, 27 percent think management deals effectively with poor performers, and 36 percent indicate leaders spur high motivation among employees.

In addition to the challenge of replacing retiring workers, federal government managers face the challenge of retaining and motivating existing employees.

Source: Adapted from Davidson 2002, C. Lee 2003, reprinted with permission from AIPCO and the *Washington Post*, respectively; and USOPM (2008a, 2008b).

identified and pursued collaboratively through dialogue with relevant stakeholders; that is, everyone who has any kind of a stake in particular public policy outcomes. Empowered administrative officials still have limited discretion, but they remain accountable to the citizens via elected political leaders and administrative oversight. Employee job boundaries are flexible and skill sets are versatile. The transition from the old to the new style of providing services has altered the role of the public sector, "emphasizing collaboration and enablement rather than hierarchy and control" (Salamon 2002, vii).

The new system has been referred to variously as "the new governance," "third-party government," "government by proxy," "indirect government," and even "the end of government as we know it" (Kamarck 2007). While fewer of those managing direct public services are government employees, George Frederickson (2003, 11) observes that those who act for the state are "clothed with the public interest" and "covered with a public purpose." The managerial challenges presented by these changes are substantial and are both similar to and different from those faced earlier. They are the same in the sense that many of the dominant values from earlier eras—efficiency, economy, fairness, and performance—continue to be important, together with renewed emphasis on values associated with citizenship, public interest, ethics, transparency, and broad democratic values of accountability, equity, and responsiveness. The challenges are different in that the production and delivery of goods and services increasingly involves two streams: (1) government as a direct provider and (2) delivery by those who act "indirectly" on government's behalf. Public officials have experience with direct delivery, but must quickly adapt to the demands of indirect government (Kettl 2002a, 2002b).

As government bureaucracies reinvent themselves and share service provision with multiple agencies, nonprofit groups, and commercial organizations, there is less emphasis on following rules and more on performance and productivity (Kamarck 2007). The transition from command-and-control decision making based on hierarchical authority structures to indirect, weblike relationships requires a new set of managerial skills: the ability to establish networks and public-private partnerships, write contracts, oversee service providers, compete for scarce resources, save costs without undermining productivity, disperse funds and audit finances, measure and review performance, and master the technicalities and legal implications of new employment and salary schemes. Kettl (2002a) singles out five skills that require special attention when managing indirect programs: goal setting, negotiation, communication, financial management, and bridge building (Chapter 4). New tools that will become more commonplace as a result of increasingly "fuzzy boundaries" of indirect government include contracting, grants, vouchers, tax expenditures, loan guarantees, and government-sponsored enterprises (Salamon 2002).

These skills and tools will be considered in greater detail in subsequent sections of this book; here it is important to stress that a new skill set is required for today's public servants, who increasingly operate in an environment where indirect government is the norm rather than the exception.

It is, perhaps, inevitable that sweeping changes to the government bureaucracy involving internal operations and the outsourcing of public services result in criticisms and complaints on the part of civil servants long used to the routines and prestige of advancing through the traditional ranks. Some changes since the introduction of the National Performance Review (NPR) and the Government Performance and Results Act (GPRA) during the Clinton administration thus encountered resistance. Although these measures, designed to make government service provision more efficient and effective while motivating employees to excel (Gore 1997), did not result in comprehensive civil service reform, they did accord departments latitude to experiment with personnel policies and performance guidelines (Thompson 2001). Some agencies responded by phasing out the traditional General Schedule grades (GS 1 through GS 15) used in hiring, pay, and promotion, in favor of occupational broadbanding and salary pay-banding (Thompson 2008).

Broadbanding combines the old GS grades into wider categories of job classifications that allow new hires to skip the traditional GS ladder by being placed in a broader band of occupational levels. Pay-banding is a merit pay or pay-for-performance system that offers flexibility, at the expense of predictability, in human resource (staffing) and personnel (performance and promotions) management. Some governmental employees resist these reforms, not only because they run counter to the traditional way of doing things and increase job insecurity (Bowman and West 2006), but also because they appear to weaken a unique occupational, pay, and promotion structure that generated pride in the civil service (Underhill and Oman 2007).

There is also resistance on the part of some civil servants to the outsourcing and privatization of services. On a practical level, those who work in government bureaucracies fear that new service strategies will cost them their jobs or even eliminate entire agencies or departments to which they have dedicated their professional careers. On a more philosophical level, many believe that only a public service–oriented government can truly act in the national interest because, unlike commercial enterprises, it continues to provide services even if that provision does not prove to be profitable.

Civil servants and contract employees differ in several important respects. Whereas public managers assign tasks and reward or discipline the civil servants who report to them, contract managers control the reporting channels, task assignments, disciplinary measures, and rewards for contract employees. Pay and benefits are set by law for the civil servant but by the contractor for the private employee. The primary allegiance of the contract worker is to his or her employer, while the civil servant is sworn to uphold the public interest. Government officials are imbued with the agency mission and culture and must follow rules and regulations; contract employees may be unfamiliar with agency culture and are free to work outside of many rules and regulations. Contract employees are not typically bound by ethics rules, whereas civil servants are subject to conflict of interest restrictions and ethics codes. Civil servants usually enjoy a merit system, due process, and other such safeguards, but contract workers are typically employed "at will" with few whistleblower protections. In a blended workforce it behooves officials and managers to be keenly aware of these fundamental differences.

Another concern is that reforms may be used as an excuse to give government managers and political appointees more control over employees, so that not only job security but also employee rights are threatened. This was the case when Congress approved National Security Personnel System (NSPS) legislation in 2003. Former Secretary of Defense Donald Rumsfeld had spearheaded the NSPS out of post-9/11 concerns for national security (Brook and King 2008), especially in the Department of Defense and the newly created Department of Homeland Security. NSPS measures, which constituted "the most sweeping proposed changes to the U.S. civil service system since the 1978 Civil Service Reform Act" (Weir 2004), were designed to give government managers more control over personnel, policy making, and information gathering in their departments and agencies. The system introduced the new performance standards, broadbanding, and pay-banding techniques of reinvented government but added an additional element: the weakening of civil service unions, collective bargaining, and employee access to independent mediators in labor disputes (Thompson 2007). Several civil service unions, including the American Federation of Government Employees, rebelled and took the government to court. Eventually a district court struck down the personnel rules related to collective bargaining, saying that they violated the rights and protections granted to employees (Pear 2005). The Defense Authorization Act, passed by Congress in January 2008, authorized the new performance, pay, and occupational banding components of the NSPS but rejected any weakening of employee collective bargaining rights.

Clearly, then, the move to reinvent government and craft a new public service is a work in progress in which the benefits of improving performance and the quality of public service must be balanced with the rights and interests of those who provide that service. As in every period of change, the challenge will be to balance the courage to move forward with the wisdom to know when to stay in place. While the gradual transition from the old to the new public service alters both the role and the operation of government, one thing remains constant: the professionalism that assumes pride of place in organizations charged to provide public services is in constant tension with the ever-present rough and tumble of that mainstay of democracy—politics. This subject is the focus of the next section.

Public Service: Politics and Professionalism

American democratic traditions reflect a tension between political and professional control of the public service. This tension was especially evident in the old (government-run) public service, but it is present in the new networked public service as well. It plays out differently at various points in the nation's history. In the first four decades following President Washington's inauguration, appointed officials in government were drawn from the gentlemanly, aristocratic ranks and "fitness" for public service was a key criterion for making appointments. Well-educated, wealthy, white, male landowners—in short, the privileged elite—were thought to be best suited to positions of high government office. The Jacksonian revolution gave greater weight to partisan politics with regard to decisions on whom to hire. Jackson helped democratize public service and diminish elitism by hiring those from diverse class and geographic backgrounds. Such appointments were consistent with Jackson's view that government work was so simple that virtually anyone could do it. Implementing his rotation-in-office principle broke the hold of aristocratic entitlement to government offices. During the mid to late nineteenth century this rotation meant that the practice of "to the victor go the spoils" was followed. With each election, many civil servants were hired based primarily on party affiliation; corruption was rampant.

The Pendleton Act of 1883 attempted to depoliticize public service by instituting a merit system at the federal level. Parallel policy initiatives in many states and localities introduced civil service reforms thereafter. Gradually, over the next several decades, what you know (merit) replaced who you know (partisanship) as the key consideration in personnel selection and merit systems became more established. Renewed emphasis was given to rationality, expertise, and professionalism. Today civil service systems, ideally based on merit principles, are found at all levels of government; however, they too have become the subject of harsh criticism because they may fall short of the principles they espouse (Pfiffner and Brook 2000). Indeed, states like Georgia and Florida have recently radically reformed their civil service systems, reinstituting at-will employment, a policy whereby employees can be let go at any time. At-will employment not only undermines job security, but also has the potential to replace merit with a spoils-like system of job placement (Condrey and Maranto 2001; Bowman and West 2007). Furthermore, in most jurisdictions, even those purportedly based on merit, politics has not been removed entirely from the selection process. In many cases, personal connections and prior service as well as partisan considerations and competence are factored together in making staffing decisions. Officials making appointments often seek a blend of loyalty and ability in their new hires.

Merit principles are ideals intended to undergird merit systems. These principles encompass open recruitment, fair employment decisions, and equitable pay. They help infuse concern for the public interest, foster efficiency and effectiveness, and ensure retention based on performance. Such principles provide employees with protection against favoritism and unfair reprisals; they also endorse training and education. Merit systems, however, do not always reflect merit principles. The media continues to report on prohibited personnel practices. Discrimination, employment decisions clearly not based on skills or abilities, and political coercion make headlines (Bowman and West 2009). Nepotism, unauthorized employee preferences, and obstruction of employment competition are egregious but less visible examples of prohibited personnel practices. Reprisals sometimes occur for whistle-blowing or exercising appeal rights and merit principles or veterans' rights are sometimes violated. Managers in public service cannot be ambivalent and must remain vigilant in ensuring that merit systems operate according to well-established merit principles.

Historically, the public has been ambivalent about "politics versus professionalism" as a controlling influence over government appointments. Professionals are admired for their training, expertise, and autonomy, but they are held in lower esteem if they work for government organizations. Political appointees connect government to the rest of society in ways that professional bureaucrats do not, as noted by Dionne, who stresses that "citizen service is essential to the health of civil society" (2001, 9). However, citizen servants appointed to political positions and the bureaucrats in the civil service are too often described as either hacks or bumblers. Despite such an overdrawn characterization, in part reinforced by scandal-seeking media and bureaucrat-bashing politicians, the clear trend has been for increased professionalism in the public sector workforce. Government employs a disproportionately large number of white-collar workers who fall into the professional, technical, and administrative U.S. census categories. This increased professionalism is necessary due to the growing complexity of the work to be done. Andrew Jackson's view of government work as "simple" has not been accurate for many generations.

The American political system continues to rely heavily on politically appointed "citizen servants," who, while amateurs, bring fresh ideas and reinvigorate governmental operations when a newly elected chief executive enters office (Radin 2007). A powerful, professional ruling class has not emerged in the United States as it has in other countries. Furthermore, in an era where privatization, partnerships, and outsourcing are increasingly common, we count on both citizen service and professional civil service to oversee the network of those who directly deliver public services; indeed, many of these service providers are professionals themselves. Nonetheless, cozy politics sometimes surrounds decisions to privatize or contract for public services (Kobrak 2002), challenging professional values and norms of operation.

The issues of politics and professionalism have captured the attention of contemporary commentators on today's public life. Thomas Frank (2008, 138) highlights the commitment of George W. Bush's administration to competition, which resulted in half of federal positions being open to bids from the private sector, and how agencies are graded based on how many federal jobs were privatized. Contractors have become, in his words, the "fourth branch of government" and professional civil servants are "dispirited," "depressed," "afraid," and "thinking about leaving." He cites John Threlkeld, assistant legislative director of the American Federation of Government Employees, who said: "Every now and then I'll hear [people] say if their job's not going to get contracted out or if they're not going to get stripped of their collective bargaining rights, then they're going to lose their civil service protections against politics and favoritism." After pointing to the low morale of federal employees he notes their diminished career prospects as government functions are parceled out to the private sector: ". . . there's an increasing emphasis on federal employees having very short-term careers and then going back out to the private sector . . . I think to some extent it's designed to reduce the independence and autonomy of the civil service" (quoted in Frank 2008, 137).

Naomi Klein (2007) provides numerous examples of this "hollowing out of government," which exacerbates what some have called a human capital crisis. As AFL-CIO President John Sweeney observes, " . . . under the banner of 'efficiency,' the nation could well return to a latter day 'spoils system.' The real possibility exists that in the future, lucrative service contracts paid for by taxpayers will be doled out in ways the civil service system was created to prevent" (AFGE 2008). Cautionary comments about privatization are not limited to labor leaders. Indeed, David Walker, U.S. Comptroller General, in 2007 spoke of the need to recognize the value of professional civil servants and how their duties differ from those of contractors: "There's something civil servants have that the private sector doesn't. And that is the duty of loyalty to the greater good—the duty of loyalty to the collective best interest of all rather than the interest of a few. Companies have duties of loyalty to their shareholders, not to the country" (quoted in Klein 2007, 388). Balancing professionalism with politics and public interest with private interests requires artful juggling in a changing public service environment.

Paradoxically, flat organizational structures, decentralized service delivery, employee empowerment, and virtual organizations (all part of the New Public Management movement, which began in the 1990s), simultaneously provide opportunities and threats for professional public servants. The independence, autonomy, and expertise associated with professionalism are given freer rein under the more flexible arrangements found in the new public service. At the same time, the loss of traditional controls provides opportunities for corner cutting, self-interested behaviors, uneven or inequitable service delivery, and conflicts of interest. New Public Management reforms have exacerbated "professional career versus political appointee" tensions (Bowman and West 2009) in several ways: new personnel systems may allow loyalty to trump professional expertise in hiring processes and employee evaluations, pay-for-performance measures may turn into awards for political allegiance, appointees could have wide discretion in overseeing agency regulations, and overall politicization of the career service could undermine the professionalism so critical in serving the commonweal.

Government oversight is crucial to curbing excesses, as evidenced by massive accounting fraud at flagship corporations (e.g., Enron, Global Crossing, WorldCom, Tyco), and epic mismanagement of investment banks in 2007 and 2008 (Chapter 5). The challenge of today's public servant, whether located inside or outside of government, is to be politically adept and attuned to the conflicting currents that must be navigated. Public servants must also be professionally astute, possessing the requisite technical, ethical, and leadership skills to do right things and to do things right. This challenge is the focus of the next section.

The Competencies Triangle

Figure 1.1 depicts the Competencies Triangle, which provides an analytical framework for the remainder of this chapter and those to follow. Today's public service requires the skills that make up three comprehensive competencies: technical, ethical, and leadership. Their mastery is essential for the consummate professional.

Figure 1.1   **The Competency Triangle of Public Service Professionalism**

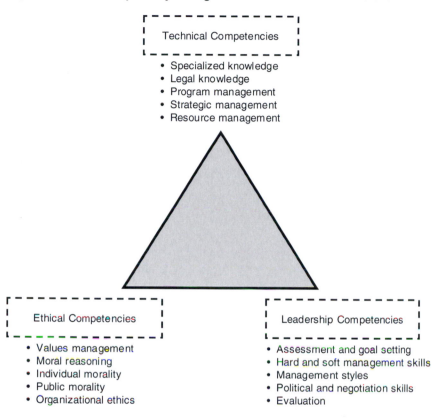

The following content appears in and around the triangle figure:

Technical Competencies

- Specialized knowledge
- Legal knowledge
- Program management
- Strategic management
- Resource management

Ethical Competencies

- Values management
- Moral reasoning
- Individual morality
- Public morality
- Organizational ethics

Leadership Competencies

- Assessment and goal setting
- Hard and soft management skills
- Management styles
- Political and negotiation skills
- Evaluation

The Technical Competency

Competence in one's chosen field is a hallmark of professionalism. Technical competence includes expertise in a functional field and a range of "hard" (goal-oriented) and "soft" (process-oriented) management skills. Functional expertise refers to specialized knowledge that allows an individual to master a particular job (e.g., budgeting) in a certain field (e.g., health care), as well as an understanding of a set of legal requirements and restraints within which that job is performed. Technical management skills include program management (with an emphasis on organizational savvy and productivity), strategic planning (with an eye toward sustainability), and resource management (as applied to finances, personnel, and information). Mastery of all these skills is essential for public servants, especially in a post-9/11, results-oriented environment. Citizens reasonably expect competent performance from all those engaged in promoting the common good; incompetence undermines the legitimacy of the public service.

The whole range of technical functional and management skills is examined in Chapter 2. Here, four skills within these categories are briefly highlighted: (1) job task mastery, (2) knowledge of information technology, (3) project management, and (4) productivity improvement. Given the vast array of public services provided, these areas are deliberately broad and involve skills that cut across sectors, organizations, and roles. Citizens, elected public officials, boards of directors, stockholders, and stakeholders evaluate professionals in the new public service based, in part, on their skills in these areas.

First, job task mastery is expected of all managers and employees regardless of their positions or employers. In the scenario that opened this chapter, Maria Rodriguez learned that she must acquire new knowledge if she was to have a professional edge in her new position as chair of her hospital's ethics committee. In this case, the ethical questions surrounding new medical technologies are emerging at a fast pace and must be addressed if patient rights are to remain inviolate. In confronting the question as to whether meeting the reimbursement requirements of third-party payers in the health care field violates patients' privacy rights, Maria must master the ethical, financial, and legal complexities that intersect with her responsibilities as chair of the ethics committee. This case makes clear the benefits that accrue to public servants when they have broad educational and/or professional experience to draw from when they need further training to master new job skills.

Second, IT developments influence all aspects of management. In the opening vignettes, Joshua Bennett had mastered the requisite skills during his probation period, but several months later he felt ill equipped to meet his growing responsibilities. Virtual technology applications in Joshua's field now involve use of software for many tasks, including payroll and benefits, job analysis and job descriptions, performance appraisal, and position classification (West and Berman 2001). Web-based training, computer-based personnel testing, training management software, as well as webcam interviews and electronic background checks, are used in many government, private, and nonprofit organizations. People are now able to "work together apart" from distant locations, and virtual interactions can occur without all parties being physically present. Use of e-mail and blogs, for example, often changes the way work is done and increases opportunities for "boundary spanning," an important advantage in the collaborative work of the new public service.

Increasingly, training in state-of-the-art IT communication is essential if public servants are to be properly prepared for the transition from traditional to virtual human resource management.

Third, competencies in program and project management are necessary for those in the new public service, and these competencies are now more complicated as informal teamwork and collaboration blur the lines among departments, organizations, sectors, and jurisdictions. One of the examples at the beginning of this chapter, Regina Blackstone, is a corporate research analyst who was used to working alone, not in teams. She has excellent skills in data analysis and the technical components of her job, but these skills are not sufficient to give her a professional edge in her new position directing her commercial firm's government contract to provide a city service. Her new job requires her to work with public and perhaps nonprofit sector managers and employees in order to successfully manage the city service project. This necessitates a whole range of management and leadership skills: from knowing how to organize and evaluate cross-sectoral cooperation to mastering communication skills in unfamiliar environments. Dedicated public servants in Regina's position can prepare themselves for challenges like this by learning management skills, such as organization planning, scheduling, budgeting, risk management, logistics, and evaluation. They can prepare themselves for leadership positions and the need to set goals, adapt their management styles, motivate employees, effectively negotiate, and evaluate themselves and their teams by taking part in leadership development programs (Chapter 4) whenever the opportunity arises.

Project and program management is especially challenging in the new public service environment. Matrix organizations and cross-institutional project collaborations complicate management and planning. Administrators must be familiar with planning processes and the tools associated with them. Time and cost estimates, as well as user surveys and needs assessments, must be conducted at the outset. Project implementation requires assigning responsibility for each task with its attendant costs and the time frame within which it must be completed. Professional project managers should be able to use tools such as Gantt charts, which break down tasks according to time frames, and Program Evaluation and Review Technique (PERT) charts, which indicate the interaction of tasks and their time frame for completion (Appendix 2.1 at the end of Chapter 2). Acquiring tool sets such as these early in their careers will enable public service professionals to meet the challenges of project and program management in the reinvented public sphere.

Finally, technical skills related to productivity improvement are crucial in both the old and new public service. Professionals must first know how to define productivity in their organizational environment and then develop ways to measure it and strategies to improve it. The traditional definition of productivity—the ratio of the output of goods and services to the input of factors of production—emphasizes efficiency. While this definition provides relatively clear guidelines for measurement and improvement in terms of costs, it is "too limited to do justice to the nature of many public service goals" (Berman 2006, x). An increasing focus on effectiveness (the outcomes of projects and programs), equity (fairness in outcomes), and the "people component" (worker empowerment) has led to an emphasis on overall performance or "managing for results" in evaluating projects and programs (Ingraham 2005; Light 2006) and on ways to improve that performance through best-practices benchmarking (Chapter 2).

Efficiency, effectiveness, and equity are longstanding productivity-related values that are emphasized in business, nonprofit, and public administration. With the increase in public-private partnerships that cut across the three sectors, mutual adjustments in the relative emphasis of these fundamental values will have to be made. As Berman notes:

> Productivity is defined as the effective and efficient use of resources. Effectiveness is typically of great importance in the public sector, and nonprofit organizations often emphasize effectiveness and efficiency in equal measure. Public sector organizations also value providing services to all population groups, that is, ensuring equity (2006, 9).

The crucial role of employees in improving performance is attested to by the increased attention paid to human resource and personnel management, because "effective performance and efforts to measure it are—at their heart—about people: having the right people, with the right skills and talents, where and when they are needed" (Ingraham 2005, 392). Government administration has been slow to recognize the importance of performance in staffing, promotion, and pay and the challenge will become more difficult when managers must assess performance in a "blended workforce"—"across contract/noncontract workers, across full-time/part-time workers, across organizations, and across jurisdictions" (393). Generational differences also affect understandings of performance and productivity. Cam Marston, typecasting employees according to generational monikers, writes:

> Generation X and New Millennials will almost always cite productivity, not time spent working, as a standard of measurement for the work done.

This is a deep source of frustration to many of their Boomer bosses, who don't necessarily cite productivity as a requirement when evaluating performance for rewards (bonuses, promotions, raises). . . . Boomers, you've got to face the facts: Generation X and New Millennials work smart during the day so that they can complete the job on time and get back to their lives (2007, 120).

Public service professionals, then, need to combine mastery of productivity improvement strategies with the ability to optimize efficiency, effectiveness, equity, and employee performance in different settings and across different generations.

The Ethical Competency

The second point of the Competencies Triangle refers to ethical capacity and the moral foundations upon which it is built. While the terms *moral* and *ethical* are at times used interchangeably, here moral refers to the values and principles used to decide what is right and what is wrong and ethical refers to behavior or decisions based on those values and principles. To cope with the changes in the external and internal environments, public servants need to buttress technical skills with the ethical competency, such as moral reasoning, values management, and prudent decision making (West and Berman 2006). Social scientists and journalists are fond of displaying thermometer charts showing the decline in public trust in government since the 1960s. Indeed, the drop in confidence has been dramatic—from more than 75 percent who in the mid-1960s said they trusted government in Washington to do the right thing "most of the time" to 29 percent four decades later (*Brookings Institution* 2002). While there was an increase in trust immediately following 9/11 (30 percent in 2000 vs. 64 percent in September 2001), just six years later a Gallup poll showed that levels of trust in the federal government were the lowest they had been in the previous decade (Jones 2007).

Those in the public service can help to rebuild citizen confidence by further demonstrating to the populace that they are worthy of their trust. They can further reinforce confidence by ensuring that those delivering services— inside or outside of government—are in compliance with professional best practices. Adhering to high standards of conduct, minimizing partisanship, avoiding scandals, spending money wisely, and being responsive to citizens are also helpful. Perhaps the most important thing they can do is to exercise their discretion wisely by making prudent decisions. In other words, those in the professional public service need to do the right things.

Table 1.1

A Six-Step Model of Ethical Decision Making

Steps		Questions to be considered
1.	Gathering data	What are the facts? What is the ethical issue? What is right or wrong in this situation? Must anything be known before considering a course of action?
2.	Developing alternatives	What can be done? What is the moral tension between alternatives? Do options detract from the organization's mission? Do options strengthen relationships with stakeholders? Is each alternative consistent with the decision maker's personal ethics?
3.	Forecasting outcomes	What will happen? What would make the situation right? Have all probable outcomes been identified?
4.	Applying criteria to the outcomes	What should be done? What ethical principles would justify the action? Are they of equal importance?
5.	Selecting an action	How should it be done? What course of action is feasible? How do organizational policies and the law affect the decision?
6.	Evaluating behavior	What difference did the action make? Did it have the desired outcome? What follow-up is needed?

Sources: Adapted from Anderson (1996); Aulisio, Arnold, and Youngner (2000); Wartick and Wood (1998).

Chapter 3 outlines five components of the ethical competency, illustrating their central role in public service: values management, moral development and reasoning, individual ethics, public versus private morality, and organizational ethics. Here, four specific skills are highlighted: (1) moral reasoning as the foundation of ethical decision making, (2) recognition of ethics-related conflicts, (3) rejection of unethical behavior, and (4) application of ethical theory.

The literature on principled moral reasoning is voluminous, attesting to its importance as a skill to be mastered. Lawrence Kohlberg (1981) holds that people differ in the way they respond to dilemmas and that their thought processes can provide the basis for categorizing them into one of three levels (each with two stages of moral development; Chapter 3). Diagnostic instruments have been developed that can help identify one's stage of moral development. Such knowledge is useful because challenging ethical issues require the mastery of moral reasoning. While conventional skills (interpersonal, legal compliance) will always be important for those in public service, principled reasoning is critical when confronting the perplexing "right vs. right" decisions (see Brousseau 1998) that are so frequently encountered today. Table 1.1 outlines a model of ethical decision making.

An aptitude for moral reasoning and ethical decision making depends on the ability to identify ethics-related conflicts. It is important to distinguish between an ethical problem and an ethical conflict. An ethical problem involves "a situation with ethical content, requiring individual choices," while an ethical conflict entails "dissonances among principles of right (do good) or among principles of wrong (cause no harm)" (Wartick and Wood 1998, 119). Thus, an example of an ethical problem might be a contemplated action that is right or wrong ("Should I embellish my accomplishments by unfairly claiming credit for my colleagues' successes and blaming others for my own failures?"). An ethical conflict, by contrast, is more difficult and could involve competing principles of right action (refraining from sharing privileged information vs. refraining from doing harm to others), when, for instance, failing to share the information results in avoidable harm (Lewis 1998). A second distinction is between internal and external ethics conflicts. While an internal conflict exists inside a person's head ("Should I or should I not apply this or that principle or take this or that action?"), an external conflict occurs between two or more persons who disagree about an ethical issue ("I disagree with you that the action I am taking is unethical").

Assessment skills also are needed to recognize and analyze the ethical issues found in particular settings. It is important not only to distinguish the ethical dimensions of a situation from other overlapping considerations (e.g., legal, economic, technical), but also to weigh a variety of appropriate alternatives and their likely consequences. When conflicts are simple and straightforward, basic skills may be sufficient, but for complex cases advanced skills are needed. Here intuition, luck, and surface knowledge will not be sufficient to resolve tough dilemmas; professional training and development are imperative. It is also useful to have ethics resources available (e.g., ombudsperson, ethics committee, hotline).

Another skill is the ability to say "no" when asked to do something unethical. This is not always as simple as it sounds. It is difficult to tell a superior that his or her instructions cannot be carried out because they may be unethical. It takes a secure person who is aware of his or her core values to refuse to engage in dubious acts. Empirical evidence shows that those exposed to coursework in ethics are better able to withstand pressure from superiors to engage in untoward acts (e.g., Jurkiewicz and Nichols 2002). Dennis Thompson provides wise counsel to public servants by identifying three paradoxes of ethics:

- Because other issues are more important than ethics, ethics is more important than any issue. The central importance of ethics is a precondition for good government and a way to maintain or restore citizen confidence.
- Private virtue is not necessarily public virtue. This paradox distinguishes between personal morality and political ethics, cautioning that those in public life must conform to more restrictive standards of behavior (e.g., financial disclosure, post-employment restrictions).
- Appearances are just as important in public service as underlying reality because of the crucial role played by trust in public life. Those seeking to build public trust, ensure compliance, and make prudent decisions need to avoid actions that are, or could be perceived to be, unethical. Headline scandals illustrate the salience of ethical decision making, the distinction between private and public virtue, and the importance of appearances (Thompson 1998, 255–257).

Finally, ethical theory can provide insights that help guide actions. If higher order moral reasoning skills are important, then knowledge of ethical theory (e.g., consequentialist vs. nonconsequentialist or principle-based vs. casuistic) is crucial to resolving those complex ethical conflicts that call upon advanced skills. Contextual knowledge can also be helpful. For example, professionals working in health care should be knowledgeable about bioethical issues (informed consent, confidentiality), the clinical setting, institutional characteristics (structure, policies, services, resources), beliefs and practices of patients and staff, as well as relevant ethics codes and laws that might impinge on decisions (see Aulisio, Arnold, and Youngner 2000). Professional associations such as the American Society for Public Administration (ASPA) and the Council for Excellence in Government have developed general ethical principles for public servants. Familiarity with moral values, principles, and development, as well as ethical theories, codes, and practices, can help professionals think through and hopefully resolve the mind-bending dilemmas found in today's work environment. Improved ethical decision making can help to restore citizen confidence and trust in public service.

The Leadership Competency

Leadership defines the third point of the Competencies Triangle. The shift in the environment of public service from hierarchical, bureaucratic, government-run programs to networks of goods and service providers in the public, private, and nonprofit sectors demonstrates the need for new forms of leadership. Top-down, command-and-control styles, while not necessarily a thing of the past, are gradually giving way to collaborative approaches to shared leadership. Leaders need skills in assessment, negotiation, and change management, and these skills can be learned. Regina Blackstone, mentioned at the beginning of this chapter, had the technical expertise required for her research position, but was thrust into a leadership position that called for skills that she had not yet developed. Leaders of the new public service, such as Regina once she has retooled, will be able to accurately assess, effectively negotiate, and creatively manage change.

Chapter 4 analyzes five components of the leadership competency: assessment and goal setting, hard and soft management skills combined with personality traits, management styles, political and negotiation skills, and evaluation of personal and organizational behavior. Highlighted here are four specific examples of hard (goal-oriented) and soft (process-oriented) leadership skills: (1) the hard skill of organizational and systems management, and the soft skills of (2) communication (3) negotiation, and (4) symbolic leadership. Organizational and systems management require hard skills in the areas of budgeting, information systems, human resource administration, and planning processes. It is crucial that professionals understand the functioning of the various systems that constitute the multisectoral, interorganizational, and multijurisdictional environment in which they operate. The coordination of these systems, which requires integrated adjustments, ensures order and organizational continuity; system dysfunctions can lead to serious service breakdowns. Leaders need not be technical experts in budgeting, IT, human resources, or planning, but they must understand how decisions are made and services are provided. The network arrangements of the new public service, which often comprise informal project teams, prove especially challenging; leaders must have the assessment skills to identify responsibility for decision making and the managerial acumen to diagnose problems and make things happen in these multidimensional work environments.

Next, some leaders are adept at dealing with systems, but have a serious deficiency in the soft skill of communication, which is crucial to fostering productive interpersonal relations and cooperative participation in shared goals. Indeed, according to Jeffrey Neal, a respected human resource professional at the Defense Logistics Agency, "the so-called 'soft' skills are really the hard skills. They are part of the ethical requirement of being a good supervisor" (Bilmes and Gould, 2009, 73). Leadership involves facilitating cooperation, mediating among conflicting interests, and resolving conflicts, thereby putting a premium on persuasive powers, people skills, the ability to inspire confidence, and knowledge of how to promote consensus and collaboration.

No longer can leaders outside of military and paramilitary settings expect to issue orders to subordinates in a command hierarchy who then immediately comply. They must be mindful of amassing facts, articulating goals, working effectively with a range of stakeholders, inspiring trust, cajoling, and embracing public involvement.

Third, the importance of political and negotiation skills cannot be overstated. It is imperative that leaders, whether working alone or with others, be adept at bargaining, competitive resource acquisition, stakeholder relations, and conflict resolution competencies. Good interpersonal abilities can help in gaining consensus and managing change, but conflict is inevitable when stakes are high and resources are scarce. Knowledge of alternative dispute resolution techniques is often required to resolve conflicts over priorities and strategies and to forge consensus. Facilitative leadership by politically savvy public servants is a glaring need when building alliances, coalitions, and networks with prominent actors and interest groups. Leaders must use their political abilities both within their organizations and in dealings with those outside their institutions if they are to be effective change managers.

Finally, symbolic skills buttress knowledge of systems, people, and politics (Bolman and Deal 2008). These include vision, knowledge of both human organizational cultures, awareness of institutional routines, and cultivation of collective identity. Leaders need to provide clarity of direction, cultivate shared vision, and evoke inspiration from others. Chances of success increase as they become better informed about the various decision-making processes in collaborating organizations, the values and interests of key stakeholders, the standard operating procedures of relevant institutions, and the extent of employee loyalty and commitment to organizational routines and goals. This requires familiarity with changes occurring in public service because government is privatizing and significant segments of the private sector are "governmentalizing" (Kettl 2000). Unlike the old public service where knowledge of one's own organization—its routines, standard operating procedures, and culture—was often sufficient for success, the new public service requires a broader awareness of collaborating partners operating in different settings.

Government leaders are crucial to effective public service. Bilmes and Gould (2009, 102–103) identify several unique challenges facing these officials. Unlike business leaders, who often enjoy considerable autonomy in decision making, public administrators are subject not only to the authority of Congress and the executive branch, whose members sometimes give conflicting direction regarding spending and service delivery, but also to the courts, which constrain and guide officials' actions, and to internal agency actors, including political appointees, civil servants, and program managers, who influence policy implementation. Government leaders are mandated to serve diverse constituencies in an equitable manner, but in contrast to their corporate counterparts, they often have little control over selecting the people they serve. Their performance objectives and measures are often ambiguous, making accountability difficult, and they are often hampered by a lack of good information or restrictions on sharing it. Further, public leaders have less latitude and discretion than business leaders in seeking to achieve results; their decisions and actions are constantly scrutinized by multiple stakeholders, who often have conflicting perspectives, and by members of the media, who frequently make judgments based on short-term political assessments rather than on longer-term program accomplishments. Effective leadership in today's public service environment requires recognition of sector differences and the development of skill-sets that differ from those that may have been suited more toward a traditional hierarchical bureaucracy.

While there are significant leadership challenges unique to government, in a networked environment it is important to cultivate analytical, technical, and managerial competencies that are common to both public and private sector work. Donahue (2009) emphasizes the need to harness the flexibility and creativity of the private sector to assist in producing public value. One way to do this, he suggests, is to encourage cross-sectoral collaboration and movement of personnel. He decries the habit of disparaging government workers, but recognizes the need to improve the image of public service if it is to attract the best and brightest. Increasing the pay and prestige of government service might make cross-sectoral careers—a portion of an individual's work life in government and another in the private or nonprofit sphere—more attractive to the ablest Generation Xers and Millennials. This would be more realistic, Donahue points out, if public sector recruitment and hiring were less cumbersome and if business schools and public policy and administration programs were to emphasize skill requirements common to both arenas so as to prepare students for mixed-sector career paths. Cross-sector collaboration, in Donahue's view, would require those in government to "understand both private motives and private capabilities, and to deploy incentives and influence to focus private energies on public missions" (163).

The leadership challenges and skills addressed here barely scratch the surface. A former cabinet officer, Donna Shalala, provides additional insights in her top ten lessons for managing a complex public bureaucracy. A number of these are relevant for work in any sector: know the culture of the organization, choose the best and let them do their job, stitch together a loyal team, stand up and fight for the people who work for you, set priorities and stick with them, look for allies where you do not expect to find them, and do not expect to win every time (Shalala 1998, 284–289). Other important skills involve managing for results, facilitating personal and professional growth, and emphasizing citizen service. The chapters that follow will address some of these in greater depth.

Conclusion

The only sure constant in today's environment is rapid change. This fast-paced change poses new challenges for public service. It is no longer acceptable to rely unduly on bureaucratic machines, hoard knowledge at the top, and dispense instructions to those lower in the hierarchy to be carried out by protected employees engaged in preestablished routines. This formalistic, static, state-centric approach is outmoded and ineffective in an era of dynamic change. Earlier meanings of public service need reformulation. Hierarchically based merit systems are gradually giving way to decentralized performance-oriented evaluations. The advent of networks and public-private partnerships has broadened the locus, focus, and skills required of professionals.

Tensions resulting from the interplay of politics and professionalism have ebbed and flowed from the earliest development of public service to the present. Fitness for public service, partisan spoils, and merit have each been ascendant as a criterion for government staffing during different historical periods. The transition from the old to the new public service continues to witness this tension. Political appointees as "citizen servants" work alongside career professionals and both groups collaborate in partnerships with nongovernmental public servants. While political-professional tensions have not abated, indirect or "third party" government puts a premium on politically sophisticated and professionally qualified public servants.

The consummate professional in today's public service must acquire the skills that make up technical, ethical, and leadership competencies. Technical competence helps public servants make correct decisions; ethical competence leads them to make good decisions. Leadership is needed to compel others to do the same by harnessing the energies of disparate service providers and orchestrating their efforts to advance the public interest. Citizens will be well served by public servants who possess these skills in rich abundance. However, having the right skill set alone does not capture the essence of public service: a commitment to making a difference in the lives of citizens, upholding democratic values, and demonstrating compassion in service to others. Anthropologist Margaret Mead (2001) said it well: "Never doubt that a small group of committed people can change the world; indeed, it is the only thing that ever has." The following chapters assume that competencies, as important as they are, must be buttressed by a deep and abiding commitment to work for the good of all citizens.

Figure 2.1 **The Competency Triangle of Public Service Professionalism**

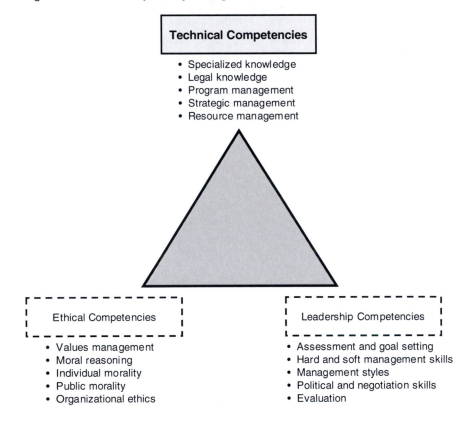

Technical Competencies

- Specialized knowledge
- Legal knowledge
- Program management
- Strategic management
- Resource management

Ethical Competencies

Leadership Competencies

- Values management
- Moral reasoning
- Individual morality
- Public morality
- Organizational ethics

- Assessment and goal setting
- Hard and soft management skills
- Management styles
- Political and negotiation skills
- Evaluation

Chapter 2

The Technical Professional
Developing Expertise

Practice does not make perfect. Only perfect practice makes perfect.
—Vince Lombardi

Technical expertise is a hallmark of public service professionalism. Citizens and employees expect service providers and their managers to be skilled in doing their jobs. If the task is to offer child welfare services, then counselors must understand which types of interventions are most effective and appropriately implemented, how to use resources efficiently, and how to deal with inevitable problems when treatments go awry. Because stakeholders demand high levels of technical skill, administrators should be exemplars of excellence. Members of the Senior Executive Service (SES) were recently asked: "What is the percentage of your current work that you consider to be of a technical/professional nature?" Survey results showed that in nearly nine out of ten agencies, on average, a majority (88 percent) of the work is technical (U.S. Office of Personnel Management (OPM) 2008d).

This chapter discusses the technical competency skills that are required to excel in public service. It begins with skills related to knowledge in a specialized field and the field's legal environment and then turns to expertise in program and organizational management, strategic planning, and resource management, focusing on finances, personnel, and information. Central to all of these components is education. Technical competency successes, failures, and conundrums are illustrated through examples such as the space shuttle *Columbia* calamity, terrorist attack challenges, U.S. Department of Homeland Security missions, strategic planning problems, and unconventional organizational methods.

Technical Expertise

Technical expertise includes the scientific knowledge necessary to perform a task (how to ensure safe drinking water), an understanding of the legal requirements related to one's field of expertise (how a city government secures bids to contract out water services), and the institutional savvy necessary to attain objectives (how to find ways to purchase the best and most cost-effective computers to monitor water quality).

Scientific mastery is critical because most services (e.g., road construction, emergency management, public health, and information technology) are built on such knowledge. Although many managers do not have a technical background, they must have a sufficient overall awareness of the technical aspects of their job to know how to identify those who can bring expertise to bear. Detailed knowledge of legal requirements is also essential because laws and regulations establish program standards and guidelines for conduct; they dictate the importance of treating citizens and employees fairly and may specify steps to be taken (e.g., investigating an employee or citizen complaint). The use of litigation and mediation methods to settle differences further increases the importance of understanding the legal environment surrounding one's field of work.

Finally, technical management skills involve knowing how to accomplish tasks inside an organization, especially program management, strategic planning, and resource management. To attain their goals, government agencies, nonprofit organizations, and businesses employ formal and informal procedures, from buying equipment to getting a definitive answer on a new proposal. Knowledge of organizational procedures, including past practices, is crucial for public service professionals because knowing why departments have operated a certain way in the past can enhance the efficient use of resources in the present, once the reasons for their use are rediscovered. On the other hand, managers must also know how to apply "best practices benchmarking" tools to assess whether past practices should be altered in order to improve operational efficiency and overall performance. Benchmarking is a comparison of the application of procedures and use of resources in one organization or agency with those of others, mostly within the same sector, but increasingly across sectors, to determine best practices. This process entails thinking outside the box or shifting organizational paradigms in order to enhance performance.

Managers must know how to apply these best practices to their own organizations, coping with potential psychological resistance to changes in the way "things have always been done" as well as overcoming operational hurdles when introducing new procedures. Benchmarking can dramatically improve strategic planning processes and delivery of services when it is properly and creatively applied. It was a central feature of the Clinton-Gore National Performance Review and GPRA of the 1990s (Chapter 1), when government agencies embarked on a cross-sectoral and intergovernmental benchmarking process to more effectively provide citizen services:

[G]overnment agencies are hard at work identifying how some of the best organizations, both public and private, listen to the voices of their customers. As part of this consortium benchmarking study, 17 federal agencies have collaborated with 13 corporations, two cities, a state, and a nonprofit organization to identify the best practices, technologies, and skills that can be used by the government to conduct strategic planning (Federal Benchmarking Consortium Team 1997).

Managers in the new public service will have to understand how to balance longstanding organizational cultures and procedures with new benchmarking techniques in order to maximize performance and establish the most productive relationships with their customers.

Technical competency, as defined by the skills highlighted in the three dimensions of scientific knowledge, legal acumen, and organizational management, is a defining feature of professionals. Administrators must have the technical skills to hire competent personnel, implement appropriate technology, understand how their subordinates work, and create financially sound programs. They need to plan program activities, build support from stakeholders, and anticipate opposition. Those who have these talents are positioned to ensure that programs flourish and impact communities productively. Knowing, adhering to, and applying scientific, legal, and organizational technical skills gives public servants a professional edge in achieving success and leaving their mark on the commonweal.

The Road to Expertise

Education continues to play a valuable role in developing the crucial baseline necessary to acquire a professional level of technical and legal knowledge and the management skills essential to making that knowledge bear fruit. It offers exposure to the following:

- Relevant social and political trends
- The technical language of a field of expertise
- The range of professional skills and standards in a area of expertise
- Alternative perspectives on issues and problem solving
- Ethical norms

Yet education can do no more than introduce a vocation. It is impossible to replace the hands-on, capacity-building, and character-forming experiences that are found on the job (Bok 1986; Bloom 1988). Thus, for many, the process of acquiring professional-grade knowledge is at least a four-year journey: two years in graduate school to acquire specific skills and knowledge and two in practice to hone targeted abilities.

Indeed, most professions resemble a craft in which knowledge and skills are gained through practice with support of others proficient in the field. Consider the following comment from a recent graduate, looking back:

> Well, I know that higher education doesn't cover everything. Overall I'd say that the knowledge, however gained, was very important. It provided the basis for some things I did after that, and it qualified me for better jobs. But it is true that there was a lot that was not covered in class. From others or sometimes just by figuring things out on my own, I had to learn many things to make my job work. I also had a few people who really helped me and, without them, well, I doubt things would have worked as well as they did.

Education seldom provides this kind of comprehension and most university internships are too short-term to develop genuine expertise.

More in-depth exposure is provided by postgraduate job experiences, many of which entail unguided, on-the-job experience rather than formal training. Those who expect such "advanced training" may be disappointed. Even if on-site professional handbooks describing procedures and standards are available, for example, they may be too voluminous to comprehend, too vague in regard to which standards apply to specific tasks, or even out of date. Employees do well to take an individualized, proactive approach to developing the technical knowledge and skills they need to excel. Seeking out a well-regarded mentor (such as an experienced employee or manager) can be a significant step in one's career (Facer et al. 2008). Mentors work closely with new employees or interns to help them assimilate relevant organizational values, negotiate interpersonal conflicts, overcome technical challenges, and become productive employees. Table 2.1 presents ideas on how to develop a mentorship program and Emerson (2003) provides a description of the U.S. Department of Labor program.

There has been an explosion of both hands-on and cyberspace mentoring programs in the last decade as educational institutions, companies, state governments, and federal agencies have begun to realize the benefits of mentoring. A recent survey of the federal Senior Executive Service asked: "Since becoming a member of the SES, have you had a mentor advising you for developmental purposes?" One in five said that they had received such advice. Over a third (37.4 percent) of SES members in the National Regulatory Commission received such advice, but only 4 percent in the Small Business Administration had mentors (U.S. OPM 2008d). The *Mentoring*

Table 2.1

Mentoring Program Components

Component	Specific Elements
1. Statement of purpose and a long-range plan	Details about activities to be performed; input from stakeholders; needs assessment; operational plan; goals, objectives, timelines, funding.
2. Recruitment plan for both mentors and participants	Assessment of expectations and benefits; marketing and public relations; needs-based targeted outreach; volunteer opportunities; link to program's statement of purpose.
3. Orientation for mentors and participants	Program review; eligibility description; screening process and suitability requirements; level and type of expected commitment; accountability requirements; expected rewards; and targeted focus.
4. Eligibility screening for mentors and participants	Application and review process; interviews; reference checks for mentors (e.g., child abuse registry, driving record, and criminal record checks where legally permissible); review of suitability criteria; pre-match training and orientation.
5. Readiness and training curriculum for all mentors and participants	Training staff; orientation to program and resource network; cultural sensitivity training, job and role descriptions; guidelines; confidentiality and liability information crisis management/problem-solving resources; communications skills development; ongoing sessions
6. Matching strategy	Link to program's statement of purpose; commitment to consistency; grounding in program eligibility criteria; rationale; pre-match social activities between mentor and participant pools, team-building activities.
7. Monitoring process	Meetings with staff, mentors, and participants; ongoing tracking activities; written record, input from relevant stakeholders; grievance mechanism.
8. Support, recognition, and retention activities	Formal kickoff event; ongoing peer support groups for volunteers and participants; ongoing training; issue discussions; networking; social gatherings; annual recognition and appreciation event.
9. Closure steps	Confidential debriefing exit interviews: participant and staff, mentor and staff, mentor and participant without staff; clearly stated policy for future contracts; assistance for participants in defining future steps to attain goals.
10. Evaluation process	Outcome analysis of program and relationship; assessment of program criteria and statement of purpose; stakeholders' information requirements.

Source: Adapted from National Mentoring Partnership 2008.

Handbook of the U.S. Department of Transportations's (DOT) Department of Human Resource Management highlights the benefits of mentoring to the mentee (opportunity to express new ideas and frustrations, smoother transition into the workforce, quicker adjustment to DOT culture, chance to work on challenging and interesting projects), as well as to the Department (gains a well-rounded employee with expanded skills, prevents employee career stagnation, creates a continuity of organizational culture, encourages employee loyalty, increases the chance that DOT will retain quality employees in an era of career mobility (U.S. DOT 2009). The U.S. Air War College has identified mentoring as a "fundamental responsibility of all Air Force supervisors" (U.S. Air War College 2009), and the state of California has developed a statewide professional mentoring program for dietitians based on six steps to match those with advanced skills with those seeking to develop those skills (Schatz et al. 2003). Those who make an active effort to find mentors and to further all forms of their educational and professional development may find more success than those who adopt a passive and reactive stance.

This activist posture positively affects the three areas of technical expertise (scientific, legal, organizational). Engineers need to know how to build actual bridges and counselors need to know how to deal with real client problems. Answers to questions such as "What approach works best, and why?" may be found through mentors and colleagues as well as by immersion in the specialized literature and professional association networking. Professionals who take responsibility for their careers seek out challenges and create opportunities to expand their experience and make an impact. A proactive stance also helps professionals acquire legal and institutional knowledge. Rules and regulations are necessary to ensure compliance and limit liability (Exhibit 2.1).

Organizations tend to be unforgiving of those who break rules, but it is sometimes unclear which rules are important and what it takes to excel (as well as to avoid trouble). Administrators must know, as a case in point, which questions they are allowed to ask job applicants and which are illegal (Exhibit 2.2).

Institutional wisdom comes from experience, which requires time and determination. Because a majority of senior managers in the federal government soon will be eligible for retirement, a valuable knowledge base will erode, competence levels may decline, and opportunities for corruption could increase. Finding ways to retain organizational memory will be crucial, and bringing back retirees to advise and mentor new employees may prove incomparably useful. Indeed, each of the three types of technical expertise may already be at risk, as indicated by the 2003 *Columbia* shuttle tragedy (Exhibit 2.3).

Exhibit 2.1

Technical Expertise: Legal Knowledge

Law is fundamental to professional proficiency. It sets out basic values or principles that society must follow (e.g., treating individuals with dignity); provides protections and assurances that help get the job done (e.g., assisting in contract enforcement); dictates how managers conduct their job (e.g., receiving three bids from vendors); and furnishes due process rights that managers are required to recognize (e.g., protecting employees from arbitrary administrative actions).

Professionals should adopt both broad and narrow perspectives on the law. The broad view focuses on inspirational purposes that provide guiding principles, norms, and values. The narrow view helps managers understand specific legal requirements, how to avoid legal entanglements, and how to prevail in those that cannot be avoided. Both perspectives are essential. Understanding the spirit of the law enables professionals to move forward when the law is unclear and encourages them to refrain from searching for technical loopholes. Yet the broad view alone may be insufficient because professionals must know and follow specific rules and regulations.

The following are some values that are embodied in laws:

- Respect for the rule of law
- Respect for the freedom of others to pursue their interests and beliefs
- Good faith in the pursuit of all activities
- Fairness
- Accountability for actions
- Respect for human dignity (see also American Bar Association Model Rules of Professional Conduct in Windt et al. 1989).

Not surprisingly, this list reflects widely held values in American society, since law tends to reflect social norms.

But specific knowledge of the law and related actions are also important. No one wants to become embroiled in legal controversies, yet the potential is clear when dealing with issues such as employee performance, supervisory discrimination, contract enforcement, service delivery, access to public information, and contract bidding.

Professionals, then, should expect to deal with legal matters sometime during the course of their careers. Accordingly, it is prudent to be familiar with statutes and cases that have been applied to one's organization (e.g.,

(continued)

Exhibit 2.1 *(continued)*

citizen eligibility for program participation, personnel administration issues, regulatory and licensing procedures) as well as new laws and court decisions that affect citizen, employee, and organizational rights. Furthermore, professionals must ensure that administrative procedures are scrupulously followed (failure to do so risks due process violations) and that supervisors act to prevent and correct violations by subordinates. They seek legal counsel before taking action and investigate the availability of agency and/ or private professional practice insurance (Wise 1996). Generally, there are two types of justice: procedural (due process) and distributive (fair outcome). Ensuring that people are treated fairly enhances the probability that the result will also be fair.

Incorporating the legal dimension into work provides better information and skills to protect the rights of citizens, employees, and professionals and to achieve institutional goals while reducing susceptibility to lawsuits. As Wise points out, "courts have not excused administrators from having to know the judicial interpretations applied to various aspects of administering public programs" (1996, 731). Quite apart from legal obligations, public service professionals need to represent the highest values of the nation.

A substantial body of literature discusses a legal system that "is not consistent across levels of government, and is not consistently defined for different governmental sectors nor for different types of public officials" (Wise 1996, 713). Sources that provide general overviews are available (e.g., www.law.emory.edu/erd/index.html; www.nolo.com/), as well as those that deal with specific topics such as liability (Wise 1996; DiNome, Yaklin, and Rosenbloom 1999) and personnel management (Rainey 1997; DelPo and Guerin 2003). HR.com's eBulletin examines a wide range of current issues, such as pending and recent legislation, case studies, and labor relations. *The Lawsuit Survival Guide* (Matthews 2003) may also be useful.

To sum up, technical expertise requires scientific knowledge, legal acumen, and organizational management skills, and the process of achieving this level of specialization requires graduate education as well as on-the-job experience. Statistics emphasize the importance of education and training in the civil service: "Nationally, 50 percent of government jobs are in occupations requiring specialized training, education, and job skills, compared to just 29 percent in the private sector" (Walters 2002, 8).

Exhibit 2.2

Discerning Between Legal and Illegal Questions

Knowledge of employment law is an important technical requirement. Managers at all levels frequently conduct job interviews. Because there are many questions that are not appropriate to ask during an interview, knowledge of employment law is an important technical skill.

Half of the questions listed below may be asked legally; the other half may not. Read the questions carefully and determine which are legal and which are not. Circle L for "legal" or I for "illegal." Correct answers appear in the footnote below. .

1. Have you served in the armed forces before?   L I
2. Do you have or plan to have children?   L I
3. What days are you available to work?   L I
4. Are you willing to work the required 10 hours per day, 4
   days per week?   L I
5. Do you have any disabilities?   L I
6. Is your spouse employed?   L I
7. If hired, can you furnish proof of age?   L I
8. Have you ever been disciplined for your behavior at work?   L I
9. Have you had any recent or past illnesses or operations?   L I
10. Have you worked for this organization under a different name?   L I
11. How much longer do you intend to work before you retire?   L I
12. Who referred you for a position here?   L I
13. What arrangements have you made for child care?   L I
14. How would you perform this particular task?   L I
15. How tall are you?   L I
16. If you get pregnant, will you continue to work? Will you
    come back after maternity leave?   L I
17. How long have you lived in [name of city]?   L I
18. You'll be required to travel or work overtime on short
    notice. Is this a problem for you?   L I
19. Have you been arrested?   L I
20. How many days of work did you miss last year?   L I
21. Of what country are you a citizen?   L I
22. Have you ever filed or threatened to file discrimination charges? L I

Source: Adapted from HR World 2007; MTU 2009.

Note: The following interview questions can be asked: 1, 3, 4, 7, 8, 10, 12, 14, 17, 18, and 20. The questions that cannot be asked are: 2, 5, 6, 9, 11, 13, 15, 16, 19, 21, and 22.

Exhibit 2.3

Technical Expertise, NASA, and the *Columbia* Catastrophe

The U.S. National Aeronautics and Space Administration (NASA) created its $25 billion space shuttle program in the 1970s, as the successor to America's moon-landing feats. The viability of the program relied on relatively low operating costs, which offset high development costs. It also set unrealistically high goals of as many as sixty flights a year. Almost from the start, the shuttle program was plagued by design failures, cost overruns, delays, fraud, and mismanagement within NASA and among its network contractors.

Many problems were hidden from the public until 1986, when the shuttle *Challenger* exploded during reentry over Texas. Faulty welds, which a subcontractor had concealed by falsifying X-rays in order to avoid repair costs, went undetected until auditors received tips from former employees. Investigators learned that NASA had cut corners on safety testing, design, and development almost from the time the program began. This was a far cry from the earlier *Apollo* program, in which each component had been designed, built as a prototype, and tested. By the time an *Apollo* spacecraft was assembled for a test, researchers and engineers were confident that it would be safe.

The space shuttles were built under much less stringent processes. To save money, major components and systems were built before they were fully tested. Over time, there were reductions in the number of inspectors and so problems with critical equipment were often not detected. In the swirl of investigations that followed the *Challenger* disaster, it was learned that NASA had misled Congress about costs and schedules, had withheld critical documents, and had violated federal codes in many instances. Billions of dollars had been misspent. It was discovered that between 1977 and 1979 NASA engineers had warned that O-ring joints of the shuttle's solid fuel rocket boosters were faulty. The agency had done nothing to correct this. Even after the discovery of the O-ring problem that followed the *Challenger* disaster, similar problems were observed with the later shuttles. In addition, shuttle program participants had been worried for years about problems with the silica tiles that cover the vehicles. Defects in these tiles apparently caused the 2003 explosion.

Tight budgets and poor planning continue to be a major cause of technical problems. Other problems are the result of an aging workforce, insufficient management, and the increasing complexity of projects. In 20 of 28

(continued)

Exhibit 2.3 *(continued)*

missions, the space shuttle *Columbia* experienced mechanical or technical problems that led to more flight delays than for any other orbiter. Since *Columbia* was the oldest of these spacecraft, NASA relaxed maintenance standards. But in spite of numerous studies that have pointed to systemic flaws in the shuttle program, NASA continues to deny that safety measures and quality control has slipped.

There are plans to retire the shuttle program in 2010, which causes concern among some that there would no longer be an "American way" to reach the international space station.

Sources: Adapted from McFadden 2003 and Flaherty et al. 2003; see also Columbia Accident Investigation Board 2003 for withering criticism of three decades of failure to reconcile the cost, schedule, and safety goals of NASA.

Technical Management Skills

Administrators cannot be entrusted with multimillion-dollar programs unless they are practiced in the tools and techniques of the profession. The stakes are simply too high, and the public too skeptical. Accordingly, key skills—strategic planning, program management, and resource management (financial, human, information)–are briefly reviewed below. These tools are expected to be used in ways that are compatible with contemporary values such as citizen service, openness and accountability, and high productivity (Holzer and Callahan 1998; Stenberg and Lipman 2007; Berman 2006).

Strategic Planning

An organization is the structure through which goals are accomplished. To organize is to determine the relationship of people or departments to each other (i.e., who is responsible to whom, and for what?). To plan is to decide what gets done. It also involves determining which people or departments are best positioned to ensure that work is accomplished and providing them with the necessary resources. These are daunting tasks, as shown in two cases involving domestic security.

Few managers have the opportunity to design a large agency de novo. In the aftermath of the 9/11 terrorist attacks, the Transportation Security Agency, with 70,000 employees, was quickly created to ensure air travel safety. Deciding which departments—and the interrelationships among them—should meet multitudinous objectives was a substantial task. Even after planning and goal setting, formidable questions remained: How will technology needs be met? What sources of intelligence will be used and how will they be coordinated? How can cooperation with foreign governments be achieved? Similar questions pertained to the Department of Homeland Security (DHS), which was established a year later. The agency, with a staff of more than 170,000, is composed of more than twenty preexisting departments (totaling eighty personnel and pay systems), each with its own organizational culture. Many employees were concerned about losing their jobs, taking pay cuts, and having no protection against partisan pressures—one-third of all federal personnel considered leaving government (Kaufman 2003). Only the future will tell whether this "ultimate management challenge" (Blair 2002) will produce a cohesive department that can secure the nation's borders and transportation infrastructure. In 2003, five senators released a report card on the DHS, giving it a grade of D+ in meeting its goals (Mintz 2003) and others have critiqued DHS reforms (Underhill and Oman 2007).

The crux of planning is to identify goals and resources, and to ascertain how and when resources are used to accomplish objectives. Strategic planning is a technique used to define the major purposes and specific activities of an organization (Bryson 1995; Kaye and Allison 1997; Berman 2006). Such planning can be undertaken by just a few managers, or used to solicit the input of hundreds of employees, thereby increasing openness and shared decision making. It is a stepwise process that first requires organizations to define their mission (what is our purpose?) and vision (what do we want to become?). Then, institutions take inventory of major defining challenges and opportunities in their environment, as well as the unique strengths and weaknesses that affect how well they can respond. Against this information, goals are put forward and selected that best further the mission and respond to the challenges and opportunities identified. Finally, to attain articulated goals, agencies establish specific objectives and devise workable strategies to achieve them. In sum, strategic planning is a process that clarifies the mission and provides specific strategies for achieving goals.

Such planning is an important, widely used technique. In the late 1990s, three-quarters of cities with populations over 50,000 utilized strategic planning in at least one of their departments within the previous twelve months (Berman and West 1998). Agency directors or senior managers usually direct the activity, but it involves many departments and offices. Units within the organization contribute information and frequently participate in strategic planning through employee teams. Many senior managers prefer a participatory process because it increases employee commitment and the quality of results. In local government strategic planning, community participation is just as important as employee involvement, as dramatically illustrated by the strategic planning process designed to revitalize the city of Benton Harbor in Michigan (Exhibit 2.4).

Goals sometimes remain undefined or underdefined, especially when legislatures enact broad guidelines without clarifying specific objectives or methods for attaining them (e.g., funding for social services to promote drug rehabilitation with no mention of specific types of services or performance levels to be achieved). Explicit goal setting is also crucial because agencies experience a plethora of competing—and conflicting—demands and priorities. Interest groups, citizens, other organizations, and elected officials are likely to express contradictory views and agencies must learn how to take these into account in the planning process. For example, should drug treatment programs target teenagers or working mothers? Should treatment centers be located in low- or high-income areas? Should faith-based therapeutic interventions be used? Should funds be shifted from prevention to rehabilitation—or the reverse? Should services be available to those outside the service area? Should they be privatized? The lack of a clear plan can lead to mission drift and goal displacement if objectives are not focused on the intended aim.

Sustainability is also crucial to the strategic planning process. Leaders and managers must consider the viability of their goals, both short-term (building a new bridge to alleviate traffic congestion) and long-term (a Big Dig project, such as in Boston, to modernize the transportation structure). Even if funds are available now to build a bridge, for instance, will future resources be sufficient to maintain repair and upgrade the structure in the years to come? In the case of long-term infrastructure projects, how will managers cope if builders go over budget? Are there sufficient numbers of trained emergency personnel to respond to building construction failures? Is available equipment up to code or will it need to be upgraded during the life of the project? A series of infrastructure and construction failures, such as the collapse of a major bridge in Minneapolis in 2007 and deadly building crane collapses in Houston, Oklahoma City, Quincy (Massachusetts), and New York City in 2008, illustrates the centrality of sustainability in the strategic planning process.

Planning is also affected by the availability or absence of resources, which greatly affects spending priorities. Managers have limited time and staff. They are responsible for many different aspects of their programs, such as personnel recruitment, quality control, interdepartmental coordination, and community relations. They have to plan a timeline and determine who will execute it. Macro-level planning, such as determining which sector—government, nonprofit, or commercial—can most efficiently and effectively provide a certain service, will be affected by policy-maker ideology, bureaucratic inertia, and

Exhibit 2.4

Community Strategic Planning

Benton Harbor is a small city along the shores of Lake Michigan. Its landscape includes acres of pristine sand dunes that are part of the Jean Klock public park and look out over the lake's sparkling waters, offering a peaceful setting for locals and tourists to enjoy recreational activities along the shore. . The dunes provide the only public access to the lake's shore in Benton Harbor.

By the early 2000s the beauty of the dunes was overshadowed by Benton Harbor's devastating economic decline, its postindustrial polluted wastelands, and violent racial tensions. Once a thriving manufacturing center anchored by the Whirlpool Corporation, Benton Harbor declined as companies either left the city or downsized their workforces. In 2000, half of all households with children were living below the poverty line. Retailers abandoned the city, drop-out and crime rates surged, and a cash-strapped and politically divided City Commission could not find the funds to support adequate police or firefighting units. African Americans made up almost 90 percent of a shrinking population that felt itself bereft of opportunities and support. In 2003, a black motorist was killed in a police chase and a week of riots ensued. Television reports showed rioters torching buildings and cars and throwing rocks and bricks at police and firefighters. The negative publicity seemed to seal the fate of an already demoralized city. Losing old businesses and unable to attract new ones, the population would continue to shrink, crime rates would continue to rise, and tourists would continue to shun Benton Harbor.

To turn the tide, Governor Jennifer Granholm created a task force comprised of local politicians, police, business leaders, and youths. The group was charged with preparing a community development plan that would spearhead a turnaround. The group worked diligently and produced a proposal to turn Benton Harbor into a community-oriented tourist center with amenities that would benefit residents. At the same time, the State of Michigan and the Whirlpool Corporation were developing their own strategic plan, called Harbor Shores, which focused more on high-end tourism geared toward out-of-state visitors. Both the S State and Whirlpool had a strong interest in transforming Benton Harbor from a postindustrial wasteland into a mecca for upper-income tourists. Whirlpool feared that it would not be able to convince executives and skilled workers to relocate to Benton Harbor.

(continued)

Exhibit 2.4 *(continued)*

Harbor Shores would develop 530 acres of land in and around Benton Harbor after ridding the land of waste and contaminated debris. The complex would include 860 residential units, a hotel/conference center, commercial and retail space, and—the cornerstone of the project—an eighteen-hole Jack Nicklaus signature golf course. Twenty-two of Jean Klock park's 73 acres, including the dunes with their spectacular view of Lake Michigan, would be given over to the deluxe golf course. In return, Harbor Shores would donate dozens of acres of land, much further from the lake, to the park, pay rent to the city for use of the parkland (in effect leasing the public land), and pay the park's maintenance expenses. In addition to generating millions of dollars in tax revenues and thousands of jobs, Harbor Shores promised community development through literacy programs, job training, housing renovation, and improved social services. The State contributed $120 million to the project, including tax credits and funds for environmental cleanup and road construction; Whirlpool contributed $12 million and land. The project was buttressed by a host of federal and state grants and official support at all levels of government, as well as by local congressional representatives and business leaders.

Because the project depended on public funding, Benton Harbor's City Commission had to approve it. In June 2005 the commissioners gave the go-ahead to proceed with Harbor Shores planning, even though some commissioners complained that detailed information had not been provided to the commission or the general public. Indeed, during the two-year initial planning phase, planners did not make an effort to engage the local community in discussions about Harbor Shores, seeming to ignore residents' efforts to devise a local-oriented development plan.

When the project's development plans were made public after the commission's vote, Benton Harbor residents saw for the first time that the dunes were to become part of the golf course. The dunes would still be "public," but would now be subject to high fees for access. Some residents and local community leaders were incensed. Fueling citizen anger was the history of the park. John Klock had donated the 73 acres to the City of Benton Harbor, stipulating that the land would always be open to its residents, to whom he had said, "This is your park; it belongs to you." Opponents to the Harbor Shores project were also frustrated that it had been presented to them as a fait accompli, with no public input or concerns solicited in the planning stages. Opposition groups sprang up in the city and many residents expressed their outrage to the city commission. Several of the nine city

(continued)

Exhibit 2.4 *(continued)*

commissioners either left the commission or were subject to recall votes as a result of the controversy.

At the same time, a review by the National Parks Service (NPS) put another spoke in the wheel of Harbor Shores. The NPS had to approve the project because of the transfer of public park land. Benton Harbor had received a $50,000 grant from the NPS in the 1970s to build bathing facilities at Jean Klock Park. A condition was that the park had to be used for public recreational purposes in perpetuity; conversion of park land would have to be matched by land of equal or greater value to the residents. In October 2005, the NPS refused Benton Harbor's proposal to lease the dunes to the Harbor Shores project, offering two reasons: failure to solicit public commentary on the plan and failure to compensate the park with land of equal value in exchange for the dunes.

Harbor Shores proponents were shocked, its opponents were mobilized into action, and the two camps engaged in a vociferous struggle. Supporters pointed to the plan's benefits: environmental clean-up, job creation, tourism revenue, an enhanced tax base for the city coffers, and the increased standard of living and social services for residents. Opponents argued that the city's poor residents would be excluded from enjoying the land that had been dedicated to them, that new jobs would be low-wage and temporary or seasonal, that the dunes would be enjoyed only by wealthy tourists, and that local businessmen and congressional representatives were concerned mostly with having a luxury golf course for themselves, in effect creating a class and, as some said, racial divide that relegated local residents to the status of menial laborers.

In the years since the controversy began, Harbor Shores planners and a newly constituted city commission rewrote the project proposal in consultation with park officials, solicited public feedback, and facilitated workshops attended by commissioners, local government staff, and residents. On June 9, 2008, the City Commission agreed to lease the dunes to the Harbor Shores project but only on condition of greater public input. The proposal was then sent to state authorities who would then decide whether or not to approve it and send it to the NPS for review. Many city residents continued to bitterly oppose the project even after the vote.

Five years after state and local business leaders developed the strategic plan, the local government and city residents made it clear that any master plan would rest in their hands. Lack of communication, failure to solicit public commentary and community input, and the subsequent perception of

(continued)

Exhibit 2.4 *(continued)*

lack of respect for residents' concerns wasted valuable time and potentially millions of dollars in income and services.

Exercise. Discuss the following: What technical skills—in terms of scientific, legal, and organizational expertise—come into play in this case? How would you evaluate the trade-offs between the benefits and drawbacks of the Harbor Shores project in terms of community development? What would likely have happened if planners had included public input and city commission involvement at the beginning of the planning? What role could ethical considerations and leadership skills play in the Benton Harbor controversy? What are the lessons here with regard to strategic planning?

Sources: Berrien County Community Development Department 2008; Dumke 2008; Governor's Benton Harbor Task Force 2003; Melzer, 2008.

shifting empirical evidence. Professionals must develop the planning skills to determine which sector has the resources necessary to attain goals and how to creatively utilize those resources to advance the common good.

Program Management

Planning is carried out at program and individual task levels. One useful tool in this process is a Gantt chart (Appendix 2.1), a timeline that specifies each activity of a program, tracks its progress, and notes when it is scheduled to finish. This timeline can span a few months to several years, depending on the nature of the project (Ammons 2002; Frame 2002; Berman 2006; Harrington 2006). It also shows the current status or phase of each project, insofar as some activities occur early in a project and others take place toward the end.

After managers articulate program goals and objectives and then identify the functions that are required to attain them (e.g., field support, scientific assessment, information technology management), they need to pose the following questions: Who is responsible for ensuring that each task is carried out and its goal realized? What support capabilities and resources must be at the ready for both planned and unplanned phases of the program? What is the quality and quantity of these resources? What kind of collaboration is needed between other programs and agencies? What adjustments may be required? In a homelessness program, by way of example, activities may include screening for health, applying for welfare assistance, placing clients in job-training programs, monitoring job searches, and searching for alternative funding sources if government funds dry up. Managers then determine whether functions (such as access to medical facilities for health screening), staffing (in terms of both quantity and quality), and resources (such as a database of clients) are available. Finally, synchronization between activities and personnel is required (a client's medical condition, for example, may affect her job search efforts).

External relations are often just as critical as internal organization. Programs must build and maintain support among stakeholders, funding organizations (including other governments), elected officials and boards, and the public. The homelessness program mentioned earlier must ensure that employers are willing to cooperate and that the community as a whole considers it effective. The challenge of program coordination is evidenced in federal environmental protection efforts: twenty-nine different agencies have responsibility for clean air, safe water, and solid waste management. Collaboration is a central feature of other programs as well: early childhood programs involve eleven agencies and twenty offices, economic development efforts are included in 342 programs, and job training appears in forty different programs (National Commission on the Public Service 2003). At the local level, emergency management responses to the 9/11 attacks illustrated the difficulty of coordination and the crucial importance of technical, in addition to ethical and leadership, competencies (Exhibit 2.5).

The significance of good organization cannot be overemphasized. Once a project is organized, it becomes possible to accomplish goals by determining how tasks get done, and how well they get done. Project employees depend upon one another to achieve mutual objectives. Because personal understandings and relationships tend to persist—regardless of outcomes—ongoing planning is important to reassessing the importance of different goals as well as finding leaders who can help people and their projects adjust to new needs.

Managers have basic tools to assist them in organizing. An organizational chart identifies functions, the people responsible for carrying them out, and lines of accountability. It may be a hierarchical pyramid, a matrix format (people or units reporting to more than one unit), or star-shaped (every unit reporting to the same center). It can also show working relationships among organizations. In any event, it is a telling reflection of management philosophies. Some agencies have traded in the traditional pyramid structure for a more domelike organizational chart that emphasizes internal communication and networking among various departments and levels of authority. These

Exhibit 2.5

9/11 and Local Emergency Management

Although the federal government is charged with heading up the response to large events such as wars and disasters, most crises are handled at the state and local levels. Indeed, just as New York City residents would normally call their local 911 number for fires, medical emergencies, and rescue needs, residents relied on their city government in the wake of the terrorist attacks on the World Trade Center on September 11, 2001. The tasks of response and recovery were immense after the buildings collapsed. They included the following:

- Setting up a remote command center; the planned hub of operations for emergencies had been inside the World Trade Center
- Restoring communication systems that had been ruptured by the attack
- Providing a sense of order amid the chaos of the catastrophe
- Securing the city from further aggression
- Evacuating tens of thousands of individuals, some injured, from inside the buildings and approximately half a million from lower Manhattan
- Discovering and removing dead bodies
- Setting up medical facilities for the injured and furnishing morgues for the dead
- Offering a vast array of disaster services, such as temporary housing, medicines, clothing, counseling, hotlines, and insurance and claims assistance
- Coordinating the efforts of a vast network of agencies, levels of government, and individuals

Despite the enormity of the events and setbacks—the horror of the acts of terrorism, the unprecedented collapse of super-skyscrapers, and the loss of the emergency command center itself—the city government responded heroically. Mayor Rudolf Guiliani acted as the chief local coordinator, the national communicator, and an individual comforter at countless funerals. Police Commissioner Bernard Kerik directed the successful evacuation efforts of lower Manhattan. Deputy Fire Chief Peter Hayden commanded the immediate evacuation of the twin towers after the loss of the Fire Chief. Together, they later commanded the cleanup of Ground Zero, where 1.2

(continued)

Exhibit 2.5 *(continued)*

million tons of debris was removed in fewer than four months. Transportation Commissioner Iris Weinshall and Transit Police Chief Michael Ansbro supervised transportation for the evacuation of the area.

Meanwhile, Governor George Pataki declared the site a disaster area and quickly got a federal disaster designation. The Federal Emergency Management Agency provided a door-to-door relief effort. Congressman Jerrold Nadler introduced the Public Safety Officer Benefit Program (to compensate the families of officers killed in the line of duty), which was signed into law in just three days. U.S. Senators Hillary Rodham Clinton and Charles Schumer negotiated federal access to $20 billion for local rescue and recovery efforts. These efforts were in support of local leadership, which so brilliantly rose to the occasion despite the enormity of the calamity and the extraordinary task of coordinating so many systems amid warlike conditions (Cohen, Eimicke, and Horan 2002).

The issues involved in preparing for 1known problems (e.g., cyclical acts of nature such as hurricanes and tornadoes) as well as for completely unforeseen crises (e.g., terrorist strikes or meteor crashes) are immense: stockpiling resources, coordinating specialists (e.g., medical, emergency response, public safety, and scientific personnel), and providing plans for coordinated response. These concerns supersede technical matters and present ethical and leadership challenges, such as preventing crises without wasting resources, maintaining a sense of urgency without creating panic, and responding to unanticipated dilemmas without violating democratic ideals.

networking grids support the dome (Figure 2.2) and encourage a more collaborative effort in attaining goals than a top-down pyramid organization.

A process flowchart specifies tasks, their duration, the persons involved, and the order of completion. In the past decade, reengineering, or the rethinking of process flows, has been applied to improve business, public, and nonprofit management (Linden 1995; Harrington 2006). Work can be designed so that citizens deal with a single point of contact—one-stop shopping programs—to reduce time and frustration. They require frontline employees to be empowered to deal with multiple aspects of the job and responsible for coordinating work. Increased use of information technology has also changed work processes, in large measure because data are available to more people who are then empowered to make decisions.

Finally, contracts with nonprofit and private organizations to perform work extend the organization beyond its formal boundaries by allowing managers

Figure 2.2   **Organizational Structures**

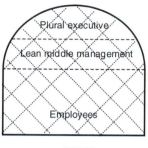

PYRAMID

- Hierarchical
- Single leader
- Dispersed information: Information flows from top to bottom
- Centralized decision making
- Highly delineated line and staff functions
- Emphasis on individual job performance

DOME*

- Internally networked
- Plural executive
- Plural information: Information flows along horizontal and vertical grids
- Decentralized decision making
- Coordination of line and staff activities
- Emphasis on teamwork

*Information on domed organizational structure from K. Harigopal 2006.

to draw on others to achieve goals. This does not release administrators from the responsibility of ensuring that the work is performed (Osborne and Plastrik 1998; Boris and Steurle 2006). Officials sometimes have advisory boards to foster community support. They also speak to local organizations to maintain such support and make sure that funding sources remain well informed.

Resource Stewardship: Finances, Personnel, and Information

Deciding what needs to be done, and then getting it done, is the essence of management. However, it is equally important to ensure that the resources necessary to get the job accomplished are readily at hand. Without money, people, and information—the acquisition of which requires considerable technical expertise—little will be achieved.

Finances

A budget is a statement about the level of resources available to each department or program during a particular period. The politics of budgeting is the process whereby departments, organizations, and/or policymakers negotiate requested funding; the practice of budgeting is as much about technical analysis (how to justify a proposed request) as it is about negotiating skills (how to acquire what is needed). The complexity of budgeting occurs not only because there are different types of budgets (for operating and capital expenses), but also because each year involves different budgets (planning for next year's expenditures, spending this year's allocations, and accounting for last year's outlays). In addition, managers rely on more than just allocation of general taxes to pay for programs; some depend on user fees, bonds, and/or grants from other organizations. State and local government agency directors thus require knowledge about creating special tax districts, such as community or downtown development, libraries, schools, water management, public health, or neighborhood beautification. Public organizations often write as many grants as nonprofit organizations. Clearly, professionals need to know about raising money as well as spending it.

Financing is closely related to accountability. People want to know (1) that dollars are being used as intended and (2) that they are getting something for their taxes. The former concern addresses issues of fraud and abuse; most public organizations have extensive controls and restrictions to ensure that spending is appropriate. Still, ethically questionable practices occur. For example, Orange County, California, invested some of its funds in high-risk stock market activities in the mid-1990s; when these investments turned sour and losses were exposed, the public was rightfully outraged. In Seminole County, Florida, tax collectors in 2002 provided knowledge of pending foreclosures to their friends and families, thus enabling the purchase of property deeds at very attractive prices. Such cases do not necessarily indicate legal wrongdoing, but they are morally dubious and highlight the need for vigilance.

Accountability for program outcomes is also a concern. Historically, most budgets accounted only for expenditures that were spent appropriately; now, budgets are often complemented by performance measures that detail specific program results (Coplin and Dwyer 2000; American Society for Public Administration 2000; Morgan et al. 2008). For example, a revenue program can gauge the number of taxpayers, those who pay, and those who should be penalized for not paying. These indicators can be compared over time and provide information to program managers and elected officials.

Personnel

Although people skills are often contrasted with technical skills, they also include technical knowledge. No matter how good one is in dealing with others (a judgment best made by someone else), employee relations provide scientific, legal, and institutional challenges in recruitment, training, compensation, evaluation, and termination, as well as employee rights and responsibilities (Berman et al. 2010).

Recruitment begins with a technical evaluation of the job opening to assess the nature of the position and determine appropriate compensation. This leads to a formal position description, including job responsibilities and the competencies required to carry them out. Job-related tests might be administered with careful attention to issues of validity (content, criterion-related, and construct) and reliability. The subsequent interview process focuses on the candidate's technical knowledge and past work experience; casual inquiries about matters that are not job-related may be discriminatory and should be avoided (e.g., asking about maiden names, religion, race, social clubs, arrest record, child care arrangements, credit history; see Exhibit 2.2). A final step involves reference and background checks, a process also infused with potential legal problems, such as character defamation and negligent hiring. Once a candidate is selected, training and development are important to ensure employee productivity. One problem occurs when technically proficient people are promoted to supervisory roles without appropriate training (Conlow et al. 2001; Belker 1997; Liff 2007); such supervisors may be deficient in required management skills.

Managing people also involves the technical skills of setting compensation rates, deciding on benefit packages, and evaluating employees. Employee compensation can be based on different philosophies reflecting employer beliefs that salaries should be below, at, or above market. Technical expertise in classifying jobs, setting compensation rates, compiling benefit packages, and conducting performance reviews is critical, especially since modern managers have become increasingly savvy about the legal rights of employees. When staff does not meet performance expectations and training does not lead to productivity improvements, "progressive discipline" begins with verbal suggestions for improvement followed by written reprimands. Providing substantiation is important because most career public employees have due process rights and cannot be terminated without just cause, and private sector workers can sue for wrongful discharge, that is, the employer violated an implied or written contract or public policy protecting employees refusing to do something that is illegal.

Finally, people have other rights as well, but these may be limited by the employer's right to workplace efficiency. For example, although citizens enjoy First Amendment freedom of speech rights, voicing dissatisfaction to the press without exhausting internal processes first may result in disciplinary action. Employees also have religious freedom, but they may be required to work on religious holidays. The right to privacy means that employers cannot intrude into their workers' private lives or work spaces but organizations can legally adopt policies that permit searches of all departmental property. Outside of the legal context of individual versus organizational rights and privileges, it is, of course, in the interest of organizations to make reasonable accommodations to their employees in order to maintain positive labor relations and encourage a productive workplace atmosphere.

Information

Public service professionals must be proficient in two types of information gathering, usage, and dissemination: inward-looking (that which is internal to the agency and designed to facilitate its organizational processes) and outward-looking (that which connects the department to customers, partners, and businesses). The former is central to all organizations; the latter has assumed special relevance in the field of public service, as federal, state, and local governments have introduced e-government initiatives to enhance communication between government and citizens (G2C), government and businesses (G2B) and different layers of government (G2G) (Coursey and Norris 2008, 535).

Employees must possess the necessary information to do their jobs and serve their organizations well. The need for effective information management is especially pronounced when multiple agencies and jurisdictions work together to administer programs (e.g., the management of environmental resources or the conduct of modern war; see Chapter 5). Decisions about which information should be shared are part of the planning and program management issues discussed earlier; they flow naturally from decisions about what gets done. But the management of the technical infrastructure for disseminating information is a relatively new function administered in some agencies. Indeed, multimillion-dollar (and sometimes billion-dollar) infrastructures must be professionally staffed. Many agencies now have a chief information officer who sets policies, advises agencies on investment decisions, and oversees staff, ensuring that the agency's networked systems are up-to-date and fully operational. The staff of central information technology departments also provides support to units and users who purchase and maintain equipment. This is a dynamic field: issues change quickly and range from system reliability, connectivity, and computer viruses to system access and data security. The only certainty is that future issues will be different and challenging, and thus demand professionals with the technical expertise to address them.

E-government—the use of the World Wide Web to provide governmental information and services to citizens—emerged in tandem with the federal "reinventing government" reforms of the Clinton-Gore administration in the mid-1990s (Tolbert, Mossberger, and McNeal 2008). Since then, federal, state, and local governments have made great strides in developing E-Government Web sites to both disseminate information and enhance citizen access to and interaction with agencies and programs. By 2008, 96.2 percent of local governments with a population of more than 10,000 had opened e-government sites, although the quality varies greatly (Coursey and Norris 2008).

At the dawn of this electronic information revolution, hopes were high that e-government might transform both the operation of government and the way it interacts with citizens. Research models predicted that this new form of information dissemination and interaction would increase citizen involvement with government representatives and agencies, enhance transparency in decision making, create a more responsive government, improve governmental efficiency and performance, and generate more trust on the part of the public in all layers of government (Coursey and Norris 2008; Rocheleau 2007; West 2005).

In some cases, research at the state level indicates that some e-government efforts have increased citizen involvement, lowered costs of public interaction with government, and helped civil servants discern their constituents' preferences (Robbins, Simonsen, and Feldman 2008). Other studies show that some local government initiatives are less successful at saving money or encouraging citizen participation (Coursey and Norris 2008). The federal government, for its part, has made a concerted effort to continue improving its Web-based information and interaction services, with the Office of Management and Budget spearheading e-government initiatives, performance management, and reporting of results expected to take hold in all federal departments and agencies (U.S. Office of Management and Budget 2009).

Initial enthusiasm concerning the transformational character of e-government has given way to more sober assessments of its progress and implications. Rather than replace governmental structures, e-government may just add another layer to the structure of government and assign another responsibility to employees (Rocheleau 2007; Coursey and Norris 2008). Of greater concern to reinforcement theorists is that e-government, far from promoting neutral dissemination of facts, will simply "support the interests of the dominant political-administrative coalitions within governmental organizations" (Coursey and Norris 2008, 533).

Whatever the case, managers will have to master the technical skill of implementing e-government (Hecks 2006) and managing what one author refers to as the "virtual State" (Garson 2006). As "e-government applications inevitably cross almost all departmental and organizational boundaries" (Rocheleau 2007, 586), professionals in the public service will have to be proficient in the technical aspects of virtual organization, as well as addressing concerns of the potential politicization of information. As with most technology, the implications of e-government depend upon the people who develop, promulgate, and decide how to use it. It is up to the professionals in the public service to ensure that it is used to promote genuinely public, and not narrowly political, interests.

Professional Technical Standards

Citizens expect public servants to be professional. This means, in part, that they have the technical knowledge to do their jobs effectively. Professionals need to have scientific skills, know legal rules and regulations, and understand institutional operations. Ongoing education and experience help individuals refresh their skills, knowledge, and understanding and ensure that they continue to meet professional standards. While the management profession is several generations old (before the 1950s, management of organizations was regarded as common sense), it generally lacks certification requirements, although the MBA and MPA degrees, which emerged in the early 1970s, may be viewed as surrogates, and postgraduate certifications in specific fields are available. University extension services in many states provide classroom training under the auspices of the Certified Public Manager program and noncredit certificates in nonprofit management can be earned at more than thirty institutions of higher education (M. Lee 2003).

The Certified Quality Manager examination, which is similar to the SAT and includes several essay questions, was created in the mid-1990s by the American Society for Quality. It provides formal peer recognition that an individual has demonstrated proficiency and comprehension of a relevant body of knowledge (Table 2.2).

The technical skill set includes strategic planning and assessment, organizational and knowledge management, project prioritization and planning, and citizen relationship management. Because such subjects are relevant to many areas, it is no surprise that the program has generated considerable interest outside of the quality management profession. The International City/County Management Association (ICMA) also has an assessment and evaluation program; in fact, the organization's code of ethics "commits members to routinely assess their professional skills and abilities." To do this, the ICMA developed a knowledge-based assessment and performance-based assessment to "identify professional strengths and pinpoint opportunities for professional development" (ICMA 2008). It's list of required skills for effective local government managers is found in Appendix 2.2. The need for such programs is illustrated by a lack of knowledge that federal managers exhibit regarding their obligations under the merit system. According to trainer Phil Varnak (2008),

Table 2.2

American Society for Quality: Certified Quality Manager Body of Knowledge

Body of Knowledge

Leadership	Organizational development, organizational culture, code of ethics, managing organizational change, conflict resolution
Team process	Team formation and evolution facilitation techniques, rewards and recognition
Strategy development and deployment	
Environmental analysis	Legal and regulatory factors, stakeholders, SWOT (strengths, weaknesses, opportunities, threats), customer/employee surveys and feedback, internal capability analysis
Strategic planning and assessment	Strategic planning techniques and models, formulation of quality policies
Deployment	Integration of strategic and short-term plans, metrics and goals to drive organizational performance
Quality management tools	
Problem-solving tools	The seven management and planning tools, root cause analysis, plan-do-check-act models, innovation and creativity tools, quality costs
Measurement: assessment and metrics	Process goals, process capability, benchmarking: internal and external
Customer-focused organizations	Customer relationship management and commitment
	Customer service principles, multiple-customer management
Supplier performance	Supplier selection strategies and criteria, techniques for assessment and feedback of supplier performance
Management	
Principles of management	Total quality management, organizational structures, business systems and independence of functions
Communications	Communication techniques, information systems, knowledge management
Projects	Project justification and prioritization techniques, project planning and estimation, project activity monitoring and measurement
Training/development	Alignment with strategic planning and business needs, training materials and curriculum development, techniques for evaluating training effectiveness

Source: Adapted from American Society for Quality 2001. Used with permission from QualityAmerica.com.

many supervisors are not acquainted with their responsibilities to follow merit system principles (retention based on performance) and to avoid prohibited personnel practices (obstruction of employment competition). Failure to fulfill such mandates places them at risk for violation of the law.

Conclusion

This chapter illustrates the importance of technical skills to public servants who aspire to excellence in their fields. Detailed knowledge of a technical specialty, familiarity with relevant rules and regulations, and an understanding of organizational structures and processes are all crucial components of the public servant's vocation. This set of technical skills is a necessary but not sufficient part of the professional edge needed to excel in one's field. Technical expertise emphasizes *what* should be done, but not *why* it should be done.

This produces an interesting paradox: the greater the demand for technical proficiency, the greater the need for ethics and leadership. Without concomitant ethical behavior, technical skills are subject to dangerous temptations of self-serving behavior that harms the public interest rather than furthering it. Without leadership, technical skills may maintain the status quo but will not further progress. Excellence in the service of the common good requires that technical skills be complemented by the moral compass needed to produce ethical behavior and the leadership qualities necessary to solve complex technical and ethical problems. It is to the ethical and leadership competencies that the following chapters turn.

Appendix 2.1. Gantt Chart and PERT Chart

GANTT CHART

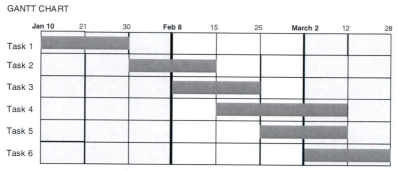

PERT CHART

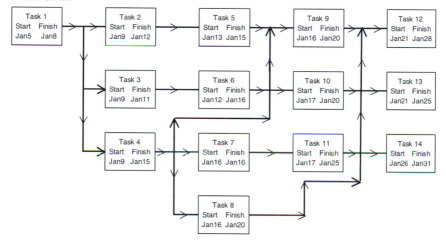

Appendix 2.2. ICMA Skills Required of an Effective Local Government Manager

1. *Staff Effectiveness:* Promoting the development and performance of staff and employees throughout the organization (requires knowledge of interpersonal relations, skill in motivation techniques, ability to identify others' strengths and weaknesses)
2. *Policy Facilitation:* Helping elected officials and other community actors identify, work toward, and achieve common goals and objectives (requires knowledge of group dynamics and political behavior skill in communication, facilitation, and consensus-building techniques; ability to engage others in identifying issues and outcomes)
3. *Functional and Operational Expertise and Planning* (a component of Service Delivery Management)
4. *Citizen Service* (a component of Service Delivery Management): Determining citizen needs and providing responsive, equitable services to the community (requires skill in assessing community needs and allocating resources, knowledge of information-gathering techniques)
5. *Quality Assurance* (a component of Service Delivery Management): Maintaining a consistently high level of quality in staff work, operational procedures, and service delivery (requires knowledge of organizational processes, ability to facilitate organizational improvements, ability to set performance/productivity standards and objectives and measures of results)
6. *Initiative, Risk Taking, Vision, Creativity, and Innovation* (a component of Strategic Leadership): Setting an example that urges the organization and the community toward experimentation, change, creative problem solving, and prompt action (requires knowledge of personal leadership style; ability to envision change, shift perspectives, and identify options, ability to create an environment that encourages initiative and innovation)
7. *Technological Literacy* (a component of Strategic Leadership): Demonstrating an understanding of information technology and ensuring that it is incorporated appropriately in plans to improve service delivery, information sharing, organizational communication, and citizen access (requires knowledge of technological options and their application)
8. *Democratic Advocacy and Citizen Participation:* Demonstrating a commitment to democratic principles by respecting elected officials, community interest groups, and the decision-making process; educating citizens about local government; and acquiring knowledge of the social, economic, and political history of the community (requires knowledge of democratic principles, political processes, and local government law; skill in group dynamics, communication, and facilitation; ability to appreciate and work with diverse individuals and groups and to follow the community's lead in the democratic process)
9. *Diversity:* Understanding and valuing the differences among individuals and fostering these values throughout the organization and the community

10. *Budgeting:* Preparing and administering a budget (requires knowledge of budgeting principles and practices, revenue sources, projection techniques, and financial control systems; skill in communicating financial information)

11. *Financial Analysis:* Interpreting financial information to assess the short-term and long-term fiscal condition of the community, determining the cost-effectiveness of programs, and comparing alternative strategies (requires knowledge of analytical techniques and skill in applying them).

12. *Human Resources Management:* Ensuring that the policies and procedures for employee hiring, promotion, performance appraisal, and discipline are equitable, legal, and current; ensuring that human resources are adequate to accomplish programmatic objectives (requires knowledge of personnel practices and employee relations law, ability to project workforce needs)

13. *Strategic Planning:* Positioning the organization and the community for events and circumstances that are anticipated in the future (requires knowledge of long-range and strategic planning techniques, skill in identifying trends that will affect the community, ability to analyze and facilitate policy choices that will benefit the community in the long run)

14. *Advocacy and Interpersonal Communication:* Facilitating the flow of ideas, information, and understanding between and among individuals; advocating effectively in the community interest (requires knowledge of interpersonal and group communication principles; skill in listening, speaking, and writing; ability to persuade without diminishing the view of others)

15. *Presentation Skills:* Conveying ideas or information effectively to others (requires knowledge of presentation techniques and options; ability to match presentation to audience)

16. *Media Relations:* Communicating information to the media in a way that increases public understanding of local government issues and activities and builds a positive relationship with the press (requires knowledge of media operations and objectives).

17. *Integrity:* Demonstrating fairness, honesty, and ethical and legal awareness in personal and professional relationships and activities (requires knowledge of business and personal ethics, ability to understand issues of ethics and integrity in specific situations).

18. *Personal Development:* Demonstrating a commitment to a balanced life through on-going self-renewal and development in order to increase personal capacity (includes maintaining personal health, living by core values, continuous learning and improvement, and creating interdependent relationships and respect for differences)

Source: Adapted from International City/County Management Association. 1991. ICMA Practices for Effective Local Management. Washington, DC: ICMA Task Force on Continuing Education and Professional Development.

Figure 3.1 **The Competency Triangle of Public Service Professionalism**

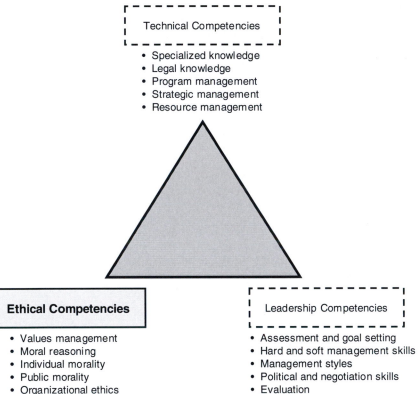

Technical Competencies

- Specialized knowledge
- Legal knowledge
- Program management
- Strategic management
- Resource management

Ethical Competencies

- Values management
- Moral reasoning
- Individual morality
- Public morality
- Organizational ethics

Leadership Competencies

- Assessment and goal setting
- Hard and soft management skills
- Management styles
- Political and negotiation skills
- Evaluation

Chapter 3

The Ethical Professional
Cultivating Scruples

In matters of style, swim with the current.
In matters of principle, stand like a rock.
—Thomas Jefferson

Ever since George Washington required "fitness of character" in his public servants, service to country has been regarded as more than a matter of mere technical skill. Competence also included personal honor, a view shared by Theodore Roosevelt, who believed that "to educate a man in mind but not in morals is to create a menace to society." This component of the professional edge—excellence in ethical bearing as well as technical ability—has long been a hallmark of governance. The obligation and privilege to uphold this ethos continue in today's multisectored public service. When representing the state, officials in government, nonprofit, and business sectors alike are stewards of the common good. The concern about ethical behavior, then, is founded upon the capacity of government (and its agents) to exercise power, a function that is moral in nature insofar as policy decisions are the authoritative allocation of societal values.

Accordingly, public servants must not only do technical things right; they must also do ethically right things. Leaders without basic ethics skills are professionally illiterate. This is what makes the recent execrable scandals in corporate, nonprofit, and governmental organizations so devastating—the worst form of incompetence is more than just not knowing how to do something; rather, it is not knowing why something should or should not be done. Many professionals in a variety of fields—management, law, securities, policy, accounting, banking—have demonstrated a lack of understanding of this fundamental precept. Muriel Siebert, the first woman appointed to the New York Stock Exchange, described an emblematic episode:

> I basically feel that Enron was a case of total moral bankruptcy. It was not just the company and its executives. It was not just the accountants. They had to get legal opinions from a law firm. They had to get the derivatives

[i.e., a security or financial asset, such as an option or futures contract, whose value depends upon the performance of an underlying security] from banks and Wall Street firms. One group alone could not have done it. The money was vast, and the money was fast (Holdstein 2002).

The centrality of ethics in management in all sectors of the economy is undeniable. It is not an imposition or constraint, but the foundation of everything a professional is or does. Exhibit 3.1 presents an overview of ethical skill and knowledge areas.

Exhibit 3.1

Sample of Ethical Skill and Knowledge Areas

Skill Areas

1. Capacity to build moral consensus
2. Ability to listen well and to communicate interest, respect, support, and empathy to involved stakeholders
3. Talent to educate involved stakeholders about the ethical dimensions of the situation
4. Versatility to elicit the moral views of involved stakeholders
5. Understanding how to represent the views of involved stakeholders to others
6. Ingenuity to enable the involved stakeholders to communicate effectively and be heard by other parties
7. Capability to recognize and attend to various relations barriers to communication

Knowledge Areas

1. Moral reasoning and ethical theory (e.g., consequentialist vs. nonconsequentialist, or principle-based vs. casuistic)
2. Relevant codes of ethics, professional conduct, and guidelines of accrediting organizations (e.g., ASPA, ICMA, NASPAA)
3. Ethical issues and concepts that typically emerge in public service work environments
4. Organizational systems (e.g., governmental, nonprofit, and private)
5. Institutional context in which work is done (e.g., organizational culture and climate)
6. Local institution's policies that are relevant to ethical decision making
7. Beliefs and perspectives of interested stakeholders where one works

Source: Adapted from Aulisio, Arnold, and Youngner, 2000.

Because controversy is inherent in decision making and there is no single best way to deal with ethical quandaries, professional practice requires that moral criteria be integrated into policy making. The technical ability to analyze problems must be complemented by the capacity to grasp those problems in a manner consistent with professional rectitude. Yet professionals may be unprepared to deal with conflicts between ethical values (e.g., honesty, integrity, keeping promises) and nonethical values (wealth, comfort, success).

FBI agents not heeding terrorist warnings, firefighters setting fires, questionable Red Cross fundraising and blood safety practices, clergymen abusing children and their superiors covering up the problem, preemptive war making, Olympic judges rigging scores, stock analysts giving biased ratings, and corporate officers "restating" record numbers of audits all demonstrate that ethics is key to the identity and legitimacy of any organization. In the latter case, for instance, "the core purpose of accounting is, after all, to verify authenticity, to certify to the public the integrity of the accounts of a business or public agency" (Frederickson 2002, 9). Instead, these professionals, unlike hospital financial officer James Alderson (Exhibit 3.2) who uncovered the largest Medicare scandal in history, sacrificed the independence they claimed to possess.

Ethics, then, is not something mysterious and far removed from ordinary life; instead, it is about people making decisions every day. There is no doubt that everyone encounters ethical dilemmas; the only questions are when, and whether they are prepared.

The management approach to the subject must include an understanding of why people behave the way they do. To assume that anyone with good character can act honorably in professional situations is no more sensible than suggesting that someone can function as a physician without special training. While values are imprinted at an early age, the real question is how they are applied at the workplace. Professional socialization can equip leaders to anticipate problems, recognize when they occur, and provide frameworks for thinking about issues; it affects not only ethical awareness but also moral reasoning and behavior (Rest and Narvez 1994; Menzel 1997; Menzel and Carson 1997; Bruce 1996). Without this preparation, individuals may rely on technical proficiency (in fact, doing things right can become a dominant *moral* code), unexamined personal preferences, passive obedience to authority, and/or unquestioned organizational loyalty. Those serving the public may bring any combination of idealism and cynicism to their work. This chapter aims to reinforce the former and minimize the latter by briefly defining values and ethics, and then examining (1) values management, (2) moral development and reasoning, (3) individual morality, (4) public versus private morality, and (5) organizational ethics.

Exhibit 3.2

Hundreds Knew But Did Nothing; One Person Did Something

Our lives begin to end the day that we become silent about things that matter.

—Martin Luther King

James Alderson was an unassuming financial officer for a hospital in northwest Montana. Yet he would blow the whistle on the fraudulent Medicare practices of one of America's largest hospital conglomerates, Columbia/HCA, and one of its subsidiaries, Quorum. Alderson's actions would lead to the uncovering of the largest Medicare scandal in U.S. history. For Alderson, the decision to undertake the arduous fight was based on his determination to fulfill his professional duty and personal ethics.

From 1984 to 1990, his professional life was uneventful. "It was a late September afternoon in 1990, about two months after Quorum had assumed management of the hospital," Alderson remembered. He was meeting with a consultant who helped prepare the hospital's government cost report when Clyde Eder, a Quorum administrator, stepped into the room. Mr. Eder asked the two men whether they usually prepared two cost reports. They were uncertain what he meant. "No, we just prepare one cost report," recalled the consultant. "I thought he was talking about maybe preparing one for Medicaid and a different one for Medicare."

But Mr. Eder meant something quite different. Quorum submitted aggressive cost reports to the government, claiming the largest possible number of expenses. But in case a later audit rejected those claims, the company also assembled a second set of more conservative reports for its internal use. Several days after the awkward encounter, Alderson was informed that he had been dismissed. In 1992 he started conducting legal research in a local library and drafted a letter outlining his lawsuit. It accused Columbia/HCA Healthcare Corporation and Quorum Health Group of defrauding the Medicare program and other health insurance programs—a case that would involve more than 200 hospitals in thirty-seven states. There could be little doubt that preparing multiple sets of cost reports was a nationwide practice that was engaged in by numerous professionals.

By 1997, there were raids of Columbia/HCA hospitals in six states and the FBI arrested several executives. On October 2, 1998, the U.S. Justice Department accused Quorum and Columbia/HCA of the following wide-ranging charges:

(continued)

Exhibit 3.2 *(continued)*

- Filed claims and received reimbursement for nonallowable costs, such as for marketing, advertising, and unrelated investments, by mischaracterizing them
- Billed Medicare for idle space in hospitals by claiming it was being used for patient care
- Concealed overcharges and Medicare auditing errors that favored HCA facilities
- Shifted costs to home health rehabilitation and other facilities that Medicare reimbursed at higher rates

By the end of 2002, a tentative settlement was reached requiring HCA to pay the Justice Department $631 million. Previously HCA had paid $250 million to resolve other cost report issues as well as $840 million to settle other whistleblower cases and criminal fines. As one official said, "James Alderson had a solid belief that this was wrong and a determination to do something about it. It's a truly amazing example of how one [individual] can make a difference."

Source: Adapted from Ventriss and Barney 2003.

Values Management and the Practice of Ethics

The most important thing in life is to decide what is important. Values are the things, such as principles or qualities, that matter to an individual or group. They reflect who we are and what matters to us. They shape a person's worldview and define the character of the individual and ultimately the community; shared values bring people together. Exhibit 3.3 displays universal and democratic values.

Conflicts are inevitable, even desirable; governance is about maintaining conditions in which civilization is possible. Indeed, the root for *ethics* is the Greek word *ethos,* which emphasizes the perfection of the individual and the community in which he or she is defined.

Ethics is a philosophy that guides the way values are practiced. Ethical behavior is a process of inquiry (deciding how to decide) and adherence to a code of conduct (a set of standards governing behavior). Ethics is a system that determines what is right or wrong in society and provides a means by which individuals can behave accordingly. It is a quest for, and understanding of, the "good life." Ethics, therefore, is not primarily about staying out of trouble; it

Exhibit 3.3
Universal and Democratic Values

Universal Values

In the late 1990s (Kung 1998), 6,500 representatives from a wide variety of world religions reached agreement on a global ethic; a council of former heads of state and prime ministers then ratified the statement. Delegates from both groups articulated two universal principles: Every individual must be treated humanely and every person and group must respect the dignity of others. These principles led to commitments to a culture of nonviolence and respect for all life, solidarity and a just economic order, tolerance and truthfulness, and equal rights and partnership between men and women. Global standards emerged from another international gathering (Kidder 1994): love (compassion), truthfulness (honesty), fairness (evenhandedness), freedom (pursuit of liberty), unity (the common good), tolerance (appreciation of variety), responsibility (care for self, the community, and future generations), and respect for life (reluctance to kill). See also the 1948 United Nations Declaration of Human Rights. For a report on emerging public management standards in a transnational world see Cooper and Yoder (2002).

Democratic Values

Democratic values in the American context have a minimum of six major elements. At least two are fairly universal among all democratic societies throughout history. The first is the belief in systematic governance that enables various issues to be brought into the public domain (or sent out of it) through an authorized process. A second value is representation, which is the belief that a system of elected representatives should decide upon the major policy questions affecting the public good. This is important because direct democracy is rarely feasible except in limited cases such as town halls and miscellaneous voter referenda.

A third value of American democracy is the division of political power in a federal system: horizontal separation of the powers of the national government into three branches checks the power of any one branch by the other two, and vertical separation divides power between the national government and the states. A fourth significant democratic value is the protection and celebration of individualism. In particular, the Bill of Rights protects numerous personal rights such as the freedoms of speech, press, and assembly,

(continued)

Exhibit 3.3 *(continued)*

freedom to bear arms, freedom from military billeting, unreasonable search and seizure, self-incrimination, and double jeopardy, rights to due process, a speedy trial, legal counsel, and a jury trial, among others.

A fifth firmly held right is religious choice. Separation of church and state ideally functions to protect the individual's freedom of religion without making religion a universal way of life. Finally, while it is often unrecognized as such, a sixth American democratic value is the pursuit of a relatively pure form of capitalism. This is a creed to have the least government intervention possible, while still providing—and therefore balancing issues leading to—a stable, humane, and safe environment. Thus while American society allows and encourages income disparities based on individual initiative and market mechanisms, it discourages system distortions such as insider trading or information monopolies.

Specific administrative values flow from some of these democratic values. There is a general understanding that public managers should implement policy but not usurp the process or amass power themselves (serve and facilitate rather than preside). There is a belief that they should be efficient and effective with the public's resources (conservation). There is a credo that administrators should support the citizens' right to know the public's business (openness and transparency). A similar value is that managers should support the public's right to be involved in governmental business through forums such as public hearings, citizen surveys, focus groups, and advisory boards.

is about creating strength in individuals and organizations. Grounded in values and predicated upon ethics, professional responsibility demands the discretion of practitioners. But upon what foundation are decisions made?

Professionals and Moral Development

The key theory of moral development was formulated by Lawrence Kohlberg (1971, 164–65). This hierarchical, inclusive taxonomy posits that individuals develop moral maturity by moving gradually through stages organized in three levels:

- Preconventional level moral reasoning reflects punishment avoidance (stage 1) or an instrumental orientation (stage 2); the person is self-interested and either fears or uses others.

- Conventional level thinking regards right behavior as conformity to expectations of significant others (stage 3) or allegiance to the broader social order (stage 4); the person's point of reference is a group, either small and personal or large and political.
- Postconventional judgments are derived from the moral autonomy that results from critically examined values in the social contract upon which the social order is constructed (stage 5) or from adherence to transcendental ethical principles (stage 6); the individual is an independent actor. Moral precepts trump the social expectations found at stage 2 and the self-interests in stage 1.

Growing from stage 1 to stage 2 is a common, though not inevitable, psychological development requiring little deliberation. Levels are not skipped, and evolution can stop at any point. Actual reasoning tends to reflect one dominant stage, although it may sometimes occur at one stage higher or lower. Kohlberg believed that most people are at the conventional level because the postconventional level requires an uncommon commitment and contemplation.

It is fitting, therefore, that professionals strive to make decisions at the highest level of moral development. They cannot form judgments solely from the self-interested perspective of the first level. Second-level thinking also may be inadequate because some social roles are unjust (e.g., law enforcement officials in the Jim Crow South in the United States; physicians in Nazi Germany). Third-level reasoning, however, prevents abuse of professional skills for one's own advantage or for that of one's social group. The idea is not to deny self or collective interest, but to temper them in light of a higher claim of human dignity (Snell 1993). Professionalism, in short, requires both dedication to technical excellence and exemplary ethical behavior. It is unthinkable for the professional to behave otherwise when grappling with important problems.

Professionals and Individual Ethics

Approaches to Ethics

The essential issue of ethics is, as Socrates said, "What ought one to do?" However, no unified theory and no single secular approach resolves all moral dilemmas. In deciding what to do, it is likely that people have always considered potential outcomes of their decisions and/or followed relevant guidelines to determine what was right. It follows that cognitive schools of thought generally contend that matters of right and wrong are a function of either (1) the expected results of an action (consequentialism or teleology) or (2) the application of pertinent rules (duty ethics or deontology).

In consequentialism, the best decision results in "the greatest good for the greatest number"; what is right is that which creates the largest amount of human happiness. In duty ethics, however, certain actions are inherently right (truth telling) or wrong (inflicting harm), irrespective of supposed consequences; one must see one's obligation and do it. Actions must conform to moral rules. In deciding what rule to apply, one asks, "Would I want everyone else to make the decision I did?" If the answer is "yes," then the choice is justified; if "no," it is not.

The claimed strength of these two approaches to ethics is that they are superior to an intuitive understanding of right or wrong—to say nothing of sheer expediency. In weighing expected results, the decision maker acts as an engineer calculating the costs and benefits of an action; in choosing among rules, she plays the role of a judge. Yet these theories have undue confidence in the power of reason: predicting consequences in human affairs is hazardous and choosing among conflicting duties is daunting. Moreover, both can be seen as rationalistic efforts that ignore the person making the decision. Ethics involves more than following general norms such as consequences or duty (Bowman 2003). Since antiquity, people have also relied upon their personal characters to guide them when confronted with dilemmas.

In the latter theory, known as virtue ethics, the primary faculty is moral intuition, not intellect. Reason may be essential in decision making, but the source of morality is human sentiment. Ethical questions are not simply technical ones to be resolved by projecting assumed results or established rules to a situation. Virtue ethics is a way of life, not merely a method of analysis. It is about right character more than right procedure. Indeed, reason may easily lead to error insofar as many do not have the capacity or training for discursive reasoning (consider the convincing—and opposing—jury closings on any number of television courtroom dramas).

Virtue ethics is a more personal, subjective approach to morality than cognitive ethics. Answers to questions of "What to do" have little to do with results and rules, and everything to do with what kind of person is making the decision. An individual must *be* before he can *do*. Personal character is forged through experience by developing praiseworthy habits. The role of theory is not to get professionals out of a jam, but to help build their moral fiber. Excellence in character ensures that the professional has "the right stuff" to do the right thing at the right time.

Yet no general theory of human virtue exists; virtues seem to vary from time to time and place to place, as some virtues may not apply to all people or groups (e.g., male vs. female, young vs. old). Further, the virtue school lacks a theory of action. Virtues may generate instructions for action (the virtue of justice, for instance, provides the motivation to act justly), but what does a just person do in a given dilemma? The theory, finally, lacks integrity: one may *be* good without knowing how to *do* good. Worse, confusing moral rectitude with ethical behavior can easily lead to self-righteousness: if an individual believes in his own goodness, he may wrongly assume that his actions are equally as good.

The Ethics Triangle

If philosophers cannot agree on competing models (results-and-rules cognitive approaches vs. virtue ethics), then why should public servants? The reason is that they must be able to defend their judgments: professionals, by definition, are obligated to develop virtues, respect rules, and consider results. A decision-making tool, the "Ethics Triangle" (Svara 1997, 2007), recognizes that the imperatives in these three schools of thought are complementary and interdependent. It emphasizes that cognition without virtue is as insufficient as virtue without cognition (Figure 3.2).

Figure 3.2   **The Ethics Triangle**

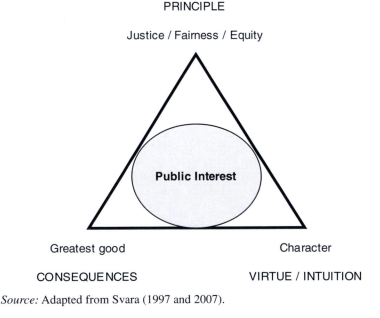

PRINCIPLE

Justice / Fairness / Equity

Public Interest

Greatest good   Character

CONSEQUENCES   VIRTUE / INTUITION

Source: Adapted from Svara (1997 and 2007).

Each point of the Triangle provides a distinct filter to clarify and reframe different aspects of a situation. Operating inside the Triangle helps to prevent the shortcomings of each approach as its angles inform and limit one another. Consider these examples:

- Exaggerating advantages of a proposal to secure support
- Insisting on one's own way at the risk of unit cohesiveness
- Cutting corners in established processes
- Showing disloyalty when times are tough
- Concealing errors
- Engaging in favoritism
- Failing to report violations of agency policy
- Denying responsibility for a mistake

Considering the results point of the Triangle, "the greatest good for the greatest number" is achieved by refusing to engage in these kinds of actions because of the negative consequences of their exposure. Using a rules-based interpretation, the duty to avoid such behavior is clear. Under virtue ethics, finally, excellence in individual and community character is nourished by doing the right thing in each case.

Complex issues—such as the genuine ethical dilemma that follows—produce more interesting, sometimes conflicting, findings.

> Bob has heard from his supervisor that their organization's staff will soon be downsized; it could be as little as 5 percent or as much as 30 percent of the workforce. The supervisor told Bob that "we're all under strict orders to keep this quiet," so that the organization's best employees would not seek other jobs. Ron, one of the finest professionals in Bob's unit, had heard rumors of the downsizing measures and told Bob that he was certain he could get a job currently advertised at another organization if a reduction in workforce did occur. Ron needed to know right away, however, because the application deadline for the new job was close at hand. Ron asked Bob: "Will there be layoffs here?" (Bowman and Knox 2008)

Exhibits 3.4 and 3.5 present other ethical dilemmas that call for the application of different points in the Ethics Triangle.

Generally speaking, when considering the results point of the Triangle, the critical question is, "Which decision has the most utility in serving the greatest good for the greatest number?" In contemplating duty-based ethics from the rules part of the Triangle, the key question is "What decision best carries the weight of universality?" (i.e., "What if everyone did that?") Finally, from the

Exhibit 3.4

The Ethics Triangle: Career Interests versus Doing the Right Thing

A young captain in the military had the responsibility of submitting monthly Unit Readiness Reports (URRs) to his superiors. The URRs had to be signed by him, a staff member from the unit, and the unit commander, who was responsible for ensuring that his unit maintained 80 percent combat readiness every month, in terms of training and successful physical fitness tests for the unit soldiers.

If actual combat readiness fell below 80 percent, it was common practice for unit commanders to overstate the number of training hours to which unit soldiers had been subjected in order to meet the established quota. The captain noticed that the unit had reported an increase in combat readiness even though concomitant requirements had not been met. He knew that commanders and staff would often create training events on paper ("pencil whip" events) that never took place in order to buttress their claim of meeting URR quotas. One month, the captain refused to sign off on the URR report, which had been signed by a staff member and the unit commander, who had recently instructed a mandatory military ethics class. The captain told the commander that the numbers were incorrect; the commander replied, "Don't worry; we'll make it all up next month."

Assume that the unit commander is a highly respected career military member, responsible for writing assessments of the young captain, who intends to make his career in the military. Under which part of the Ethics Triangle does his ethical dilemma fall? What risks does the captain take in continuing to refuse to sign the report? What risks does he take in signing the report? What elements would go into your decision making about this dilemma if you were in the captain's shoes?

Exercise. Search news reports for examples of ethical dilemmas represented in the Ethics Triangle: those involving justice/fairness, the greatest good for the greatest number, and integrity. Cast a wide net by looking in the arenas of politics, government operations, business, the nonprofit sector, and academia. Be prepared to explain the dilemma in terms of how it evolved, the choices faced by the people involved, and the potential consequences of each choice.

Exhibit 3.5

**The Ethics Triangle: Private Business versus
Department of Homeland Security**

Mary owns a meat-packing plant in Arizona. A significant number of her employees are illegal immigrants who surreptitiously crossed U.S. borders in order to create a better life for themselves and their families. Many of these illegal immigrants have families living with them in Arizona; others send their earnings home to relations outside the United States. It is against the law for U.S. employers to hire illegal immigrants. U.S. law has imposed sanctions on employers who hire illegal immigrants since 1986.

The law was almost universally ignored by politicians, employers, and the legal authorities for decades because of the reluctance to lose a source of cheap labor and the unwillingness to devote the resources necessary to impose the law. However, after the terrorist attacks of September 11, 2001, as well as the increasing concern about identity theft, the U.S. government started to compel compliance to the law. They devoted more resources to enforcement and imposed stiffer fines on noncompliant employers. Responsibility for enforcement was transferred in 2002 to the newly created Department of Homeland Security (DHS). DHS requires employers to verify that job applicants and current employees are in the country legally though its E-Verify system, which matches the social security numbers provided by applicants and employees against its national database. The goal is not only to uphold laws against illegal immigration but also to enhance national security by tightening border security and to prevent identity theft by illegal immigrants who often use false social security numbers to get jobs and drivers licenses. Beginning in 2007, the Immigration and Customs Enforcement (ICE) section of DHS began to intensify its raids on businesses suspected of employing illegal immigrants. The raids resulted in steep fines for the employers, arrest and detention of some of the illegal immigrants, and immediate deportation of others who were sent home, while their families, usually wives and children, were left to fend for themselves in the communities where they had made their homes.

Mary does not comply with the law for several reasons: First, she believes that her illegal immigrant employees came to the United States to work hard to improve their lives and she sees nothing wrong with hiring them. These workers work long hours for low wages. Since these are conditions which no U.S. citizen would accept, Mary does not believe that by hiring illegal

(continued)

Exhibit 3.5 *(continued)*

immigrants she is taking jobs away from American citizens. Second, the low wages paid to her employees means that she can sell her services more cheaply to retailers, who can then sell their products more cheaply to the American public. Mary believes that she is doing the American economy and the American consumer a favor by employing these illegal immigrants.

Third, the wages she pays keep her costs low so that she can turn a profit and stay in business. In a competitive economy, especially one experiencing a downturn, higher wages and generous benefits might mean that she would have to go out of business. Fourth, most of Mary's competitors hire illegal immigrants. If she abided by the law, this would put her at a severe disadvantage and would adversely affect her business. Fifth, Mary knows that the law was effectively disregarded for two decades; she doesn't see why all of a sudden she should change her practices according to the whims of politicians; if they could ignore the law for so long, why can't she? She has gotten to know dozens of her employees who have worked for her since the 1990s and she doesn't want to suddenly turn them in to the authorities. Sixth, Mary believes that the law is inhumane because it causes undue stress on terrified workers who fear being arrested or deported and breaks up innocent families. Mary continues to defy the law, despite the increased risk of ICE raids and the consequent threat to herself, her employees, and her entire business.

Mary is breaking a federal law that is being promulgated to uphold immigration laws, protect national security, and prevent identity theft through the appropriation of individual social security numbers. She claims that she is justified, for moral, pragmatic, and commercial reasons, in breaking the law.

Exercise. Discuss the following: What components of the Ethics Triangle does this case involve? What is your opinion? What are the consequences of each of Mary's choices in this situation? What is the proper approach to an ethical dilemma posed by disobedience to a law that one considers to be unjust?

virtue ethics angle, one might ask, "Who am I?" "What would a person of integrity do?" or "How can I best achieve excellence in this circumstance?"

Although the synthesis developed from this triangular analysis does not explain what to do or how to do it, it offers guidance about how to handle the situation.

- Because all schools of thought in the Ethics Triangle imply that confidential information is to be respected, an honest answer to Ron's question might be, "I don't know what the level of reduction will be, but some reduction will occur. Ron, I want to keep you and help you, but you must decide what to do."
- Given that duty and virtue ethics emphasize the importance of telling the truth, the fair treatment of individuals suggests that the information Bob has should not be withheld, especially for organizational convenience and expediency; it follows that Bob should tell Ron what he has heard.
- Deliberation stimulated by applying the Ethics Triangle could foster moral imagination, whereby an individual seeks solutions that both respect privileged organizational information and honor individuals. Promoting ethical behavior through open communication, for example, could help Bob deal with his manager (pointing out that a dearth of information results in negative rumor-mongering), while demonstrating personal integrity (telling only Ron and not the entire staff would be improper and unfair). After suggesting to his manager that he issue a statement to quell rumors, Bob could tell Ron that he will seek clarification from his superiors, the only ones who have the authority to provide the relevant information.

This analysis, then, is useful in teasing out the underlying logic by which actions are justified.

Of course, none of these strategies will satisfy everyone, but that is hardly the point; the Triangle cannot produce a final, perfect decision applicable to all seasons. Instead the decision-making process highlights a key function of ethical management: generating alternative viewpoints, systemically evaluating them, and crafting a considered judgment. The result is not a muddled compromise but a conscious attempt to reconcile conflicting values. It is because this is so difficult that decisions are not easily made. This eclectic technique for adjudicating matters of right and wrong is very demanding. Ethics requires not just rectitude but also resourcefulness to devise options. In light of the shortcomings that may appear at each point of the triangle, there is little alternative; such an ethic is necessary given the complexity of the human condition. When choices are guided by benevolence, creativity, and an ethic of compromise and social integration—a moral tenet of democracy—there is at least the satisfaction that the problem has been fully examined and that the result can be rationally defended.

The goal is to strive for balance; governance is not geometry, but the art of the possible. It is an imperfect world where no one gets everything he or she wants. In ethics, as in the rest of life, there are no magic answers. Differences among theories, nonetheless, should not lead to despair or the conclusion that one is just as good as another. Better to have an imprecise answer to the right question than a precise answer to the wrong question.

Indeed, a narrow, overreaching application of a single approach at the extremes of the Triangle at the expense of the others holds considerable dangers: expediency (consequentialism), rigid rule application (duty ethics), and self-justification (virtue ethics). Attempts at rationalizing the eight dubious behaviors listed earlier illustrate these risks. Instead the task is to consider the issues from each viewpoint and make an informed judgment. Professionals can do no less. Ethical quandaries are maddeningly intractable—and hauntingly unavoidable. Still, the difficulty in conclusively resolving these dilemmas demonstrates how fundamental they are; the fact that decisions are difficult does not stop them from being made.

The Ethics Triangle, then, like a good map, offers choices, not formulas. Just as a map outlines a journey, the Triangle provides help in making the inevitable compromises. As Aristotle admonished, do not expect more precision from the subject matter than it can allow. Professional ethics is more like an art than a science; instead of expecting definitive technical solutions, an aesthetic perspective appreciates that conflict is essential and productive. "Great art is beautiful precisely because of tension, not in spite of it" (Anonymous 2002). Like the artist, the professional creatively combines differing influences. The need for judgment is not eliminated, but rather the Triangle enables the skilled management of ethical ambiguity and independent thinking.

Professionals and Public versus Private Morality

Complicating the issue of how to know what is right and to act upon it ethically is the professional's need to distinguish between two distinct spheres of moral standards and the ethical behavior that follows: private and public. In private life, individuals are guided by their consciences to make a distinction between right and wrong and to behave ethically in respect to the people with whom they interact. Once engaged in public life as a consumer, citizen, employee, or political representative, individuals must be guided by a set of laws and regulations that may not always coincide with their own moral precepts or their idea of what constitutes ethical behavior. Those involved in public life are charged with acting in the name of an entity larger than the group of people with whom they themselves interact. Corporate employees act in the interest of the business and its customers; nonprofit personnel act in the interests of particular groups of people or specific causes; public servants are charged with supporting the "common good" of constituencies of varying sizes.

Thus, while an individual may hold family support and loyalty as his highest moral value, he may not use his public power to pull strings to get a family member hired over some more qualified person or to steal from his company to provide a better standard of living for his family. A pharmacist who is against birth control for religious reasons may refuse his underage daughter access to birth control methods but is not justified in refusing to fill a prescription for birth control pills at a public hospital pharmacy. A pro-life U.S. senator may nonetheless support pro-abortion legislation if a majority of her constituents are for it. Public servants may be called to either (1) subjugate their own views out of adherence to the law of the land, agency regulations, and court rulings or (2) change them through established processes. Whether acting on the status quo or promoting change, public servants must develop consistent ethical standards to guide their actions at every stage of the decision-making processes that engage them in their professional lives.

Conversely, citizens should also make a distinction between private and public morality when judging the actions of career civil servants and elected officials. The standard should be accountability, not to an arbitrary set of personal values, but to the legal, institutional, and political standards to which professionals commit themselves. Research shows that public servants take professional ethics and integrity very seriously and that professional codes of conduct play an important role in government agencies (Bowman and Knox 2008). Civil servants should be judged by the standards of these codes as well as broader legal and institutional rules. An overemphasis on the private lives of public servants and politicians undermines the quality of democratic discourse and may lead to what Dennis F. Thompson calls "the rut of smut." He argues that "[p]ublicity about the private lives of public officials can damage the democratic process by distracting citizens from more important questions of policy and performance of government" (Thompson 2001, 165).

The boundaries between private and public morality are not always stationary or well-defined, especially if they involve hypocrisy—a palpable disjunction between an official's publicly expressed private morals and his public behavior. But it is necessary to try to identify those boundaries in order to establish consistent standards by which professionals are held accountable and to encourage a democratic discourse that centers on performance.

Professionals and Organizational Ethics

Individual-centered ethics is necessary, but not sufficient, for understanding the full scope of professional ethics. Because employees are susceptible to workplace influences, organizations are also important (recall the Greek emphasis on the citizen and community). People may make judgments based on personal standards, but institutions define and control the situations in which decisions are made (see the discussion of the nonprofit sector in

Appendix 3.1). That is, organizations are major agencies of social control; ethical behavior is as much a sociological as a psychological phenomenon. As Myles's Law of Bureaucracy dictates, what employees ought to do is affected by their organizational roles ("Where you stand depends upon where you sit").

Some resist acknowledging institutional factors for fear of diluting personal moral responsibility, but this concern is based on a false dichotomy. Recognizing the role of organization does not exculpate wrongdoers; it simply recognizes that "no man is an island," and that both the individual and the collectivity of which he is a part share important obligations. In order for either one to exercise responsibility in an informed manner, their interdependence must be acknowledged and acted upon.

Kohlberg's six stages of individual moral development can also be applied to organizations. Stage 1 institutions focus on survival as their moral beacon; any strategy will be employed to ensure it. Those in stage 2 define success by manipulating others; victory justifies the tactics used. Stage 3 companies, nonprofits, and public agencies conform to the practices of peer institutions; prevailing industry customs dictate what is right and wrong. Stage 4 organizations take direction from legitimate authority to determine standards; their moral compass is based on society's legal structure. Units representing the next stage rely on tolerance, open discussion, and participatory management in upholding—or changing—the social contract under which they operate; standards are derived through critical analysis and consensus. Finally, stage 6 businesses, nonprofits, and governmental departments profess ideals such as justice and individual rights; balanced judgment among competing interests, based on universal principles, determines right behavior. When laws violate these principles, principles ultimately prevail.

For purposes of analysis, these stages can be condensed into two organizational approaches, as shown in Exhibit 3.6.

The personal, negative, punitive, "low road" compliance strategy derives from Kohlberg's lower stages. This policy is clearly important, for without it a comprehensive ethics program may lack credibility. Yet it concentrates on individuals, defines ethics as staying out of trouble, emphasizes "symptom-solving," and often uses ethics to control behavior instead of to encourage improvement. If this approach represents the lowest common denominator, then the "high road" strategy symbolizes the highest common denominator. In the latter approach, a structural, affirmative, commitment system based on the more mature stages of Kohlberg's framework is aimed at deterring rather than merely detecting problems by promoting right behavior. Instead of stressing blame and punishment, the approach focuses on reform and development. A robust ethics strategy, as described in the following paragraphs,

Exhibit 3.6

Comparing Organizational Strategies

Low Road

Ethos: Conformity with external standards
Objective: Prevent criminal conduct
Leadership: Lawyer-driven
Methods: Training, limited discretion, controls, penalties
Assumption: People driven by material self-interest

High Road

Ethos: Self-governance according to chosen standards
Objective: Enable responsible conduct
Leadership: Management-driven
Methods: Education, leadership, accountability
Assumption: People guided by humanistic ideals

Source: Adapted from Paine (1994: 113).

would likely include elements of both plans, although not necessarily in equal proportion.

Creating an ethical institutional culture is no more easily achieved than resolving individual moral conundrums (White and Lam 2000; Trevino et al. 1999; Gilman 1999; West and Berman 2006). In an organizational age, instruments of leadership are often corporate in nature. Indeed, the cornerstone of a comprehensive ethics program is a code of ethics (West 2009). While some may question their value, codes can play significant aspirational and operational roles when viewed as a means to a greater end. The real issue is how the codes are developed and enforced in order to make them meaningful in daily management. Like any organizational initiative, the impetus to create (or reinvigorate) an agency code must have authentic leadership support (Bowman and Knox 2008). A meaningful code of ethics should be produced and implemented by a representative employee taskforce. It begins with a self-generated assessment of needs to gather information, encourage participation, and create a shared vocabulary. Depending on the results, the initiative could include the following:

- Advice mechanisms and reporting channels: establishing an independent advisory ethics board, grievance procedures, whistleblower mechanisms (hotlines, confidential communications), due process support structures, an ombudsman
- Decision-making tools: appointing an "angels' advocate" to raise ethical issues in staff meetings, formulating ethical impact statements prior to major decisions
- Promotion activities: posting the code of ethics in the department, as well as reprinting it in agency newsletters and reports; recognizing exemplary cases in an awards program
- Personnel system changes: revising recruitment, training, and performance evaluation processes, including identification of ethical dimensions of jobs in position descriptions and whistleblower protections against retaliation
- Periodic ethics audits: conducting document reviews, vulnerability assessments, employee interviews and surveys, evaluations of existing systems, etc. to provide an ongoing appraisal of program effectiveness

The objective is to make the code a living document by offering opportunities to participate in its development and evolution, infusing its values into the routines of the organization, providing procedures for its interpretation, and ensuring its enforcement.

While it may be true that very few things of importance occur without participation by individuals, it is also true that little is lasting without institutions. A number of steps can be taken to show that managers are serious about ethical conduct within an organization:

- Appoint an independent ethics officer to whom all employees, including the CEO, are accountable
- Hook up an ethics hotline in the executive's suite
- Encourage top management to play an active role in fostering an ethical culture
- Increase executive exposure to criminal and civil liability
- Include outside directors on nonprofit and business boards
- Create "open book" management systems
- Rotate auditors on a periodic basis
- Strengthen conflict-of-interest rules
- Adopt a "three strikes and you're out" corporation "death penalty" (revocation of the corporate charter with the third criminal conviction)
- Support the formation of a national commission on white-collar crime

What is needed, in short, is an actual commitment to an ethical infrastructure rather than just an announcement about a commitment (see Appendix 3.2 for a meaningless announcement of a code of ethics and Exhibit 3.7 for a real commitment).

An employee of the Defense Supply Center noted the difference: "Each organization is different and has diverse motivations. We should ask ourselves if ethics initiatives are more for public relations than for establishing an ethical organization. For those of us who have been around for a while, and watched programs du jour come and go, one develops a healthy skepticism about the intentions of organizations" (Interview with DSC employee, January 26, 2003).

While no strategy will be without criticism, improvement is unlikely if all proposals are rejected until perfection is guaranteed. Public and private organizations should plant and cultivate standards by which a professional can measure his or her behavior, encourage correction of deficiencies, and minimize institutional conditions that lead to unethical behavior. The issue is not whether norms of conduct will develop in an organization, but rather what these norms are, how they will be communicated, and whether all are fully conscious of the ethical dimensions of their work. The idea is to nourish a transparent institutional culture by offering incentives for ethical behavior, reducing opportunities for corruption, and increasing the risk of untoward conduct.

Like the cover of a jigsaw puzzle box, such an initiative can provide a point of departure and serve as an enabling device to strive for professional ideals. It must have the leadership's dedication, be "home grown" by employees themselves, and include a clear policy statement, explanatory guidelines, due process procedures, and employee training, as well as sanctions and rewards. That is, there must be top-down commitment to, and bottom-up participation in, processes designed for continuous improvement in realizing ethical ideals (West and Berman 2004). Such a program makes common rationalizations of questionable behavior (e.g., "What I want to do is not 'really' unethical" or "Because the action will help the organization, I will support it") much more difficult (Gellerman 1986). Organizations, paradoxically, are at their most dangerous when they are successful because people become arrogant and that prevents learning. In the absence of an ethics initiative, business-as-usual expediency and an "anything goes" mentality is likely to dominate, condoning questionable behavior, reinforcing amorality or even immorality, and discouraging ethical action.

Exhibit 3.7

Organizational Ethics:
How to Produce a Culture to Correspond to the Code

The U.S. government has established an independent executive agency, the Office of Government Ethics (OGE), to develop ethical standards and foster ethical behavior in all governmental agencies. Each agency has a Designated Agency Ethics Official (DAEO) to oversee training and oversight. Following is the OGE's mission statement, as noted on its Web site:

> The Office of Government Ethics (OGE), a small agency within the executive branch, was established by the Ethics in Government Act of 1978. Originally part of the Office of Personnel Management, OGE became a separate agency on October 1, 1989, as part of the Office of Government Ethics Reauthorization Act of 1988. . . . The Office of Government Ethics exercises leadership in the executive branch to prevent conflicts of interest on the part of Government employees, and to resolve those conflicts of interest that do occur. In partnership with executive branch agencies and departments, OGE fosters high ethical standards for employees and strengthens the public's confidence that the Government's business is conducted with impartiality and integrity.

Each agency is responsible for developing its own standards of ethical behavior and the means to instill them in its employees. All agencies are required to illustrate promotion of ethical behavior through the development of a culture of ethics that is practiced and promulgated by agency leaders.

Strategies Used by Various Agencies to Teach and
Monitor Ethical Standards

- A training regulation that requires a written ethics briefing distributed to employees with a mandatory follow-up questionnaire to be returned in an enclosed prestamped, postage-paid envelope.

The questionnaire, entitled "What Would You Do?" is comprised of seven scenarios requiring employees to use their understanding of laws and regulations to answer ethics-related questions. Employees who incorrectly answer questions or illustrate a lack of knowledge about relevant laws and regulations are contacted by the DAEO and the ethics policy is reviewed. In addition to ensuring that employees have an active knowledge of ethics rules, the questionnaires allow DAEOs to identify problem areas that need to be addressed on an agency-wide basis.

(continued)

Exhibit 3.7 *(continued)*

- Interactive CD-ROMs to train and provide information to agency staff
- Biweekly ethics training sessions for new employees
- Loose-leaf ethics policy binders for all employees that allow for updates and communication of actual ethics-related problems confronted by agency employees
- Periodic publications on agency ethics that include quizzes
- E-mail delivery of monthly ethics updates

The OGE realizes that in addition to these training techniques, a culture of ethics must be encouraged by agency leaders if ethical behavior is to become part of standard operating procedure. Toward this end, OGE promotes an ethical culture whereby agency leaders "identify concrete actions. . . . to promote an ethical culture and to support an agency's ethics program." OGE offers specific ways in which commitment to an ethics program can be demonstrated:

- Communicate the importance of ethics (e.g., enhance the visibility of the ethics office by ensuring it is clearly reflected in the organizational chart of the agency)
- Underscore the consequences of unethical behavior (e.g., post possible penalties for violating the ethics laws in public areas)
- Promote awareness of the ethics training program [e.g., have ethics officials brief senior staff (on content and participation in training programs)]
- Demonstrate the emphasis placed on ethics training (e.g., participate in an ethics training session alongside employees)
- Demonstrate the emphasis placed on an ethical culture (e.g., make managers and supervisors accountable for the actions of staff who fail to fulfill their ethics requirements)
- Demonstrate personal ethics behavior (e.g., model a "Should I do it?" versus a "Can I do it?" mentality)
- Demonstrate vision (e.g., incorporate ethics elements in the agency emergency preparedness plan)
- Promote an ethical culture of transparency, efficiency, and accountability (e.g., solicit employees' ideas on how to maximize involvement in ethics)
- Emphasize the importance of follow-up and accountability (e.g., emphasize to employees the importance of reporting observed misconduct).

Sources: Adapted from United States Office of Government Ethics (http://www.usoge.gov/pages/about_oge/background_mission.html); http://www.usoge.gov/ethics_docs/agency_model_prac/agency_model_prac.aspx; http://www.usoge.gov/ethics_docs/agency_model_prac/looseleaf_handbook.aspx.

Should this occur, beware of statements such as:

"Corruption is everywhere." The claim not only is self-defeating, but also assumes something that is, in fact, contestable. Poor health is common, but no one concludes that treating it is a bad idea.

"Dealing with corruption requires difficult changes taking many years." While evil has been present for a very long time, so has honor. There is no time like the present to close loopholes, create incentives and deterrents, and augment accountability. The objective is to change the perception of corruption from low-risk, high-profit to high-risk, low-profit.

"Worrying about corruption is pointless; with free markets, corruption will disappear." Corruption can easily damage markets as the Savings and Loan, Enron, and subprime/credit crises have clearly demonstrated; the scandals exposed widespread misdoings, exploding the myth of self-regulating markets. Markets, as imperfect human-created constructions of reality, eventually may be self-correcting, but not without considerable damage to society (see Klitgaard et al. 2000).

It is critical, then, that invalid reasons for ignoring corruption be recognized and rejected.

Conclusion

Moral development theory and the strengths and weakness of three major approaches to ethics—results, rules, and virtue—are part of the mosaic of understanding moral philosophy. The Ethics Triangle model emphasizes the interdependence of these approaches and can assist professionals in making good decisions. As Stephen K. Bailey (1965) believed, the dilemma—and glory—of public service is to be consistent enough to deserve respect from others (and oneself) and pliable enough to accomplish ethical objectives. Each person, in short, should strive to become ethically competent. This means being committed to high standards, possessing knowledge of relevant ethical codes and laws, engaging in ethical reasoning, acting upon public service ethics and values, and promoting ethical behavior in organizations (Menzel 2009).

Ultimately, the challenge of every public servant is to resolve to act solely in the public interest and to shun the many opportunities that threaten this resolve. The quest to improve social circumstances and ultimately to fulfill human potential, is to lead the "good life." The state of mind required to achieve this has been eloquently described by Max Weber:

> [I]t is immensely moving when a mature person . . . is aware of a responsibility for the consequences of his conduct and really feels such responsibility

with heart and soul. He then acts by following an ethic of responsibility and somewhere he reaches the point where he says: "Here I stand; I can do no other." That is something genuinely human and moving. . . . In so far as this is true, an ethic of ultimate ends and an ethic of responsibility are not absolute contrasts but rather supplements, which only in unison constitute a genuine person—a person who can have the "calling" for politics (Weber 1991, 127).

Individual ethical behavior revolves around values and recognition of the tension between public and private morality. Organizational ethics involve an understanding of the vitality inherent in conflicts and the capability to harmonize opposing interests in praiseworthy ways. Moral development theory establishes organizational guidelines for ethical infrastructures. Such guidelines, or codes of ethical behavior, can lay the foundations for an organizational ethical culture but they cannot create it—that remains the function of leadership, the subject of the next chapter.

Appendix 3.1. Organizational Ethics in the Nonprofit Sector

Bonnie Feinman, founder of Special Families (San Diego, California), with Levi F. Robinson and Bruce Hillman

American society was created with a basic distrust of government, and that suspicion remains as a large part of the national culture. As a direct result, these 1.5 million nonprofit arts, environmental, human services, civil rights, and other organizations have gained considerable power and respect; because they do not distribute profits, they are exempt from taxes by virtue of being organized for public purposes. They not only provide services, but also promote such values as community justice, compassion, and social responsibility. Given their altruistic purpose, many people do not question the behavior of these organizations. This public reverence is matched only by outrage at such scandals as

- Exorbitant salaries paid to United Way of America (and some other nonprofit) executives in addition to a series of highly publicized fraud cases;
- Overhead expenditures twice the average for charitable organizations on the part of the U.S. Olympic Committee; and
- Chronic quality control problems, fundraising and distribution inefficiencies, as well as a diversion of substantial 9/11 funds for administrative purposes on the part of the American Red Cross.

Indeed, the general assumption that nonprofits promote ethical conduct, the public's limited attention span, and a willingness to forgive obfuscates the need for ethical training in the third sector. In addition, important barriers to the incorporation of ethical values in daily operations include the following:

- Compliance with legal constraints and regulations, and publication of an admirable mission statement are often regarded as sufficient.
- A pluralistic staff, representing multiple professions (each with their own ethics code) establishes a territorial attitude that may support conflicting standards, a situation that complicates identification of common values.
- Performance is judged by volunteer board members with a business, bottom-line orientation.
- An attitude that because staff members must deal with "difficult" populations, nonprofits "earn" a tolerance for less than exemplary management.
- Tight budgets common to nongovernmental organizations restrict dollars available for training.

Leadership is, of course, a significant factor in setting an organization's moral direction. In one example, a nonprofit agency serving emotionally disturbed children had CEOs with social work background for most of its more than 100 years of existence. With rare exception, the social work ethos carries a moral dimension that places the highest priority on helping people. Beginning in 1990, the required professional background of the CEO changed from social work to business administration.

With this change came a shift in focus: The first priority was the bottom line, which took on a moral dimension because only then could children be helped. This had a domino effect on decision making throughout the organization as it took the "low road" to organizational ethics. The primary question for personnel issues, program planning, and daily child care decisions became "Is this cost effective?" rather than "Is this helping a child?" Licensing regulations were regarded as necessary evils; the goal was to avoid fines and bad publicity. Quality standards were something to prove to the accrediting organization with the proper documentation. Other nonprofits were regarded as competition and offers of collaboration were viewed with suspicion. Given this perspective, the organization represents Kohlberg's stage 2 of moral development.

With uneven accountability, access to donated funds, and a client base comprised of the neediest members of society, the potential for abuse cannot be overlooked. The first step in advancing ethical behavior is creation of clear ethical guidelines. Beyond that, there must be institutional encouragement of ethical behavior so that the principles behind the guidelines become an accepted part of the agency's ethical infrastructure. It is not enough that these organizations were created to do good work; they must do good work in an honorable manner. Because the nonprofit sector avoids much of the regulation and scrutiny found in business and government, it must develop and apply its own standards; if it avoids its responsibilities, its very purpose is negated.

Appendix 3.2. Organizational Ethics
Enron: A Code of Ethics with No Culture of Ethics

On paper, the Enron Corporation had what appeared to be one of the most comprehensive, thorough, and commendable code of ethics ever devised. In July 2000, Enron Chairman Kenneth Lay wrote a letter introducing Enron's code of ethics to employees. The sixty-five-page document laid out in detail the ethical behavior expected of all employees, from the chairman down through the entire structure (Miller 2002). The Code referred to ethical behavior in the areas of:

- Human rights (respect, integrity, communication, excellence) that transcend all boundaries
- Insider trading
- Antitrust legislation
- Conflicts of interest
- Open and honest communication

The document referred to employee actions necessary for Enron to retain its "competitive edge" but always within the framework of ethical behavior.

Every employee had to sign the certificate of compliance included in the booklet, and a set of mechanisms that appeared to be direct and transparent was put in place so that employees could report suspected violations. The Code exhorted employees to report any concerns to the compliance officer or even to "telephone or send an email addressed to the office of the Chairman of the Company" (direct phone number included). Suspicions could be voiced either anonymously or personally; the Code of Ethics contained a strong statement that whistleblowers would not be harassed or punished.

The Enron Corporation explained its company's code of ethics in a detailed, transparent, and compellingly written document in July 2000. Less than a year later, it became clear that Enron's official Code of Ethics booklet wasn't worth the paper it was written on.

The Enron Board of Directors had openly waived one component of the company's code of ethics twice in order to allow an Enron executive, Andrew Fastow, to head up two outside partnerships with which Enron would do business and from which Fastow could expect great financial gain. This was supposed to be a temporary measure, subject to annual review " . . . as to the application of the Company's code of ethics to assure that such transactions would not adversely affect the best interests of the Company."

It turned out that the "interests of the company" in the eyes of top management lay more in cooking the books in order to enrich themselves and placate worried investors than in following their own ethical guidelines. Far more serious than this supposed temporary action on the part of the Board was management's willful violation of every single component of the code of ethics behind closed doors, from insider trading, to opaque and illegal business transactions, to the sleight-of-hand approach to Enron's accounting system that made it appear that the company was flush when it was flat broke. The managers' violation of their own company's code of ethics not only destroyed the company, but lay waste to its thousands of employees, who lost their jobs and their entire pensions, and to the U.S. economy as a whole. Perhaps most significantly, in light of this very public code of ethics, the officers' ethics violation undermined the trust so necessary for a healthy economy and cultivated a new level of cynicism that was harmful to public life in America.

There is an important lesson to be learned from this disastrous episode: In order to have meaning, an organization's code of ethics must be accompanied by a culture of ethics that is promulgated and practiced from the top down and reinforced, reinvigorated, and replicated from the bottom up through daily example and a workable accountability system based on pragmatism, not puffery. Business ethics experts note than an organizational culture of ethics begins and is sustained by the commitment of managers and leaders to personally embody the organization's code of ethics.

> "People at the top tend to set the target, the climate, the ethos, the expectations that fuel behavior," says Thomas Donaldson, a business ethics professor at the Wharton School at the University of Pennsylvania. . . . Practicing good business ethics creates dividends that go beyond avoiding legal disaster. A host of studies has shown that employees who perceive their companies to have a conscience possess a higher level of job satisfaction and feel more valued as workers. The 2000 Ethics Resource Center [Washington, D.C.] study canvassed corporations and nonprofits across the country. Among its findings: Managers' efforts to instill good business ethics were welcomed overwhelmingly by workers (Wee 2002).

Exhibit 3.7 in this chapter illustrates the mechanisms by which *code of ethics* can be turned into a *culture of ethics* by examining the guidelines established by the U.S. Office of Government Ethics.

Note: The Enron Code of Ethics booklet produced in July 2000 can be found in its entirety at http://www.thesmokinggun.com/graphics/packageart/enron/enron.pdf.

Figure 4.1   **The Competency Triangle of Public Service Professionalism**

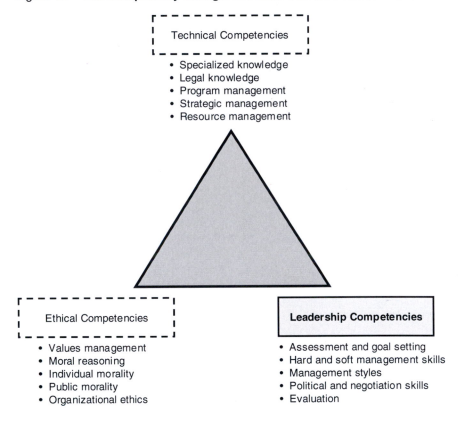

Chapter 4

The Consummate Professional

Creating Leadership

Leadership is the capacity to translate vision into reality.
—Warren G. Bennis

Public service professionals confront complex challenges in the name of the common good. They must possess technical skills in an area of specialized knowledge and organizational management. They should also have a finely honed sense of ethical behavior that compels them to "do the right thing" when charged with balancing competing interests or confronting political intrigue. These talents, however, are not sufficient to produce public service excellence. To develop "the professional edge," public servants must exhibit leadership qualities that support and give meaning to their technical abilities and ethical actions. Members of the Senior Executive Service were recently asked, "What is the percentage of your current work that you consider to be of a leadership/managerial nature?" Survey results revealed that in more than two-thirds of agencies, on average a majority of the work involves leadership and management (U.S. OPM 2008d). This chapter explores the role and nature of the complex and subtle topic of leadership.

Leadership is a challenging subject, the discussion of which ranges from generalized platitudes to sophisticated modeling techniques. Its nature varies significantly over time and from one situation to the next. Leadership competency includes a range of inherent personal traits and a set of learned skills (Appendix 4.1). New leadership development programs operate on the assumption that some inherent personal traits can also be learned, so that leaders can be "grown" as well as "born." Leaders use these traits and skills to assess the institutional dynamics of their organizations and the environment in which they operate (Van Wart 2003). They face the constraints that are intrinsic to overseeing routine tasks and the challenges of leading change. Leadership's role in an organization is crucial, as is demonstrated by the vulnerability that results from its absence.

Public service leadership is similar to that found in the private and nonprofit sectors; but it is also unique in the following ways: Public leaders are part of an administrative structure that includes career employees and political appointees; networking relationships that characterize the "new public service" cross sectoral boundaries and demand sophisticated knowledge of public and private sector organization (Chapter 1); civil service activities are subject to both horizontal and vertical oversight; and public agencies must retain the transparency that lies at the heart of a democracy.

This chapter tackles two crucial aspects of leadership: (1) its development in the civil service and (2) the traits and skills that characterize leadership competency. The latter is explored through two examples: How political skills allowed a government bureaucrat to stand up to powerful politicians and how negotiation skills can turn intractable political conundrums into mutually beneficial results. Whereas the first example required a leader to stand up to his political masters and demand recognition of the letter and spirit of the law, the second illustrates how public servants can learn to be more adept at negotiating with opponents in order to best serve the common good.

Leadership in the Public Sector

Interested onlookers have long worried that leadership in the public arena has not kept pace with leadership development in the commercial and nonprofit sectors and that the lag undermines the productivity of government agencies and the performance of their employees. Added to the problem of an aging civil service and difficulty in recruiting new young talent (Chapter 1) is the unique environment of government employment, which makes leadership more difficult to develop and sustain than in the commercial and nonprofit sectors where organizational hierarchies and goals may be more stable and clearly defined.

One key element of this environment is its two-part administrative structure, which combines officials who are elected and appointed with high-level managers in the career bureaucracy (Ingraham and Getha-Taylor 2004, 96). Career civil servants in the U.S. Department of State, some of whose expertise in a specific area spans decades and several presidents, may find themselves subordinate to a presidentially appointed ambassador with no foreign policy experience. A program manager in a state environmental protection agency who has worked her way up the ranks of the bureaucracy in the field of pollution controls may find her efforts thwarted by a gubernatorial appointee who brings different ideological assumptions or political connections to the job. A project manager who led efforts to find funding for city housing projects may suddenly find his efforts stymied by the election of a mayor who opposes public housing construction. This dual administrative structure in the public sector makes leadership development particularly problematic and unique.

A second challenge is a new public service milieu that encourages agencies to work with private firms and nonprofit organizations to attain public goals. The networking of resources and tasks, as well as the contracting out of services, means that managers and leaders must possess cross-organizational and cross-sector skills, the ability to motivate different groups of employees, the flexibility to adapt to different work environments, and the capacity to oversee the integrity of complex processes. A third environmental pressure on leaders is the cross-cutting assessment of and influence over their actions and their organizations. Horizontal oversight (e.g., court assessments of an agency's actions), and vertical influence (e.g., the need to alter local and state educational standards in order to attain federal funding), add to the external pressures faced by leaders. Democratic transparency constitutes a fourth challenge. The availability of public records, access to meetings, and media attention are all laudable features of a democratic political process; at the same time they put unique pressures on public servants in their pursuit of the commonweal.

Finally, while change is an ongoing feature of all organizations, the nature and scope of change in issues that confront public servants means that leaders must be especially adept at managing change in unstable and opaque environments. The creation of the Department of Homeland Security (DHS) after the 9/11 terrorist attacks, for instance, produced a radical change in both the organization of civil service activities and the goals to which they were directed. Dozens of agencies in many different federal departments, along with all their employees, were shifted to the new DHS. The emphasis on disaster relief efforts changed from natural disasters to catastrophic terrorism, and new channels of information had to be coordinated, filtered, and processed. The challenges to leadership in this uncertain environment were, and continue to be, enormous.

Demands on leaders are so acute that they have received dedicated and focused attention from government agencies and civic-minded nonprofit organizations. The U.S. Office of Personnel Management (OPM), for example, carried out a study of 8,000 leaders and managers in the civil service and used it to derive a set of five executive core qualifications (ECQs) that incorporate twenty-eight leadership competencies as a way to direct the hiring, development, and evaluation of leaders throughout the federal bureaucracy. These ECQs include the abilities to lead change, direct people, drive results, apply business acumen, and build coalitions (U.S. OPM 2008a). OPM has developed two methods of recruiting and training leaders that correspond to the civil service's dual administrative structure referred to earlier: Its Senior Executive Service (SES) is a group of career executives who embody the leadership competencies that make up the ECQs (U.S. OPM 2008c). In addition, the OPM publication

United States Government Policy and Supporting Positions (known as the Plum Book) advertises more than 9,000 positions that can be filled either through career civil service promotions or noncompetitive appointments (U.S. OPM 2008b). In 2006, OPM launched the Federal Government Leadership Development Program (FedLDP), which catalogues all of the leadership development programs in each agency that are designed to instill and enhance relevant skills. This approach applies to the nature of leadership in all fields; individuals must utilize and add to a set of general competencies in different ways, depending on the organizational culture in which they operate.

Nonprofit organizations have also become involved in encouraging leadership in public service. Foremost among them is the Partnership for Public Service, founded in 2001 by Samuel J. Heyman, an attorney in the Kennedy administration's Department of Justice. This group merged in 2005 with the Private Sector Council, an organization dedicated to bringing corporate leaders together with public service leaders to improve government productivity. The Partnership seeks to "fuel innovation" in government by "[i]mproving government performance. . . . [driving] change in government by providing hands-on assistance to federal agencies from both in-house experts and private sector partners. . . . conducting research to measure government performance in ways that promote transparency and accountability, and growing and training a new class of change agents within our government" (Partnership for Public Service 2008). It offers a Public Service Fellows program and works with federal agencies, corporations, foundations, and nonprofits to conduct research, further education, and promote professional interaction in order to inspire a new generation of public service–minded individuals who can meet the challenges faced by prospective leaders in the field. (For an extensive account of landmark achievements by civil servant leaders in contemporary history, see Light 2002). The 2008 recipients of the Partnership's Service to America Medals ("Sammies") are profiled in Table 4.1. This award recognizes the recipients' work to make the nation "safer, healthier, and greener" (Partnership for Public Service 2008).

The next section turns to the skills and traits that constitute the leadership competency that these individuals must develop, enhance, and master in order to excel.

Leadership Competency: Traits and Skills

As indicated by the OPM's approach, while every organization has specific needs with respect to the traits and skills one must possess in order to lead it toward excellence, there are overarching characteristics that individuals must exhibit in order to lead in any context. Some of these involve hard

Table 4.1

Winners of the Nonprofit Partnership for Public Service Awards 2008

Name	Agency	Award	Impact
Richard Greene	U.S. Agency for International Development	Federal Employee of the Year	Leadership of the President's Malaria Initiative providing prevention and treatment resources (e.g. malarial drugs, insecticide-treated mosquito nets) to 25 million African children and pregnant women.
Stephen Andersen	Environmental Protection Agency	Career Achievement Medal	Helped implement the Montreal Protocol, a treaty that has protected about 6 million lives from skin cancer and saved about $4 trillion in health care costs.
Alain D. Carballeyra	59th Medical Wing at Lackland Air Force Base	Call to Service Medal	Transformed the Air Force's only 3-D medical modeling laboratory into a state-of-the-art facility for those treating wounded service members.
Rajiv Jain	U.S. Department of Veterans Affairs	Citizen Services Medal	Leadership in reducing a life-threatening, hospital-acquired infection at 153 VA hospitals and other facilities nationwide.
Eddie Bernard	National Oceanic and Atmospheric Administration	Homeland Security Medal	Helped to prevent loss of life from natural disasters by creating a tsunami detection system that increased earlier warning time.
Steven Chalk	U.S. Energy Department	Science and Environment Medal	Leadership in federal efforts to increase the development and use of renewable energy.
Mary Katherine Friedrich	U.S.-Afghan Women's Council	National Security and International Affairs Medal	Worked with young Afghani women to clarify their career goals and the choices available to them.
Mark Pletcher	U.S. Department of Justice	Justice and Law Enforcement Medal	Leadership in halting bid-rigging, fraud and corruption among U.S. officials and defense contractors in Iraq, Kuwait and Afghanistan.

Source: Adapted from Ballenstedt, 2008b.

skills, or the ability to attain specific goals through concrete actions (such as organizing a unit to attain maximum effectiveness, overseeing a project to ensure goal attainment, preparing a budget, or implementing a new computer system). Complementing these hard skills is a set of soft skills and personality traits used to develop the constructive human interactions necessary to attain organizational goals. Soft skills—often called people skills or emotional intelligence—refer to the abilities used to control one's own behavior and relate to others in ways that compel the most desirable outcomes. Personality traits tend to be inherent or ingrained, while soft skills are more easily learned. The term "born leader" indicates an assumption that a person has inherent leadership personality traits, while the OPM's approach is that great leaders are made, not born. This distinction is important because it determines whether organizations seek leaders through recruitment or the training of current employees. While born leaders may effortlessly step into top positions because they have natural abilities to motivate people, those without such capabilities may be trained to acquire them. Whether born or trained, leaders must possess the traits and soft skills necessary to inspire others to follow their example and strive for excellence.

The Leadership Cycle

The five components of the leadership competency can be viewed as a cycle, as illustrated in Figure 4.2.

Leaders first assess their organizations and the environments in which they operate and then establish performance and outcome goals. They then use their technical and management skills to address these goals and apply their personality traits and emotional intelligence to motivate relevant internal and external actors to excel, adapting their personal leadership style to suit the context. At some point, leaders inevitably have to bring political or negotiation skills into play in order to break through roadblocks that emerge or to mediate among competing interests that threaten the realization of organizational goals. Finally, officials must evaluate their own behaviors and strategies and their concomitant effect on the organization and the realization of organizational goals. When a task is completed or a goal reached, the process begins again. Each component of the leadership competency is briefly examined here.

1. Assessment and Goal Setting

Organizational as well as environmental assessment and goal setting are the logical first steps in the leadership process. This stands out in sharpest relief when a new individual is recruited to conduct a review of a work system by scrutinizing data and interviewing employees. Effective leaders possess the analytical skills necessary to review large amounts of information and identify important operational and motivational trends. These include task skills, role clarity, innovation and creativity, resources and support services, employee

Figure 4.2   **The Leadership Cycle**

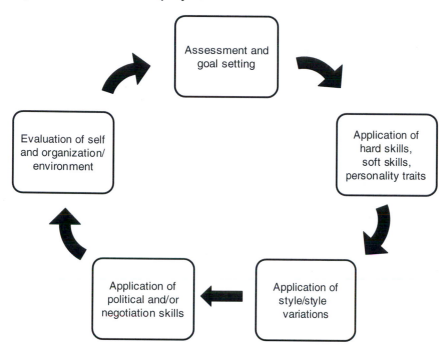

inclusiveness and productivity, cohesiveness and cooperation, work organization, performance strategies, organizational culture, and external coordination
and adaptability (Yukl 1998).

Some of the relevant questions leaders assess in relation to these trends are:
Do employees have the skills, training, and supervisory feedback necessary
to do their jobs? Do individuals and teams know exactly what is expected
of them? Does the organization encourage all employees to be innovative
and creative? Are employee pay, benefit, and workplace policies adequate
to compete in the market? Are employees supported by adequate human
resource, budgeting, and information technology administrative staff? Are
all employees invested in the goals of the institution? Are labor relations
more harmonious than hostile? Is work organized to promote efficiency and
are all personnel provided incentives to excel rather than just get by? Is the
culture of the organization such that stated goals can be attained or does the
culture need to be adapted to changing circumstances? Does the agency have
effective external links and can it react deftly when the external environment
suddenly shifts?

2. Application of Hard Skills, Soft Skills and Personality Traits

Hard skills are the technical expertise and management skills examined in Chapter 2. Technical expertise involves a field of specialized knowledge that leaders must master in order to excel at their jobs, an understanding of the legal requirements related to the position, and a keen awareness of the functioning of the organization within which that job exists. Technical management skills involve the attainment of goals through the effective management of organizational operations; they include strategic planning, project and program management, team building, budgetary operations, staffing decisions, technology implementation, and change management. Hard skills can be learned, making it easier to train current employees to perform additional technical skills or to promote an employee from a technical to a managerial position. Leaders, in particular, must master a specialized field of knowledge and the legal and organizational context within which it is applied, as well as a wide array of managerial skills, so that they can harness all the resources at their disposal to make a significant impact. Hard skills are necessary for excellent leadership but are by no means sufficient. It is the personality traits and soft skills—those components of leadership competency that are either innate or more difficult to learn—that determine whether people have the capacity to become true leaders.

Emotional intelligence, or a set of soft skills, involves the ability to use one's own emotional maturity to relate to and communicate with others. Emotional maturity includes awareness of one's own emotions, an instinct for how to balance flexibility and resolve, and the capacity to reconcile ambition with ethical standards (Berman and West 2008). Interpersonal skills, such as understanding others' interests and motivation, listening to employees' concerns, leading by example, fostering teamwork, and creating a productive work atmosphere are necessary to effectively engage coworkers and subordinates so that they work to their best capacities. Communication skills—written, verbal, and nonverbal—are crucial in ensuring that all involved parties understand the expectations placed upon their work, the goals of particular tasks, and the ultimate purpose of organizational endeavors. Increasingly, these communication skills involve what is known as cultural competency, or the ability to communicate effectively across diverse cultural groups by understanding the values and behaviors that comprise a diverse workforce (Combs 2002). Leaders must understand how to coordinate specific organizational cultures with the variety of human cultures that make up the organization. Studies have shown that, however they are labeled, emotional intelligence skills are valued and nurtured in public service managerial positions (Magala 2005).

By the turn of the twentieth century, researchers concluded that leadership varies too much by individual and situational circumstances to build a theory equating certain personality attributes with leadership ability (Stogdill 1948). It is clear, however, that certain personal traits and the ability to relate to others are essential. Pertinent personality attributes include physical comportment, self-confidence, decisiveness, resilience, flexibility, energy and drive, a willingness to assume responsibility, and a motivation to excel. It is clear from this list that these traits alone are not enough to guarantee that a leader will use them for positive ends, such as organizational excellence or perpetuation of public goods. Physical comportment—a personal presence that inspires confidence—may be used to intimidate as well as motivate. Each of the traits listed here may be directed toward aggrandizing the individual and not attaining organizational or societal goals; excessive confidence, for example, can degrade into egotism, stubbornness, or aloofness. Thus, a further set of personal characteristics used to identify positive leaders focuses on ethical behavior and integrity (Chapter 3). Studies of employee attitudes put integrity, honesty, and fairness at the top of the list of desirable leadership attributes. Because of the stewardship role of leaders, these values assume an almost hallowed stature, the absence of which is enough to tarnish reputations (Fairholm 1991; Terry 1995; Riccucci 1995).

3. Application of Personal Style

Style refers to dominant and defining behavioral patterns. Few leaders have a single, overall style that they use all the time; styles vary from one situation to the next. People tend to have preferred and secondary styles that they either adopt consciously or, more often than not, simply exhibit unconsciously. Their preferred style is the one with which they feel most comfortable and they rely upon in ambiguous situations. Secondary styles are those that they consciously employ to adapt to particular situations. Successful leaders know which styles are appropriate to which situations. They either adapt their style to the situation or attempt to change the nature of the situation in order to fit in with their preferred style (Hersey and Blanchard 1969). Scholars differ on how much a given individual can alter style or adapt to circumstances (Fiedler, Chemers, and Mahar 1976). Style change occurs, for example, when a leader switches from negotiation to confrontation to attain a goal. A situation change, on the other hand, would involve defusing a confrontation so that negotiation tactics can be employed. It is possible that an individual has a great capacity in one style only, without the ability to call upon secondary styles; in this case, effective leaders will prove capable of adapting situations to fit their behavior or to find the right person to handle a given situation.

The way people employ styles depends upon the nature and role of those with whom they interact, organizational power structure, organizational goals, and the environmental factors affecting an organization. Leaders are likely to use different approaches with new recruits than they do with long-time veterans. Large agencies may have a dual power structure, where the CEO or director focuses on external relations and a chief deputy director handles internal operations; this calls for leadership styles that differ from those used in a single hierarchical power structure. External, or "environmental," crises (such as unexpected obstacles to goal attainment from outside the organization or terrorist threats undermining national security) demand different styles than stable environments with foreseeable patterns of interaction.

Finally, the goal of organizational leadership affects how leaders adapt their styles: is the goal to maintain the status quo or to introduce changes that enhance performance or promote newly defined goals? Management activities designed to maintain the status quo call for "transactional" styles, whereas leading organizational change calls for styles that are "transformational" in scope (Trottier, van Wart, and Wang 2008), in which leaders play the role of "change agent." The transformational style is entrepreneurial (encouraging redefinition of tasks), charismatic (motivating people to adjust to changing circumstances), and visionary (clearly articulating new goals and ways to attain them). Complete the tests in Exhibits 4.1, 4.2, and 4.3 to assess your own leadership skills, styles, and personality traits.

4. Use of Political and Negotiation Skills

Individuals may possess all of the technical and personal skills and traits embodied in leadership competency and yet fail in the end if they lack two crucial abilities: to overcome inevitable opposition and to negotiate among conflicting interests, both of which can bring organizational progress to a standstill. Leaders require political skills to avert or successfully counter opposition, and negotiation skills to settle conflicts of interest that arise both within and outside of their organizations.

Only rarely can people in top positions successfully impose their vision on a hierarchical structure. More often than not, some form of opposition, whether blatant or subtle, direct or indirect, obstructs a leader's goals. This is especially true in public service, where personnel operate within a dual administrative and cross-sectoral structure that may include governmental, commercial, and nonprofit organizations. An elected official may encounter opposition from entrenched civil servants who instinctively oppose change. A seasoned career professional may encounter opposition from unqualified elected officials who pursue their own political interests, rather than those of the organization. Managers and leaders in all sectors may encounter various

Exhibit 4.1

Leadership Trait Questionnaire

Instructions: The purpose of this questionnaire is to measure personal characteristics of leadership. The questionnaire should be completed by the leader and five individuals who are familiar with the leader.

For each adjective listed below, indicate the degree to which you think the adjective describes the leader. Please select one of the following responses to indicate the strength of your opinion.

Key: 5 = strongly agree, 4 = agree, 3 = neutral, 2 = disagree, 1 = strongly disagree

1. Articulate—Communicates effectively with others	1	2	3	4	5
2. Perceptive—Discerning and insightful	1	2	3	4	5
3. Self-confident—Believes in oneself and one's ability	1	2	3	4	5
4. Self-assured—Secure with self, free of doubts	1	2	3	4	5
5. Persistent—Stays fixed on goal(s), despite interference	1	2	3	4	5
6. Determined—Takes a firm stand, acts with certainty	1	2	3	4	5
7. Trustworthy—Acts believably, inspires confidence	1	2	3	4	5
8. Dependable—Is consistent and reliable	1	2	3	4	5
9. Friendly—Shows kindness and warmth	1	2	3	4	5
10. Outgoing—Talks freely, gets along well with others	1	2	3	4	5

Scoring Interpretation: The scores received on the leadership trait questionnaire provide information about how you see yourself and how others see you as a leader. The chart allows you to see where your perceptions are the same as others and where they differ. There are no best ratings on this questionnaire. The purpose of the instrument is to give you a way to assess your strengths and weaknesses and to evaluate areas where your perceptions are congruent with others and where they are not.

Source: Northouse 2003, 31. Copyright ©2003 Sage Publications, Inc. Reprinted with permission.

forms of opposition from recalcitrant employees or outside actors determined to undermine the goals of their organization. Some of the political skills that can help leaders to be successful are: exuding a sincere belief in a set of goals, engaging others to invest themselves in attaining those goals, forging a consensus on the desirability and viability of the goals, separating self-serving

Exhibit 4.2

Style Questionnaire

Instructions: Read each item carefully and think about how often you (or the person you are evaluating) engage in the described behavior. Indicate your response to each item by circling one of the five numbers.

Key: 1 = never, 2 = seldom, 3 = occasionally, 4 = often, 5 = always

1. Tells group members what they are supposed to do	1	2	3	4	5
2. Acts friendly with members of the group	1	2	3	4	5
3. Sets standards of performance for group members	1	2	3	4	5
4. Helps others feel comfortable in the group	1	2	3	4	5
5. Makes suggestions about how to solve problems	1	2	3	4	5
6. Responds favorably to suggestions made by others	1	2	3	4	5
7. Makes his or her perspective clear to others	1	2	3	4	5
8. Treats others fairly	1	2	3	4	5
9. Develops a plan of action for the group	1	2	3	4	5
10. Behaves predictably toward group members	1	2	3	4	5
11. Defines role responsibilities for each group member	1	2	3	4	5
12. Communicates actively with group members	1	2	3	4	5
13. Clarifies his or her own role within the group	1	2	3	4	5
14. Shows concern for the personal well-being of others	1	2	3	4	5
15. Provides a plan for how the work is to be done	1	2	3	4	5
16. Shows flexibility in making decisions	1	2	3	4	5
17. Provides criteria for what is expected of the group	1	2	3	4	5
18. Discloses thoughts and feelings to group members	1	2	3	4	5
19. Encourages group members to do quality work	1	2	3	4	5
20. Helps group members get along	1	2	3	4	5

Scoring: The style questionnaire is designed to measure two major types of leadership behaviors: task and relationship. Score the questionnaire by doing the following. First, sum the responses on the odd-numbered items. This is your task score. Second, sum the responses on the even-numbered items. This is your relationship score.

Total scores: Task_____ Relationship_____

Scoring interpretation:
45–50 Very high range; 40–44 High range; 35–39 Moderately high range; 30–34 Moderately low range; 25–29 Low range; 10–24 Very low range;

Exhibit 4.3

Skills Inventory

Instructions: Read each item carefully and decide whether the item describes you as a person. Indicate your response to each item by circling one of the five numbers to the right of each item.

Key: 1 = not true, 2 = seldom true, 3 = occasionally true, 4 = somewhat true, 5 = very true

1. I enjoy getting into the details of how things work.   1   2   3   4   5
2. As a rule, adapting ideas to people's needs is relatively   1   2   3   4   5
   easy for me.
3. I enjoy working with abstract ideas.   1   2   3   4   5
4. Technical things fascinate me.   1   2   3   4   5
5. Being able to understand others is the most important   1   2   3   4   5
   part of my work.
6. Seeing the "big picture" comes easily for me.   1   2   3   4   5
7. One of my skills is being good at making things work.   1   2   3   4   5
8. My main concern is to have a supportive communica-   1   2   3   4   5
   tion climate.
9. I am intrigued by complex organizational problems.   1   2   3   4   5
10. Following directions and filling out forms comes easily   1   2   3   4   5
    for me.
11. Understanding the social fabric of the organization is   1   2   3   4   5
    important to me.
12. I would enjoy working out strategies for my organiza-   1   2   3   4   5
    tion's growth.
13. I am good at completing the things I've been assigned   1   2   3   4   5
    to do.
14. Getting all parties to work together is a challenge I   1   2   3   4   5
    enjoy.
15. Creating a mission statement is rewarding work.   1   2   3   4   5
16. I understand how to do the basic things required of me.   1   2   3   4   5
17. I am concerned with how my decisions affect the lives   1   2   3   4   5
    of others.
18. Thinking about organizational values and philosophy   1   2   3   4   5
    appeals to me.

(continued)

Exhibit 4.3 *(continued)*

Scoring: The skills inventory is designed to measure three broad types of leadership skills: technical, human, and conceptual. Score the questionnaire by doing the following: First, sum the responses on items 1, 4, 7, 10, 13, and 16. This is your technical skill score. Second, sum the responses on items 2, 5, 8, 11, 14, and 17. This is your human skill score. Third, sum the responses on items 3, 6, 9, 12, 15, and 18. This is your conceptual skill score.

Total scores:
Technical skill _____   Human skill _____   Conceptual skill _____

Scoring interpretation: The scores you received on the skills inventory provide information about your leadership skills in three areas. By comparing the differences between your scores you can determine where you have leadership strengths and where you have leadership weaknesses. Your scores also point toward the level of management for which you might be most suited.

Source: Northouse 2003, 61–62. Copyright © 2003 Sage Publications, Inc. Reprinted with permission.

---

politicking from substantive opposition, and knowing when to simply impose rules or to negotiate them.

Conflicts of interest may arise at any level of the organization and in any part of its operational environment—whether about salary negotiations, benefits packages, local government budgets and the level of property taxes, strategies to reduce global warming while not undercutting business profits, or missile defense policies among competing international powers. In all cases, leaders must possess the negotiation skills necessary to bring all of the parties to the table, encourage constructive dialogue that turns opponents into partners, and compel participants to attain mutually beneficial outcomes. William Ury, the co-founder of Harvard University Law School's Program on Negotiation, illustrated specific components of negotiation skills and provided examples of a negotiating strategy in his book, *Getting Past No,* that can turn a no-win situation into a win-win outcome. (Exhibits 4.4 and 4.5).

A historical case study from Ury's work shows how deft negotiation skills benefited the United States in its nuclear weapons standoff with the Soviet Union (Appendix 4.2) during the Cold War.

Exhibit 4.4

Negotiation Skills:
Turning the Power Game into a Problem-Solving Game

In addition to reframing a problem to encourage results, William Ury advises negotiators to avoid the temptation to engage in power games that pit opponents against each other and conceive negotiations as a problem-solving game, whereby equal partners seek mutually advantageous outcomes. The following is from Ury's book, *Getting Past No: Negotiating Your Way from Confrontation to Cooperation:*

> The best general is the one who never fights.
> —Sun Tzu

The Power Game: "You threaten or try to coerce the other side and then they back down. However, unless you have a decisive power advantage, they usually resist and fight back. They get angry and hostile, reversing your attempts to disarm them. They cling even more stubbornly to their position, frustrating your efforts to change the game. They become increasingly resistant to reaching agreement, not only because you may be asking for more but because agreement would now mean accepting defeat . . . You are thus forced at great cost to try to impose a solution on the other side. As they strike back, you typically escalate into a costly struggle. . . . you spend a great deal of time and money, not to mention blood, sweat, and tears" (p. 131).

Turn the power game into the problem-solving game:

- Instead of seeking victory, aim for mutual satisfaction. Use power to bring them to their senses, not to their knees.
- Let the other side know the consequences of not reaching an agreement. Ask: "What do you think we will do?" and "What will the absence of an agreement cost you?"
- Warn, don't threaten. Always have your Best Alternative to a Negotiated Agreement (BATNA) in mind; warn your negotiating partner how you will satisfy your interests through BATNA if an agreement is not reached
- Use the minimum power necessary to persuade your opponent to return to the negotiating table; exhaust all your alternatives before escalating.

(continued)

Exhibit 4.4 *(continued)*

- Neutralize your opponents' ability to coerce you by anticipating possible reactions and preparing for them.
- Build a coalition of supporters to help constitute a potential "third force" in the negotiations.
- Let your opponents know they have a way out. For every ounce of power you use, you need to add an ounce of conciliation.
- Let them choose. Paradoxically, just when the other side seems to be coming around, you are well advised to back off and let them make their own decision.
- Keep implementation in mind. Design an agreement that induces the other side to keep their word and protects you if they don't.
- Reaffirm the relationship. It is in your interest for your counterpart to feel as satisfied as possible at the conclusion of the negotiation. Although you may feel elated at your success, don't crow.

Source: Ury 1991, 130–156. Reprinted with permission.

The important point is that a leader must decide when to use political skills to counter opposition to stated strategies and goals and when to negotiate on redefining the strategies or even the goals themselves. In some circumstances, leaders must have the courage to cut through self-serving politicking in order to attain goals; in other cases, they must negotiate with opponents to come to mutually satisfactory conclusions. The skill of deciding which tactic to use is as important as the tactical skills themselves.

5. Evaluation

Evaluation ends one leadership cycle and begins the next. While it can occur at regular intervals, it should be an ongoing activity. First and foremost, leaders must examine the appropriate balance among technical operations, employee productivity, alignment of organizational operations, and progress toward goal attainment. The next step is to identify the areas that require primary focus in upcoming periods. In terms of transformational goals, leaders must analyze the success or failure of strategic initiatives and the specific change management strategies by which they were introduced. Is the overall initiative sound? Have the strategies used to pursue it worked as efficiently and effectively as possible? Should operational processes be altered in order to improve quality of outcomes? What are the requirements

Exhibit 4.5

Applying the "Getting Past No" Negotiation Techniques:
United States–North Korea Stalemate and Breakthrough

Relations between the United States and North Korea have been tense ever since the division of the Korean peninsula following the Korean War in 1950. North Korea became a communist state supported by the Soviet Union. It has been ruled by two dictators, Kim Il-Sung and, after his death in 1994, his son Kim Jong Il. The United States has never recognized the North Korean state and imposed economic and commercial sanctions on North Korea under the Trading with the Enemy Act. The United States had nuclear warheads aimed at North Korea during the Cold War, which were supposed to have been removed in the early 1990s. South Korea is a U.S. ally and both South Korean and U.S. troops are stationed at the demilitarized zone along the border between North and South Korea.

In 1985, North Korea signed the Treaty on the Non-Proliferation of Nuclear Weapons (NPT), pledging never to develop nuclear weapons. U.S. intelligence photos, however, showed signs of possible nuclear weapons materials, which led the International Atomic Energy Agency (IAEA) to demand inspections of North Korean nuclear facilities. Kim Il Sung refused, and announced that North Korea would withdraw from the NPT in March 1993. Two months later, a UN Security Council resolution urged Kim Il Sung to cooperate with the IAEA and also urged UN member states to encourage North Korea to abide by the resolution. No progress was made, however, and by the summer of 1993 North Korea had the nuclear reactor components necessary to produce nuclear weapons.

With tensions high, former President Jimmy Carter, acting for the Clinton administration, brought the United States and North Korea to the negotiating table, and in October 1994 they signed a Framework Agreement, which included the following provisions:

1. North Korea would freeze its plutonium enrichment program and allow IAEA to verify progress
2. North Korea and the United States would work together to safely store the spent fuel from Korea's nuclear reactor
3. North Korea and the United States would work toward a normalization of political and economic relations (extending diplomatic recognition and lifting economic and trade sanctions)
4. North Korea and the United States would cooperate to promote peace and security on a nuclear-free Korean peninsula
5. Both sides agreed to cooperate in strengthening the NPT

(continued)

Exhibit 4.5 *(continued)*

The Framework Agreement was weakened by the fact no time frame was established for each side's compliance measures, no authority was assigned to monitor implementation or compliance, and no interested third parties with political and geostrategic interests in the outcome (i.e., South Korea, Japan, China) were brought into the negotiations. Still, the Framework Agreement was a basis upon which progress could be made. By 1995, North Korea made the commitment to freeze its nuclear program and develop methods to store spent nuclear fuel. In May 2000, the United States and North Korea agreed to follow-up negotiations and proceeded to plan for Agreed Framework Implementation Talks.

Six months later, George W. Bush was elected President and everything changed. Upon taking office in January 2001, President Bush and hard-liners in his Administration rejected both the 1994 Framework Agreement and practically every single one of William Ury's recommendations for reaching a mutually satisfactory agreement between two opposing camps. Bush publicly opposed the 1994 Framework Agreement and his Administration recrafted U.S. policy toward North Korea. The United States claimed that North Korea was developing a program to enrich uranium in order to produce nuclear weapons and was concerned that North Korea would try to sell nuclear armaments to U.S. enemies in order to purchase foodstuffs to feed his population. In his January 2002 State of the Union address, President Bush characterized North Korea as one of the countries comprising an "axis of evil" threatening the interests and security of the United States along with Iraq and Iran. Bush vowed "to confront, not negotiate with" Kim Jong Il, and Vice President Cheney added, "We don't negotiate with evil, we defeat evil." Although the U.S. State Department continued to support negotiations with North Korea to attain elimination of its nuclear processing facilities, hard-liners in the executive branch who equated negotiation with appeasement won out and a standoff ensued. Bush intimated that his ultimate goal was regime change in North Korea and that the United States, acting unilaterally, would do everything in its power to accept nothing less.

North Korea subsequently tested a nuclear device, in addition to announcing its development of a uranium enrichment program, its termination of the 1994 Framework Agreement's freeze on its plutonium-based nuclear program, its expulsion of IAEA inspectors, and its intent to reprocess spent

(continued)

Exhibit 4.5 *(continued)*

nuclear fuel for the purpose of producing weapons. Evidence emerged that North Korea had sold nuclear weapon components to Syria. The United States refused to engage in two-party talks with North Korea, placed the country on its list of state sponsors of terrorism, and ratcheted up the rhetoric against Kim Jong Il's regime, leading some to fear that the Bush administration would not count out military action against North Korea, action it could hardly afford, given the deployment of military troops and the National Guard in Iraq and Afghanistan.

The standoff continued until a shift occurred in the Bush administration's approach to foreign policy. Realizing that its unilateral, ultimatum-based, war-threatening orientation was not producing the desired results, Bush made changes in his Administration and reoriented his own stance, so that the door opened to more productive negotiations from which both sides could gain. Secretary of Defense Donald Rumsfeld was replaced by the more moderate Robert Gates and Condoleezza Rice gave up her National Security Advisor position to become Secretary of State. Together with the highly respected negotiator Assistant Secretary of State Christopher Hill the team worked to establish a foundation for productive negotiations that would convince North Korea to eliminate its nuclear weapons program in return for large-scale U.S. economic aid. Hill emphasized that his negotiations with his North Korean counterparts would take place in phases, and expressed confidence that it would be possible to reach an agreement providing "mutual satisfaction."

After several rounds of talks, the payoffs started to emerge, though in fits and starts: North Korea released a sixty-page declaration of all of its nuclear activities, though six months later than the agreed-upon date, and promised to blow up the cooling tower of its plutonium-based nuclear reactor in Yongbyon, which it fulfilled on June 27, 2008 in front of CNN cameras for all the world to see. In return, the Bush administration offered food aid, lifted some commercial sanctions, and promised to remove North Korea from its list of state sponsors of terrorism on the condition that it would continue to comply with agreement stipulations. On June 30, 2008, the United States began to deliver the promised 500,000 tons of food aid.

Liberal commentators welcomed the Bush administration's newfound willingness to negotiate with North Korea as antagonistic partners rather than irreconcilable enemies. Many conservative observers were less

(continued)

Exhibit 4.5 *(continued)*

impressed with the new approach, some claiming that Bush had abandoned "Republican principles" and weakened the United States through
his policy of appeasement.

Stephen J. Hadley, Bush's National Security Advisor said simply, "I
think one of the things we did in this process, to be honest, is I think we
learned a bit." This episode only temporarily quieted tensions, however.
North Korea's defiant insistence on pursuing nuclear weapons development, as well as its detention and trial of two U.S. journalists, posed
challenges to the new Obama administration in 2009. As in most foreign
policy dilemmas, officials must decide which measures–negotiations,
confrontations, or ultimatums–best support U.S. and international
interests.

Exercise: Apply William Ury's techniques for reframing an issue and
changing the power game into a problem-solving game to this episode in
United States–North Korea relations. Show which techniques were first
rejected and then accepted and illustrate the consequences. For a more
in-depth exercise, research some instances of international diplomacy
that involved appeasement (such as the UK's notorious appeasement
policy in relation to Nazi Germany in 1938) and discuss whether what
seems to be mutual negotiation can really be a one-sided appeasement
that results in harm to one of the partners. Discuss whether there are
instances in which negotiation should not be the motor force of conflict
resolution.

Sources: Davis et al. 2004; Choe Sang-Hun 2008; Schleicher 2003.

---

for effective organizational operations, how have these evolved over time,
and what are future projections? How do these requirements fit into existing
and projected internal and external conditions? Whether managing for the
status quo or leading change, leaders must constantly evaluate the present
and projected condition of the organization within the context of its external
environment.

Finally, officials must examine their own behavior, the roles they play, the
strategies they use, and the impact (positive or negative) they have had. Do
they need to redeploy their own energies based on their assessment? Should
they employ a secondary style to adapt to a particular situation or change
their primary style to meet evolving conditions? Are they continuing to lis-

ten and learn from others and from their own mistakes? Are they prepared to consistently develop their own resources, capacities, and skills in order to perform more effectively? Just as it is important for leaders to understand when to counter opposition head on and when to negotiate, so it is crucial for them to know when to accommodate others for the sake of personal and organizational renewal.

An overview of the disastrous Savings and Loan scandal of the 1980s and 1990s (based on Riccucci 1995) illustrates how a confluence of factors created a crisis for those engaged in public service. The situation cried out for a leader who would marshal the resources of government and the commercial sectors to resolve the debacle. The response came not from powerful political leaders or politicians, many of whom were implicated in the crisis or turned a blind eye to it, but from a courageous bureaucrat who applied all of the components of leadership competency outlined in this chapter to take the lead in getting the savings and loan industry back on its feet. The Savings and Loan scandal is not an isolated incident; in fact, it was only the first act in a series of financial crises that eventually rocked the first decade of the twenty-first century, when no singular leaders emerged to help avert the burgeoning dilemma (Chapter 5).

The Savings and Loan Crisis and the Emergence of an Exemplary Public Administrator

Savings and Loan associations (S&Ls), also called thrifts, were created in the nineteenth century as a community-oriented alternative to corporate national banks. Their main purpose was to encourage home ownership. Individuals could invest their savings in a financial institution that would then use the accumulated capital to make home mortgage loans to people in the community. Borrowers would pay interest on the loans, which would in turn be used to pay depositors interest on their savings accounts. This simple two-way relationship between borrower and S&L promoted an equilibrium that would make for a healthy financial institution and a prosperous, home-owning community. The 3,800 S&Ls that had come into existence by the 1970s were a centerpiece of the American dream. The Federal Savings and Loan Insurance Corporation (FSLIC) insured depositor's savings and the Federal Home Loan Bank Board (FHLBB), a government agency, regulated the S&L industry to promote financially sound transactions and the goal of family home ownership. The government capped the interest rates S&Ls could offer depositors (to ensure capital flow and protect FSLIC obligations), and the interest that could be charged on home mortgage loans (to help middle-class Americans pay off loans for the family home).

The Savings and Loan Crisis: Anatomy of a Failure

The turbulent economic conditions that shook the United States in the 1970s put an end to this cozy equilibrium. Skyrocketing energy prices, declining economic growth, and an unusual confluence of international economic factors resulted in historically high levels of inflation. The resulting rise in interest rates upset the balance that S&Ls had traditionally maintained between their capital assets and outlays. With interest rates high and a cap on how much interest could be offered on deposit accounts, customers began moving their savings to high-interest savings and money market accounts at big banks. As S&Ls began losing significant portions of their capital assets, they still had outstanding mortgage loans that were bringing in lower-than-market interest charges because of the mandatory caps that had been imposed to encourage home ownership. This led to an "asset-liability mismatch" that caused many of the institutions to lose money, with an ever-looming threat of insolvency (Moysich 1997, 168).

In the 1980s, the Reagan administration and Congress decided that a reduction of government intervention and oversight was not only philosophically correct (government should play as limited a role as possible in the economy) but also economically expedient (private entrepreneurs have the best technical skills and motivation to produce wealth) and ethically sound (unfettered production of wealth would lead to the greatest good for the greatest number because of the "trickle down" effect). Critics argued that deregulation was a means to allow the upper classes, the traditional base of the Republican Party, to accumulate ever more wealth and that "trickle down" was merely a ruse to convince Americans that a policy designed in the interest of the elite was really a principled stand to better the lives of the masses. Whatever the case, deregulation proponents weakened government regulation of financial institutions and the number of public examiners was consequently reduced.

The deregulation of S&Ls began with two congressional laws: the Depository Institutions Deregulation and Monetary Control Act of 1980 (FDIC 1980) and the Garn-St. Germain Depository Institutions Act of 1982 (FDIC 2002). These, in conjunction with other regulatory changes, eliminated limitations on S&L interest rates for both savings accounts and loans, expanded the realm of loans from home mortgages to commercial construction and agricultural loans, allowed S&Ls to offer more financial options to customers, and opened the door to a wider range of allowable investments, heretofore prohibited in order to reduce risk. The laws also relaxed accounting and auditing reporting standards so that balance sheets could reflect higher levels of capital assets (Curry and Shibut 2000, 27). Deregulation led to radical changes in the way managers handled financial resources and investments. A whole new layer of financial players came between the customer and savings and loan associations as investment officers engaged in risky transactions with far-off commercial real estate firms, bundled their mortgage loans to sell to outside investors, and sought to enhance their capital assets using untested and complex financial instruments. Independent deposit brokers, stockbrokers at large firms, and Wall Street financiers got into the act as they tried to take advantage of this newfound pool of money.

It did not take long for thousands of these actors to find ways to play the new system to their own advantage. Corrupt deposit brokers developed scams whereby they steered deposits into S&Ls in return for loans for their clients, which they then directed to themselves or their cronies after paying their clients a fee. Some stockbrokers steered the S&Ls toward junk bonds, which resulted in huge financial losses. Many Wall Street financiers bought packages of mortgage loans from the institutions for less than they were worth, "securitized" them, and sold them as government-backed bonds, earning big commissions along the way.

Corrupt S&L officers used the new complex web of financial transactions to their own advantage by engaging in insider trading deals, defrauding their own customers and institutions, and arranging for low-interest loans for themselves and their friends. In sum, many managers as well as third-party financial players used their technical expertise in the intricacies of the financial markets to manipulate the system. They threw all ethical behavior to the wind in the interest of filling their own coffers. Even honest but inexperienced S&L managers felt they were under pressure to engage in risky and ethically questionable financial transactions in order to pump up their capital asset base. The problem was that most supervisory boards, public examiners, accountants, and financial analysts lacked the same expertise or technical skill to keep track of the depth of deception and the overextension of resources. This same technical incompetence lay at the foundation of the more comprehensive financial crisis that struck the U.S. economy in 2008 (Chapter 5).

The result of the corruption was inevitably catastrophic: S&Ls started hemorrhaging money. Their financial staff made ever riskier investments as their initial attempts resulted in dramatic financial losses; fraud and racketeering on the part of corrupt managers and Wall Street speculators drained whatever resources remained. The money that was lost ultimately belonged to the depositors who had entrusted their savings to the community associations. The FSLIC was obligated to pay these depositors insurance on their losses; 100 percent of up to $100,000 deposited. In 1986, the FSLIC was declared insolvent after paying out insurance on the lost S&L deposits and almost 300 of 3,800 organizations across the country were closed or put into government receivership by the end of the year (Curry and Shibut

2000). The news would get even worse despite attempts by Congress to stem the tide. In 1987 Congress established the Financing Corporation (FICO) to renew funding for the FSLIC through the issue of government bonds. This proved insufficient, however, to make up for the huge losses incurred. The FSLIC was abolished in 1989. Congress then created an alphabet soup of new organizations to stem the flow of losses; the only way to do this effectively was to use taxpayer funds to bail out the S&Ls, rescuing those that were salvageable, closing down those that were not, and putting the remainder under government control.

The Civil Servant as Leader: William K. Black

The only hint of leadership—of one person willing to step up and take measures that involved courage, fortitude, and potential costs to himself—came not from a well-known politician who made speeches about the common good and the importance of upholding the law, but rather from an unknown, uncelebrated civil servant who worked in the federal bureaucracy. This public servant stood up to his ultimate boss in the executive branch—the President of the United States—and to powerful members of Congress, including the Speaker of the House of Representatives—by fighting for regulations to restore the financial viability of the financial sector and the ethical accountability of its protagonists and by insisting that violators of the public trust be brought to justice. This person, William K. Black, used the leadership skills and traits examined in this chapter to bring the S&L crisis to light, avert an even more disastrous fallout, hold violators of the law responsible for their actions, and set the industry back on its feet again.

Bill Black demonstrates the professional competencies discussed in this book: technical skill, moral courage, and leadership ability. In asserting his leadership, he made use of the cycle we have examined: He assessed the hostile environment in which he worked, planned goals and backup strategies, made full use of his personality traits and emotional intelligence skills, varied his style to suit evolving situations, used his considerable political skills to take powerful financial and political leaders to task, and evaluated the results to see how improvements could be made. He exemplifies the "new public service" in that he has worked in government, the commercial world, and the nonprofit sector and has maintained strong commitment to the common good. Whether working as a public administrator, private lawyer, or academic, Black has always exhibited the same level of professional dedication in addressing pressing concerns of American citizens. He has worked in relative obscurity, despite the fact that he probably saved taxpayers between $100 billion and $200 billion. Like many unsung heroes in the field of public service, his motivation is not profit, fame, or power but rather dedication to public service, where making a contribution to the commonweal is a fit reward.

After working in the U.S. Department of Justice and in a private law firm, Black became head litigator for the FHLBB in 1984 and deputy director of the FSLIC in 1987. His assessment of the S&L environment began with his successful prosecution of a thrift in Florida. He saw firsthand how corrupt S&L presidents would try to defer government receivership as long as possible so that they could continue to squander millions of dollars without personal liability. He also saw how government kept expanding deregulation, restricting examiner access, and cutting agency budgets and staff in the vain hope that thrifts would "grow their way out of the problem." The FHLBB, a regulatory agency, would normally have had significant legal authority to hold thrifts accountable for their financial viability, but government officials and Congress, with an influential House Speaker and many powerful Senators in the 1980s, curtailed its power and resources. An honest appraisal of the situation would have left most people in Black's position feeling powerless.

But Black and his first boss at the FHLBB, Edwin Gray, refused to be complicit in a scandal that would harm taxpayers and have dire consequences for the whole economy. Employing the first category of the leadership competency (Figure 4.2), they established both short- and long-term strategies that would allow them to fulfill their obligations. In the short term, they continued to regulate S&Ls with the resources they had, dispatched FHLBB examiners to ensure the integrity of financial transactions, and executed government takeovers when necessary. At the same time, they were devising new ways to uncover massive fraud. In the long term, they had to aggressively seek means to hold financiers and politicians responsible for their actions, compel Congress to provide the laws and resources necessary to bring the S&Ls back in line, prevent political intervention in the prosecution of corruption, and resolve a scandal that was spiraling out of control. This would require a whole range of leadership traits and skills, not the least of which was a hefty amount of moral courage.

Leadership: Creative Strategies

Government regulation of the S&L industry suffered from close ties between regulators and industry actors. Under the FHLBB, twelve regional Home Loan Banks—government chartered but privately owned—regulated S&Ls in their jurisdictions; the president and senior staff of each of the Home Loan Banks acted as supervisors of thrifts in their region. This created a dual system: the FHLBB examiners charged with overseeing the S&L industry were federal employees, while the supervisors of S&Ls within each of the twelve regions were employees of the privately-owned Home Loan Banks. This arrangement "generated mistrust and disrespect" between the federal examiners and the regional supervisors (Moysich 1997, 172). The latter received much higher salaries than FHLBB examiners and were in many ways beholden to the thrifts they regulated. The extent to which they supervised S&Ls in accordance with federal guidelines was thus dependent on their individual integrity. FHLBB examiners were weak in comparison to the supervisors from the twelve regional Home Loan Banks because of constant federal budget and staff cuts. The problem was complicated by the rush of inexperienced entrepreneurs who entered the industry once deregulation created a veritable gold rush. Many states, especially California, Texas, and Florida, relaxed their rules on creating and operating S&Ls. The FHLBB was incapable of keeping up with its dwindling resources and faced increasing resistance to government oversight from industry representatives (Moysich 1997, 176–178).

Despite strong resistance, Gray and Black imposed stricter regulations in 1984 to control the level and type of investments S&Ls could make, ensure the financial soundness of S&Ls, and impose tighter accounting practices (Moysich 1997). In 1985, Gray ordered that the number of FHLBB examiners would be doubled. Black took the unprecedented step of transferring the FHLBB's examiner staff to the regional Home Loan Banks so that they would be independent of the executive branch, more generously compensated for their work, and closer to the S&Ls they were regulating.

The reaction from the industry, Congress, and executive branch leaders was fast and furious. Congress tried to delay imposition of the restrictions and controls; S&L financiers put pressure on members of Congress; and Gray came under increasing pressure to fire Black. House Speaker Jim Wright (D-TX) tried to compel Black to leave the thrifts alone and verbally attacked him in public. Charles Keating, who operated the freewheeling Lincoln Savings and Loan, told certain U.S. Senators (whose districts benefited from his business and whose campaigns he helped to fund) that it was payback time. Keating pressured Senators Cranston, DeConcini, Glenn, McCain, and Riegle (who came to be known as the Keating Five) to organize a meeting with Gray and Black to convince them to ease up on Lincoln. This was a most unusual step: a private financier demanding that members of the Senate intimidate regulators to turn a blind eye to speculative transactions and criminal activity. Even more unusual was the fact that the Senators agreed. Black attended two meetings in the spring of 1987 where Senators, in varying degrees, tried to get him to leave Lincoln alone (Black, n.d.).

Black refused to back down or allow powerful politicians to undermine his work. He countered Wright's attacks by divulging to the media the Speaker's attempt to obstruct the FHLBB from carrying out its work. Instead of being intimidated by the Keating Five, Black turned the tables on them. He told them directly that the Lincoln S&L was considered the most corrupt in America and that criminal charges would be filed with the Department of Justice against Keating and other financial operatives.

Leadership: Reassessment

Later that year, as the political intrigue was in full play, Black reassessed the situation and decided he could accomplish more outside of government. He left the FHLBB to help resolve the crisis by employing the resources of the private sector, becoming the chief legal officer in charge of regulating S&Ls at the private Home Loan Bank in San Francisco. Gray, meanwhile, had been replaced by Danny Wall, a former thrift owner who was sympathetic to the industry and deregulation, as Chairman of the FHLBB. Wall did everything in his power to get Black terminated, but Black was now protected by his status as an employee of a private Home Loan Bank and empowered by the responsibility of these regional Banks to carry out S&L examinations. Wall then tried to outflank Black by moving jurisdiction of the Lincoln S&L away from Black's region to protect Keating from criminal charges. He also tried to downplay the crisis so that it would not affect the 1988 presidential election.

Again, Black did not capitulate. Even from a less public position, he used whatever resources he could to bring the scandal to light by engaging in organizational and networking endeavors to ramp up support for exposing corruption. Black maintained public pressure by prosecuting high-profile cases, making accusations against Speaker Wright, the Keating Five, and FHLBB Chairman Danny Wall, exposing corruption, and along with a growing chorus of concerned voices, pressuring Congress to face the S&L crisis in a comprehensive way.

In the end, Black's refusal to back down paid off both literally and figuratively. As the scope of the scandal and the depth of the corruption became widely publicized, its facilitators were called to task. House Speaker Jim Wright lost his position after review by a congressional Ethics Committee. The Senate Ethics Committee also rebuked two of the Keating Five Senators, citing them for using "poor judgment" in calling regulators to a meeting. Keating was prosecuted, charged with fraud and racketeering, and sentenced to twelve years in prison; he was released after four years on a technicality (Petersen 1998). Black's dogged persistence is thought to have stemmed the flow of billions of dollars in S&L losses and saved taxpayers as much as $2 billion. More importantly, his technical skills, ethical integrity, and leadership capabilities illustrated the power of an individual, whether working as a government bureaucrat or private bank examiner, to face down a presidential administration, powerful members of Congress, and influential financiers, all in the name of the public interest.

Leadership: Skills and Style

After assessing the situation and establishing short- and long-term goals, Black employed all the resources embodied in the second category of the leadership competency (Figure 4.2). He used hard skills in financial and legal processes and organizational management to:

- build effective audit teams to tackle new types of fraud at S&Ls, which involved personnel planning, team formation, and personnel management.
- organize project teams with the set of complementary skills necessary to follow through on audits and help the teams rapidly adapt their investigative and litigating practices as the enormity of the scandal unfolded.
- take part in auditing and prosecuting teams where tasks were clearly delineated and power effectively delegated.
- manage technical innovation to give examination teams the necessary investigative tools.
- clarify and optimize the relationship between the FHLBB and the regional FHLBanks through strategic planning, networking, and creative thinking to enhance the power of S&L regulators.
- use his knowledge of government regulations and the law, as well as experience in litigation, to bring criminals to justice.

Then, Black used a whole array of personality traits such as self-confidence, resilience, flexibility, energy, drive, and motivation to excel in order to work in the hostile environment that was allowing fraud and greed to ruin the S&L industry and bankrupt many of its customers. These traits buttressed his ability to apply a set of soft skills and ensured that the application of his technical and management skills would bear fruit. He used these soft skills to:

- hire competent examiners and litigators, clarify their roles, and allow them to do their work independently.
- accurately gauge his examiners' skills and effectively communicate their tasks.
- identify and analyze problems in numerous separate S&L investigations.

- listen to examiners' assessments of a variety of problems.
- organize teams, create a productive working atmosphere among their members, prevent conflict.
- keep his teams motivated despite heavy workloads and political setbacks.
- help his teams to rapidly adapt their investigative and litigating practices.
- envision an outcome and establish a mission statement to achieve it.

In addition to applying hard skills, personality traits, and soft skills, Black made use of the third category of the leadership competency by engaging a variety of styles (Figure 4.2) to adapt to various stages of the S&L crisis. When first hired under Gray, he adopted a pragmatic style, focusing on technical and personnel issues. As evidence of fraud increased, he became increasingly task-oriented, actively pursuing litigation and organizing his staff to carry out the FHLBB's mandates. As an entrepreneurial leader, he devised new ways to make examiners more effective by instigating unusual and untested organizational changes. His people-oriented approach compelled him to train and consult with bank examiners, help examiners develop their skills in handling complex cases, and effectively network to create a base of support against political and industry opposition. His charisma imbued a sense of team spirit in the embattled examiners, motivated his staff even in the face of setbacks, and convinced outsiders of the seriousness of the S&L crisis. Black used this variety of styles effectively, even though he often stayed in the background, making frequent recommendations to Gray about organizational strategies, for example, while not seeking the limelight.

Applying the fourth category of the leadership competency, in order to prevent being intimidated by the governing administration, powerful congressmen, and influential financiers, Black adeptly used political skills to:

- exude a sincere belief that government, operating through its own agencies and its publicly chartered private FHLBanks, should effectively regulate the S&L industry to prevent fraud and irresponsible financial transactions and prosecute those who violated the rules.
- convince others across a wide organizational span to invest themselves in putting an end to the corruption and flagrant violation of the law.
- forge a consensus on the desirability and viability of regulating the S&L industry, despite the ideological, political, and pragmatic emphasis on deregulation.
- identify opposition to regulation efforts as self-serving politicking used to protect congressional backers in the S&L industry.

- insist on upholding the law and the rules of the game when pressured by members of the Senate to give in instead of negotiating away his own power or that of the FHLBB.

In 1989, Congress finally began to act. That year it passed the Financial Institutions Reform, Recovery, and Enforcement Act (FIRREA) to refinance the government-backed S&L industry and implement new enforcement powers to clean up the mess. The FHLBB and FSLIC were abolished because of a lack of confidence in existing structures and a loss of personnel. Congress created the Office of Thrift Supervision (OTS) in the Treasury Department to oversee the S&L industry, along with a number of other temporary and permanent agencies to restore order and integrity to the system.

Leadership: Self-Evaluation

Black also applied the fifth category of the leadership competency: evaluation. His assessment of the likely impact of his own endeavors, as well as a scanning of the political environment, compelled him to leave government to work in the commercial sector. Black decided that he could use his experience and skills to help assess the causes of the S&L crisis and prevent it from recurring in the future. In 1990 he became senior deputy chief counsel in the OTS, where he helped to systematically reform government regulatory policies. From 1992 to 1993 he served as deputy director of the National Commission on Financial Institution Reform, Recovery, and Enforcement, which was established to support FIRREA. In the late 1990s, he switched sectors again, entering academia to teach and write about, among other things, his experience in the S&L debacle (Black 2005). An objective evaluation of how personal skills impact a constantly changing environment helps leaders chart new directions in tackling challenges.

By 1995, government agencies had closed 1,043 thrifts holding a total of $519 billion in assets (Curry and Shibut 2000, 26); 3,700 senior executives and owners of failed thrifts served time in prison. The combined direct and indirect costs of the government bailout are estimated at $152.9 billion, with taxpayer losses accounting for 81 percent of total costs, or $123.8 billion, thus producing "the greatest collapse of U.S. financial institutions since the Great Depression" (26). Bill Black did more to clean up the disaster than any other individual (Riccucci 1995). He often had to work at odds with the most powerful men in America. Despite the extraordinary feat of serving the public in both public and private employment to resolve the crisis, Black remains virtually unknown and unacknowledged. He is one of the unsung heroes of public service who direct their unshakeable commitment, mastery of technical and management skills, ethical integrity, and leadership traits and skills to serve the common good. In the words of one analyst, Black was a leader who exhibited the "willingness to 'speak truth to power,' regardless of the consequences for himself" (Tonon 2008, 18). This willingness, backed up by the technical, ethical, and leadership competencies outlined here, defines the consummate professional.

Conclusion

Civil servants such as Bill Black and the new generation of public service leaders encouraged by federal agencies and public-spirited nonprofits will face increasingly complex challenges brought about by new technologies, the distribution and cost of limited natural resources, continued debates about the role of government in the commercial and private spheres of life, and the disputed role of networking and outsourcing for the provision of public services. In addition to new challenges, leaders must find new, creative, and effective ways to deal with the same old problems: corruption, fraud, private gain at public expense, and the moral hazard involved when government steps in to bail out financial institutions. Moral hazards—the temptation to engage in unethical behavior when the cost of risk-taking is assumed by others—can span decades, as the next chapter illustrates. Chapter 5 highlights challenges, some with roots in the past and some with implications for the future, faced by public servants and asks how they can be met by the creative application of technical, ethical, and leadership competencies that are examined in this book.

Appendix 4.1. The Leadership Competency Cycle

I. Assessment and Goal Setting

- Identify operational and motivational trends
- Ensure employees have the skills to excel at tasks
- Encourage innovation and creativity
- Guarantee appropriate resources and support services
- Ensure employee inclusiveness and productivity
- Promote cohesiveness and cooperation
- Organize work effectively
- Establish performance strategies
- Identify organizational culture
- Ensure external coordination and adaptability

II. Utilize Hard Skills, Soft Skills, Personality Traits

Hard Skills

- Excel in a specialized field of knowledge
- Know legal requirements and constraints
- Understand functioning of organization and environment
- Manage organizational operations
- Plan strategically
- Direct programs and projects; delegate management
- Build effective teams
- Oversee budget
- Coordinate staffing and evaluation
- Supervise information technology systems
- Identify and manage change

Soft Skills

- Be aware of emotions
- Balance flexibility and resolve
- Reconcile ambition with ethical standards
- Understand others' interests and motivations
- Listen to others' concerns
- Lead by example
- Foster teamwork
- Create a productive work atmosphere
- Develop written, verbal, and nonverbal communication skills

III. Apply Personal Styles to Suit the Situation

- Pragmatic: focus on technical and personnel issues
- Task-oriented: complete specific tasks in specified time frame
- People-oriented: focus on verbal communication to clarify tasks and strategies; network
- Entrepreneurial: devise new and creative strategic and organizational methods to handle problems
- Charismatic: motivate employees to adjust to changing circumstances
- Visionary: articulate new goals and ways to attain them

IV. Apply Political and Negotiation Skills

Political Skills

- Exude a sincere belief in goals and strategies
- Engage others to invest themselves in your goals and strategies
- Forge a consensus on the desirability and viability of goals and strategies
- Distinguish self-serving politicking from genuine opposition
- Know when to impose rules and negotiate about the rules

Negotiation Skills (Appendix 4.2)

- Ask problem-solving questions
- Question "Why?"
- Consider "Why not?"
- Ask "What if?"
- Request your partner's advice
- Ask "What makes that fair?"
- Make your questions open-ended
- Tap the power of silence

V. Evaluation of Self and Organization/Environment

- Review balance between technical operations, employee productivity, integration of organizational operations, and progress toward goal alignment
- Consider the condition of the external environment
- Project future conditions of organization and external environment
- Identify areas that require primary focus
- Examine own behavior strategies, impact on employees and organization
- Decide whether and how to alter personal/organizational behavior

Appendix 4.2. Negotiation Skills
Reframing the Problem with an Opponent-Turned-Partner

When dealing with an intractable problem, leaders and managers often have to take creative steps to break an impasse or prevent the breakdown of negotiations. One approach recommended by William Ury in *Getting Past No: Negotiating Your Way from Confrontation to Cooperation* is to reframe the problem in order to get one's negotiating opponent invested in a mutually beneficial outcome. As a good beginning, view your "opponent" more as a "partner." Reframing consists of the following steps:

1. Pose problem-solving questions. Instead of making demands, ask questions that help your partner help you.
2. Ask "Why?" Treat your partner's stance as an opportunity rather than an obstacle.
3. Wonder "Why not?" If your partner won't directly answer "Why?" propose your own solution and ask "Why not?" thereby eliciting your partner's concerns and interests.
4. Consider "What if?" Lay out a list of possible solutions without undermining your partner's position and engage in a mutual brainstorming session.
5. Ask for your partner's advice. Acknowledge your partner's competence and status by asking his/her opinion as a way to establish trust and help him/her become invested in a mutually beneficial outcome.
6. Ask "What makes that fair?" If your partner makes what seems to you to be an unreasonable proposition, don't reject it outright; rather ask why he/she considers that to be fair. This establishes an expectation of fairness and puts the burden on your partner to justify his/her stance.
7. Make your questions open-ended. Use words such as *how, why, why not, what,* or *who,* rather than *is, isn't, can,* or *can't,* which can be answered with a simple negation and lead nowhere. Open-ended questions require answers that produce more information that can help you negotiate a mutually beneficial solution.
8. Tap the Power of Silence. Allow your partner creative time to answer your questions. Avoid the temptation to jump in and help break what are sometimes uncomfortable silences. Both the time and the discomfort may result in information that can further the negotiations

The above was adapted from Ury (1991, 80–89). Reprinted with permission.

Ury provides an example of how a U.S. Senator successfully reframed a serious international problem using these techniques.

In 1979, the Strategic Arms Limitation Talks (SALT II) arms-control treaty was up for ratification in the U.S. Senate. To obtain the necessary two-thirds majority, the senate leaders wanted to add an amendment, but this required Soviet assent. A young U.S. Senator, Joseph R. Biden, Jr., was about to travel to Moscow, so the senate leadership asked him to raise the question with Soviet Foreign Minister Andrei Gromyko.

The match in Moscow was uneven: a junior senator going head-to-head with a hard-nosed diplomat of vast experience. Gromyko began the discussion with an eloquent hour-long disquisition on how the Soviets had always played catch-up to the Americans in the arms race. He concluded with a forceful argument for why SALT II actually favored the United States and why, therefore, the U.S. Senate should ratify the treaty unchanged. Gromyko's position on the proposed amendment was an unequivocal *nyet.*

Then it was Biden's turn. Instead of arguing with Gromyko and taking a counterposition, he slowly and gravely said, "Mr. Gromyko, you make a very persuasive case. I agree with much of what you've said. When I go back to my colleagues in the Senate, however, and report what you've just told me, some of them—like Senator Goldwater or Senator Helms—will not be persuaded, and I'm afraid their concerns will carry weight with others." Biden went on to explain their worries, "You have more experience in these arms-control matters than anyone else alive. How would you advise me to respond to my colleagues' concerns?"

Gromyko could not resist the temptation to offer advice to the inexperienced young American. He started coaching him on what he should tell the skeptical senators. One by one, Biden raised the arguments that would need to be dealt with, and Gromyko grappled with each of them. In the end, appreciating perhaps for the first time how the amendment would help win wavering votes, Gromyko reversed himself and gave his consent.

Instead of rejecting Gromyko's position, which would have led to an argument over positions, Biden acted as if Gromyko were interested in problem-solving and asked for his advice. He reframed the conversation as a constructive discussion about how to meet the senators' concerns and win ratification of the treaty.

Source: From William Ury, *Getting Past No: Negotiating Your Way from Confrontation to Cooperation.* Revised Edition. New York: Bantam Books, 1991, pp. 78–79. Reprinted with permission.

Chapter 5

The Future of Public Service

Cases and Commentary for the New Millennium

Only they deserve power who justify its use daily.
—Dag Hammarskjöld

The consummate public servant develops a professional edge: the integration of the technical, ethical, and leadership dimensions of a craft. Today, public service professionals find their responsibilities affected by a host of trends and issues: downsizing, homeland security, contracting reforms, aging staff, performance measurements, citizen demands, and the thinning of management ranks already eroded by years of cutbacks. Accordingly, they must excel at old skills and develop new ones by focusing on:

- Technical expertise (financial, human, organizational, and information resources)
- Ethical behavior (accountability, credibility, integrity)
- Leadership skills and traits (character, vision, soft and hard management skills)

Professionals confront this question: "Do I have sufficient abilities in the triangle of competencies to meet the challenges I face?" They require, for example, technical expertise to manage the installation of a cutting-edge information system, the ability to make ethical human resource judgments with respect to the operation of that system, and the leadership capacity to motivate people to effectively integrate the system and use it toward the organization's goals. Professionals rarely have the luxury of having only technical expertise while avoiding ethical decisions or shunning leadership roles. Instead they must be able to move seamlessly from one point of the Competencies Triangle to another in performing public service.

Public servants must be able to weigh competing needs and know how to reconcile the various interests and values that characterize democratic public life. Various needs that may conflict are personal (career advancement and job fulfillment), professional (goal attainment), organizational (program effectiveness), legal (adherence to laws), and public interest (protection of the commonweal) (Van Wart 1998). Some conundrums faced by public service professionals are: personal privacy versus national security, principle versus compromise as the basis of action, and government or private firms as public service providers. To sharpen their professional edge, public leaders must detect underlying value and interest issues, balance them according to the demands of specific situations, and explain their decision-making rationale.

The Competencies Triangle: Case Studies

The democratic context of public service requires a healthy and open debate about competing interests and values. The following case studies, which discuss cybersecurity and cyberwarfare, U.S. Forest Service fire control strategies, and city trash collection services, illustrate how professionals can address potentially controversial problems by applying technical, ethical, and leadership competencies.

Cybersecurity and Cyberwarfare

> Two months before any shots were fired in the Russian-Georgian war during the summer of 2008, widespread "denial of service" attacks on Georgia's Internet infrastructure, which were designed to disable the country's communication network, initiated a cyberwar that took place on a "digital battlefield." This was the first time in history that a physical attack by an army was connected to a cyberattack by unknown digital warriors (Hart 2008a, b).

National security and war used to be thought of in terms of human, material, and psychological components, such as the protection of coastlines, the defense of airspace, antiaircraft artillery, radar and sonar systems, human spies on the ground, levels of armaments and missile defense systems, numbers of troops, the making and delivery of bombs, terrorist cells, weapons caches, propaganda, and motivation. Wars have traditionally been fought by groups (e.g., tribes, nations, empires, states, ethnic/religious groups, terrorists) that mobilize a certain level of material resources to engage other groups in battle. It was usually clear who had perpetrated the aggressive actions; soon the battle lines were drawn and the balance of all resources determined the outcome.

Revolutionary developments in computer technology and the widespread use of personal computers have led security and military experts to radically rethink the very nature of national security and warfare. Hacking incidents in recent years have shown that not only large entities such as states, but also single individuals working from their personal computers, can breach national security information systems worldwide and cause potential havoc by disrupting governmental and commercial information systems. Very often it is difficult to identify the perpetrator of an assault; Internet protocol (IP) addresses can hide actual identities and "attack" computers can be trained to take over other "innocent" computers, making the latter appear to be the sources of the hostile action. If space was the new frontier for a generation of spaceships and satellite technology a half century ago, then cyberspace is an ever-expanding realm of bits and bytes that can be directed as much toward the misuse of information as toward its dissemination.

Here are some of the ways in which cyberspace has been and can be used for attack and defense in national security and warfare:

- Hacking into enemy computers to find strategic military plans
- Electronically disabling enemy strategic communication
- Electronically disrupting radar signals so that enemy planes cannot identify their targets
- Jamming enemy computer networks to disable interoperational communications
- Initiating "denial of service" attacks by manipulating "innocent" computers around the world
- Using computer-controlled drone aircraft to blow up targets
- Disabling transportation (air traffic control, subway systems), commercial (banks, the stock market), and energy (electricity grids, nuclear power plants) computer systems
- Electronically controlling and manipulating operations at manufacturing plants and public works
- Installing spyware on enemy computers, either through software or built into the hardware

Some incidents involving these methods, such as unmanned drones electronically tracking down terrorists on the run, are well known. One of the most widely reported incidents was a denial-of-service attack on Estonian government computers in 2007 that disrupted banking, media, ministerial, and parliamentary systems. The Estonian Foreign Minister charged that the Russian government was behind the assault because of its fury over the fact that the Estonian authorities moved a Soviet-era war monument from the center of Tallinn to a less populated area, thus offending the very large Russian minority living in Estonia. Other Estonian government ministers, however, acknowledged that it was impossible to identify the perpetrator of the cyberattack. In the end, many thought that the culprits were a new breed of activists who hack into computers to promote their causes, known as "hactivists" (Schwartz 2007). Hactivists attacked Radio Free Europe/Radio Liberty computers in Russia and eastern Europe in the spring of 2008, and hactivist attacks of all kinds have become increasingly active throughout the world (Mills 2008). After numerous attempts by hackers to infiltrate the Pentagon and other U.S. government agencies, former U.S. Director of National Intelligence J. Michael McConnell expressed concern in his annual threat assessment to Congress about "[t]he vulnerabilities of the U.S. information infrastructure to increasing cyber attacks by foreign governments, nonstate actors and criminal elements" (McConnell 2008).

These examples represent only isolated incidents of how cyberspace can be used to protect national security and to carry out various levels of warfare. It is a huge leap from these incidents to the development of a national strategic military plan that seamlessly integrates cyberspace into existing security and military frameworks. The government, criticized for its failure to integrate its own computer networks, has taken steps in this direction. At the turn of the twenty-first century, the Pentagon established a Cyberwarfare Center to coordinate the cybersecurity capabilities scattered among various government departments and agencies. The Center, located at Peterson Air Force Base in Colorado, is managed by the Air Force Space Command (Becker 1999). The goals were to first develop an integrated defense against outside attacks on U.S. military computer networks and then turn to offense capabilities, such as coordinating a joint forces military operation against enemy computer networks (Markoff 1999). In 2004, the Pentagon established the Network Attack Support Staff to integrate offensive operations by connecting military personnel on the ground to cyberattack experts (Bruno 2008a,b).

Still, an interagency review in 2007 disclosed that the federal government has been too slow in establishing operational capabilities in the fields of cybersecurity and cyberwarfare. This led to a funding request by President Bush for a Comprehensive National Security Initiative (CNSI) in 2008. The initiative would secure government computer systems against current and future attacks. This highly secretive project came to light during congressional hearings on the intelligence budget (Pincus 2008). The U.S. Air Force implemented its Cyberspace Command structure to "defend military data, communications and control networks, and . . . disable an opponent's computer networks and crash its databases" (Schwartz 2007). The Air Force has already added cyberspace to its mission statement: "To deliver sovereign options for the defense of the United States of America and its global interests to fly and fight in air, space and cyberspace" (U.S. Air Force 2008). There is still much work to be done. A panel of government computer experts that spoke before the Senate Committee on Homeland Security and Governmental Affairs on July 31, 2008, the same day the CNSI project was discussed, presented a dismal picture of federal agencies' ability to use their earmarked funds to carry out designated IT projects. Of twenty-eight agencies and departments examined, fourteen received a failing grade (including the Departments of Defense and Homeland Security; see U.S. Senate Committee on Homeland Security and Government Affairs 2008).

Two more incidents mobilized the Obama administration into action in early 2009. In early April, it was discovered that international hackers broke into the U.S. electrical grid and installed software designed to disrupt the system (Gorman 2009). In late April, the Pentagon disclosed that spies had penetrated its "Joint Strike Fighter" project, potentially undermining the ability to diagnose in-flight aircraft maintenance problems of the costliest Defense Department weapons system ever designed. The administration carried out a review of cybersecurity policies and proposed plans to increase funding, establish a senior White House post for coordinating policies, and establish a military command to protect government computer networks (Gorman, Cole, and Dreazen 2009).

Developing a strategic, integrated cybersecurity plan is one of the most complex and exciting challenges that lies ahead for public servants. They must resolve bureaucratic turf wars over cybersecurity policy (Hosenball 2009), tap into the wealth of knowledge, skills, and creativity of cyberenthusiasts in all spheres of society, marshal these resources into a unified national plan to protect national security, and initiate offensive operations against terrorists and enemy combatants (Sanger, Markoff, and Shanker 2009). This inevitably involves outsourcing and private-public partnerships to integrate the skills and resources of the private, commercial, and governmental sectors in the service of the nation's security. The technical, ethical, and leadership competencies discussed in this book can be applied to this endeavor as follows.

Technical

Cybersecurity and cyberwarfare plans demand the utmost in technical skills and creativity. Experts must solve current problems and imagine the nature and scope of potential threats in a realm whose dimensions are still not completely understood. They must understand the technical details necessary to solve specific problems while taking a "big picture" view of all technical capabilities in order to create an integrated government information network and a long-term strategic plan. Government cybersecurity efforts recognize that this entails public-private collaboration and government support of IT projects in the commercial and private sectors.

Ethical

It is always a challenge to ensure that ethics keep pace with technology. The ethical conundrums surrounding cybersecurity and cyberwarfare will not be completely clear until questions about the nature, substance, and methodology of the technologies are worked out. Still, it is possible to identify potential ethical problems at the early stages of development: (1) When is hacking legitimate and when is it illegal? Can an activity that is now illegal, and whose perpetrators are punished, become a legitimate tool of national security? (2) Are preventive strikes ethical? Should governments be allowed to test their operational capacity to hack into enemy computers without any provocation? How does the first-strike capability that was so contentious in the nuclear warfare debate apply to cyberwarfare? (3) Should the government be allowed to monitor Internet communications and be able to identify the source and timing of Internet traffic? If so, what legal provisions must be in place and what is the responsibility of commercial Internet enterprises? This ethical question has already caused much controversy in the contentious debate over the PATRIOT Act and the renewal of the Foreign Intelligence Security Act (FISA) in 2008. (4) What is the role of noncombatants? International law has traditionally established very specific parameters concerning the impact of military actions on civilian noncombatants in war zones; cyberwarfare creates a whole new set of problems. Is it legitimate for governments to electronically monitor and/or control commercial and production operations that would negatively affect the health and welfare of civilians in a conflict? Is it right that a government engages in the electronic manipulation of services and production that targets noncombatant civilians? (5) What are the parameters that would form the basis for a new cyberspace "just war theory"?

Unlike in conventional wars or terrorist acts, the tenets of such a theory would apply to huge numbers of people and would be much harder to apply and enforce, not only because of the numbers involved but because of the difficulty in identifying the source of hostile computer actions. The Ethics Triangle (Chapter 3) may be useful in addressing these questions.

Leadership

The development of a strategic cybersecurity and cyberwarfare plan involves more than new technical and ethical boundaries; it encompasses a unique way of thinking. It is precisely at junctures such as these, which provoke a paradigm shift, that creative leadership is so desperately needed. Leaders must craft strategic plans by integrating disparate components of cyberabilities, articulate new mission statements, and change a whole mentality that surrounds the concept of national security and warfare by combining experience with innovation. Many times experienced employees become set in their organizational and operational ways of thinking; those who emerge with creative ways to solve problems often do not have the experience necessary to understand how existing structures may affect the application of new solutions. The field of cybersecurity demands leaders who help change the culture of national security planning while understanding how current organizations and processes must be redirected to attain newly defined goals.

The U.S. government has lagged behind in terms of integrating its computer networks and preparing a cybersecurity plan (Clarke 2008). The first step in fixing this problem is finding and training leaders with a clear vision of what needs to be done and the skills to follow through.

Forest Service Fire Suppression: Debate over Technical Means

The U.S. Forest Service has always had a potentially conflicting, multiuse philosophy that includes forest sustainability, wildlife protection, support of commercial logging, and recreation (Dubnick 1998). Because of these competing interests, the Competencies Triangle must be fully engaged in order to craft effective policies in an often highly turbulent environment (Kaufman 1960; O'Neill and Christopher 2002).

One dramatic challenge confronted by the Forest Service was its controversial fire suppression policy (U.S. House of Representatives 2001). The implicit assumption that guided policy was that all fire is bad and has to be either prevented or suppressed wherever and whenever possible (Smokey the Bear's famous motto: "Only you can prevent forest fires" symbolized this approach). Yet as it turns out, the very success of fire suppression that has occurred since the 1930s has caused problems because there are different types and intensities of fire. Fires occur in nature under normal conditions because of lightning and dryness; these types of fire periodically "clean" forests of ground debris and excessive young growth that leads to crowding. Most of these fires consume excess fuel on forest floors and burn much of the younger growth, allowing larger, older trees to survive in a healthier environment. In the 1930s up to forty million acres of land burned every year as a result of these regenerative, or "cool," fires. In large part because of Forest Service philosophy, this number had been reduced to less than five million acres by the beginning of the 1990s. Though the number of fires decreased, the fire suppression policy left most forests more vulnerable to catastrophic, rather than regenerative, fires.

By the 1980s, it was clear that the suppression policy was not working well. Fires were increasingly frequent, dangerous, and uncontainable, since most of them were "hot," or catastrophic. Not only did they burn the largest trees, but the enormous amount of accumulated debris on forest floors caused the soil itself to be burned down to eighteen inches deep. This means that nature's tremendous regenerative powers were in large part eliminated. Furthermore, fires moved more quickly and the threat to people or animals in their path increased.

Suppression policies were unsustainable in the long run because of the accumulated effects of the absence of periodic fires. To respond to the emergent crisis, in 1996 the Forest Service proposed the Land and Resource Management Plan (Reuters 1996). Joined by the Department of the Interior, the Forest Service (an agency in the Department of Agriculture) supported a new National Fire Plan, which was authorized in 2000. Since then, the agency has established the goal of "enhancing the positive role fire plays in resource management" (USDA 2006).

This approach entails two concurrent policies. First, the Forest Service added a tool called the "prescribed burn" to its arsenal. Such burns allow the agency to start fires in a controlled environment where firefighting personnel are prepared to ensure safe outcomes. Unfortunately, a prescribed burn near Los Alamos, New Mexico, in 2000 "escaped" and destroyed many homes in the area, leading to intense criticism of the new policy. The second policy allowed for renewed thinning of forests—the cutting of all trees less than twelve inches in diameter—by commercial interests. This created controversy, as environmentalists expressed their distrust of the motivations and actions of commercial loggers. The Forest Service once again found itself trying to balance potentially conflicting technical approaches and competing interests: fire suppression versus prescribed burn techniques, and environmental versus commercial interests. Human lives and a wealth of natural resources depend on a clear and effective plan to prevent, control, and put out fires, as the devastation in California caused by raging firestorms in the summer of 2008 compellingly illustrated.

The Forest Service has assiduously attempted to balance its methods in light of policy outcomes and political controversies. With budgets nearly doubled after numerous catastrophic fires in the western states in the late 1990s, the Forest Service embarked on a decades-long plan to manage forests by simulating natural conditions instead of initiating prescribed burns. Each year it used a combination of methods to clean a small but growing portion of land under its stewardship through limited clear-cutting, extensive thinning, and mechanical cleaning such as piling and chipping. Along with efforts to undo past mismanagement of forest fires, the Forest Service is enhancing its capability to aggressively fight the especially dangerous "hot" fires spawned by earlier fire suppression policies. While it cannot completely reconcile competing environmental and commercial interests, the agency can gauge its political success by making sure that ecological and commercial interest groups are equally dissatisfied with its multiuse policy philosophy, while simultaneously gaining the respect of both groups for the integrity of the day-to-day practices of Forest Service personnel. Success depends on applying the Competencies Triangle.

Technical

The Forest Service is mandated to provide ecological, biological, and horti-cultural expertise by developing forest management plans that reflect state-of-the-art practices and social needs. The technical challenge is to balance fire suppression techniques with forest clearing tactics, some of which may involve prescribed burns. The agency is devoted to multifaceted research and development programs involving collaboration with other agencies, nonprofits, commercial groups, and academia to attain sustainable management of the land under its watch (U.S. Forest Service 2009). The ten-year strategic plan implemented in 2006 aims to provide the "knowledge and tools that managers use to reduce negative impacts and enhance beneficial effects of fire and fire management on society and the environment" (USDA 2006).

Ethical

The Forest Service is obligated to protect the land under its supervision and to ensure that it is used for the benefit of the population. It must weigh the environmental, commercial, and recreational consequences of this obliga-tion, acknowledge the inadequacy of past decisions, and create new ways to balance the concerns of its constituencies. The most important ethical aspect here is transparency, so that competing interest groups clearly understand both the gains and the losses that inevitably ensue from a multiuse policy that acknowledges the existence of potentially conflicting interests.

Leadership

The Forest Service must act as a leader in the field of sustainable management. The skills include the formation of a clear mission statement, the establish-ment of a dynamic research and development program, the proposal of new policies when old ones prove inadequate, collaboration with Congress and the U.S. President to build coalitions to adopt and support new policies, and the initiation of public, nonprofit, and commercial projects to encourage cooperation on the attainment of common goals.

Trash Collection: Government versus Private Service Provision

In many cases, the provision of services is vital to ensure health and safety. This includes essential, if mundane, community needs such as water supply, electricity distribution, and trash collection. Professional technical, ethical, and leadership skills are crucial in developing the most effective delivery systems and preventing disruptions in service that can negatively affect quality of life and seriously disrupt commercial transactions, medical provision, and numerous other essential services.

Public services are furnished by both the public and the private sectors, depending on local circumstances; debates about privatization have gone on for years. As governments try to downsize and local budgets shrink, questions regarding the sources of public service provision become more acute: Which delivery model is technically superior and provides the best quality? How can ethical behavior, such as accountability for cost, dependability, and cleanliness, be ensured? Who can provide the leadership necessary to engage the most reliable service provider while addressing the needs of those who receive the services? The professional edge—technical, ethical, and leadership competencies—requires the ability to understand and implement best practices when it comes to the complex task of providing public services to communities with different needs.

While focus on "best practice" has resulted in general agreement about provision of public safety (government) and human services (nonprofits), the preferred approach for basic utilities has vacillated over time and is still subject to some controversy. General arguments for public provision center on the efficiency and effectiveness of economies of scale, the dependability of the government, the ongoing expense of infrastructure development, and the relatively benign nature of public monopolies as opposed to private monopolies. Proponents of private sector provision, stressing the principle of limited government, want to restrict government intervention in the economy, marshal the superior efficiency and sharper cost-consciousness of entrepreneurs, and prevent government from monopolizing too many economic resources (see Van Wart, Rahm, and Sanders 2000 for an expansion of the arguments).

An interesting example of changing preferences is that of garbage collection and landfill services. Through the 1960s, cities assumed responsibility for trash collection and service provision was usually characterized by high quality and frequency of pickups, low cost, and cleanliness. By the 1970s and 1980s, however, some private providers were also meeting these standards just as many local jurisdictions began to look for alternative models. In the early 1980s the city of Phoenix, Arizona, for example, decided to open trash collection services to competitive bids from private firms, as well as from the city, in order to save costs and improve performance. The city lost a number of districts, forcing its workers to work harder and smarter if they wanted to make sure to keep their jobs and win back the city's role as service provider. By the end of the 1980s, the city had won back all of the districts by increasing efficiency and aggressively saving on costs, including a move to two-person trucks and the introduction of side-load automatic lifts. It seems that the introduction of competition, a key factor in improving the city's provision of services, can render local governments capable of matching or exceeding private sector performance levels (Pack 1989).

Many cities have gotten out of the trash business in recent years by privatizing collection services. In 1995, the city of Conroe, Texas, signed a ten-year contract with a private firm to collect trash and transport it to landfills. The city not only saved money in the process, it also made money by selling its garbage trucks to the private firm. In order to avoid having to lay off city workers, included in the contract was a provision that fourteen employees would be hired by the firm if the local government could not transfer them to other city jobs (*American City and County* 1998). In 2001, the city of Roxboro, North Carolina, followed suit and signed a five-year contract with a private firm to provide all solid waste removal services for residents. To avoid the criticism that private firms often pay lower wages in order to save on costs, the private service provider agreed to match the level and extent of city wages and benefits (*American City and County* 2002). In addition to public and private provision of services, some states, such as California, are enthused about the opportunities presented by public-private partnerships (P3s). P3s are designed to combine the advantages of the public sector (such as democratic input) with those of the private sector (such as increased efficiency and innovation). (See California Debt and Investment Advisory Commission 2007 for an excellent overview.)

Citizens appear to be relatively indifferent as to the source of utility services, as long as the quality remains high, costs low, and corruption absent. They expect services to be technically proficient (timely and clean) and ethically fair (costs related to services provided and no monopolization). Though comfortable with different service provision models, the public does generally expect that the government will exercise leadership in finding the best and most cost-efficient provider and in maintaining and regulating the service over time.

The question of which sector, or combination of sectors, is best at offering public services has become even more relevant and controversial over time, especially because of the crisis caused by energy deregulation in California in the early 2000s. Applying the Competencies Triangle can help determine which model of provision—public, private, or P3—will provide optimal public services to citizens in particular communities.

Technical

It is important to determine which sector can provide the best technical skills to deliver utility services. The choice involves the quality of the product (clean water, tidy trash collection, biofuels) as well as efficient and reliable delivery (no power outages, no accumulation of trash) and viable contingency plans (fair water rationing in case of drought, emergency generators if ice storms down power lines). Included in the technical competency is cost-effectiveness, especially given the pressure on government budgets. Local leaders must ask which sector can provide the best service at the lowest cost; the Phoenix example shows how inserting competitive bidding into the equation can help encourage improvement in technical skills while increasing cost-effectiveness. As this book has emphasized, however, the technical competency alone does not guarantee professionalism; it must be combined with a code of conduct in order truly to serve citizens.

Ethical

Whenever private companies participate in or take over service provision, there is concern that the gain of technical expertise will be attained at the cost of public control and accountability. The use of public funds to enhance commercial profits when utilities and services are privatized is often met with apprehension. This goes back to the ethical question referred to earlier: What role should government play in the economy and society? Proponents of limited government believe that private firms provide better service. Critics claim that privatization can involve the misuse of public monies (given the absence of oversight), a lowering of accountability standards (because private companies are more concerned with shareholders than with citizens), a reduction in wages and benefits (due to commercial cost-saving measures), and the laying off of government employees. How should these cost-benefit equations be balanced? Ethical questions that center on the fundamental role of government and guarantees of accountability, transparency, and fairness pervade discussions about public service provision. These ethical conundrums can be addressed using the Ethics Triangle discussed in Chapter 3.

Leadership

Increasingly, local and state leaders must find creative ways to solve complex service delivery problems. Leadership skills are crucial in identifying new models of service provision, addressing the ethical problems that arise, and engaging the public to generate support for what may be untested but promising methods. The examples provided in this section illustrate various leadership skills: injecting competition into the process to improve the cost-effectiveness of services, ensuring that city workers displaced by privatization or P3 models find comparable employment, and stipulating contractual obligations whereby firms hire some displaced workers and ensure comparable wages and benefits. The challenge for civic leaders is to enhance accountability and transparency when private firms participate in public policy. Especially in polarized political environments, if citizens have strong views about the role of government and justifiable fears about commercial monopolization, leaders must be able to foster confidence and support in their ability to provide for people's basic needs.

Greed, Speculation, and Debt: What Is the Role of Government?

The preceding case studies illustrate challenges that require the application of technical, ethical and leadership competencies: cyberwarfare, forest fire prevention, and provision of public services. Since the turn of the twenty-first century, public servants have had to face problems that negatively affect the entire U.S. economy and that have potentially devastating effects on a wide swath of the American population. Two such challenges are the stepchildren of the Savings and Loan debacle of the 1980s: the Enron scandal at the beginning of the first decade of the twenty-first century and a devastating financial crisis initiated by a mortgage loan fiasco, at its end. The Enron debacle involved the implosion of a corporate energy giant due to fraud, greed, and widespread deception. The financial disaster stemmed from millions of bad loans and risky speculation; it froze credit markets, toppled Wall Street investment firms, and paralyzed banking systems around the globe. These two events illustrate how the misuse of technical skills, the absence of ethical safeguards, and the failure of leadership led to dire consequences for the U.S. and world economies and devastated individual citizens. With so much at stake, the application of technical, ethical, and leadership competencies by committed public servants becomes ever more critical to the health and well-being of the American public.

The Enron Scandal

Just as the S&L crisis of the late 1980s and early 1990s is a parable of deregulation, so the Enron scandal a mere ten years later tells the tale of corporate fraud enabled by government complacency. Like the S&L fiasco, the Enron case, which involved numerous companies and the economy as a whole, reveals the nexus between the public and private sectors. More than fifty senior officials from the Enron Corporation, for example, held important posts in the Bush administration, and many members of Congress received campaign contributions from the energy giant. Politicians, on behalf of their corporate benefactors, deregulated markets, limited liability, minimized reporting requirements, underfunded oversight agencies, and intervened to protect businesses from scrutiny. The injustice revealed in the Enron scandal is that firms are rewarded for lobbying prowess and the application of cunning, but unethical, financial transactions rather than for the honest production of quality goods and services (Mallaby 2002; Wee 2002). The following is a brief look at the past details and future implications of the Enron case, including:

- The collapse of oversight and control mechanisms,
- The company bankruptcy,
- The government response,
- The failure of public leaders to protect Enron employees and taxpayers, and
- The resolution of the crisis.

The ultimate miscarriage of the Enron episode, in what *Fortune* magazine characterized as a "system failure" (Nocera 2002), is that few of the thousands of professionals involved properly exercised their technical, ethical, and leadership responsibilities.

The Perils

This scourge of white-collar malfeasance may have seemed like "business as usual." Enron's accounting firm, Arthur Andersen, for example, was involved in the S&L crisis and other scandals throughout the 1990s (Kelly 2002). But the Enron scandal was symptomatic of problems far more serious than isolated episodes of malpractice, as the financial crisis of the early twenty-first century would powerfully illustrate. Exhibiting technical, ethical, and leadership bankruptcy, Enron was both a creator and product of a system characterized by unregulated profiteering, deceptive accounting practices, offshore tax havens, money laundering, price gouging, irresponsible executive boards, insider trading, and complicit public officials.

The bursting of the dot-com bubble in 2000 had raised questions about artificially inflated profits, but the spectacular 2001 collapse of Enron, which called itself "the world's greatest company," sparked a series of corporate implosions. Over a thousand blue-chip companies had to restate their earnings and serious harm was inflicted on employees, shareholders, and the population at large. By the end of 2002, the scandals had resulted in a collective loss of some $700 billion in shareholder value (Huffington 2003) and thousands of employees saw their pension plans, and in many cases their entire life savings, completely wiped out (CNN.com 2002). The damage to the economic health and well-being of the nation, which was ushered in by the consequent worst decline in the markets since the Great Depression, was enormous. The adjective *white-collar* should do nothing to detract from the fact that the people involved in propagating the deception were criminals.

Both internal and external controls, beset with conflicts of interest, failed. The system put in place to protect the public interest was compromised by the following entities, which should have performed their attendant tasks:

- Company boards (provide oversight)
- Auditors (certify the accuracy of transactions)
- Outside legal firms (supply legal advice and oversee actions of executive boards)
- Professional associations (formulate standards of practice)
- Credit rating agencies (gauge the financial health of businesses)
- Brokerage firm analysts (furnish investment advice)
- Mutual fund and pensions managers (independently analyze business in which they invest)
- Securities and Exchange Commission (SEC) regulators (receive and review financial statements)

The path to the dereliction of duty on the part of these entities begins at about the same time that the S&L scandal came to light. Enron was founded in 1986, when energy production was a publicly sanctioned monopoly. That changed when the federal government deregulated natural gas and electricity production a few years later and Enron—honored by *Fortune* magazine as "America's most innovative company"—emerged as the seventh largest corporation in the United States and the dominant force in trading energy contracts. The fundamental problem was that large profits from energy trading could not be gained honestly and so Enron executives devised (or "fell into") a business plan predicated on deceit, insider trading, conflicts of interest, and deceptive accounting. The idea was not only to pad their own pockets, but to convince stockholders that share prices were consistently on the rise to increase the market value of the company and to guarantee enormous corporate profits. Enron had an elaborate code of ethics, but on two occasions the Board of Directors waived the code so that executives could profit from insider trading deals (Chapter 3). The company's legal firm appeared to find nothing wrong with this wanton dismissal of what turned out to be a meaningless set of ethical standards (Ackman 2002).

The corporation inflated profits and lowered debt figures through complex accounting maneuvers involving thousands of shell partnerships, thereby misleading unsuspecting investors and the general public about its financial condition. The Private Securities Litigation Reform Act of 1995 made much of this not only possible, but likely (Labaton 2002c). The accounting industry—which had to pay more than $1 billion in damages as a result of the S&L crisis—ensured that the law shielded auditors from liability for false reporting and made it difficult for shareholders to bring suit. Once exposed, it was clear that the scandal—which for a short time was the largest financial fraud in corporate history—had all the features of a Shakespearean drama including ambition, avarice, arrogance, anguish, and death (one executive, as he prepared to testify, allegedly committed suicide, and another died of a heart attack soon after he was sentenced). Company stock dropped from nearly $90 per share to less than $1, thousands of employees lost their jobs and retirement savings, and executives reaped millions by surreptitiously selling stock before the corporation's demise.

The calamity shook markets, as investors feared that other companies had engaged in fraudulent accounting practices, a fear that was realized as a long and growing list of firms came under scrutiny: Adelphia Communications Corporation, AOL-Time Warner, Bristol-Myers Squibb, Duke Energy, Dynegy, Merck and Company, Centennial Technologies, Edison Learning, Global Crossing Ltd., Fannie Mae, Halliburton, HealthSouth, Tenent Healthcare Corporation, the Home Store, ImClone Systems Inc., Kmart, Lucent Technologies, Merrill Lynch, General Electric, Martha Stewart Living OmniMedia, Phar-Mor, Qwest Communications International, Rite Aid, Sunbeam, Salomon Smith Barney, Sprint, Waste Management, WorldCom, Xerox, Tyco International Limited, and UnumProvident. Leading banks (such as J.P. Morgan, Chase, Citigroup) had also facilitated the duplicitous transactions. Greed and criminality would later spread to the nation's $7 trillion mutual fund industry. Indeed, the usual way the mass media labels a scandal (by applying the suffix "-gate" to the problem) did not apply because so many organizations were involved (for tallies, see www.citizenworks.org and www.thecorporatelibrary.com).

In 2002, Congress passed the Sarbanes-Oxley Act (also known as the Public Company Accounting Reform and Investor Protection Act), which imposed new corporate governance standards and reporting requirements on publicly traded companies, their accountants, and their attorneys; some called for a similar law covering governmental entities (Bronner 2003). New standards included forms of executive liability, compensation, conflicts of interest, and financial disclosure. Critics charged, however, that many key concerns were not addressed, such as (1) restoring a Depression-era law holding investment bankers, lawyers, and auditors liable for fraud; (2) providing for effective rules to prohibit accounting firms from selling consulting services to the same companies they audit; (3) closing the revolving door between auditors and clients; (4) establishing a new regulatory board to oversee accounting firms; and (5) dealing with energy regulation and campaign finance reform (see Labaton 2002c and U.S. PIRG, no date). Despite, or perhaps because of, the new law, a record number of shareholder resolutions seeking to safeguard investments were introduced at annual meetings (Deutsch 2003).

Effective enforcement is a critical component for any change, which requires the political will to supply more resources than agencies have or are likely to receive. In 1980, for instance, the Securities Exchange Commission (SEC) checked all company filings; in 2002, the share declined to only 8 percent because the Commission had come to rely on industry self-regulation (*Washington Post* 2002). Thus, the SEC, charged to review 17,000 companies, oversee mutual funds, vet brokerage firms, ensure proper operation of exchanges, and guard against market manipulation and accounting misconduct, did not have sufficient staff to "even read annual reports" (Nocera 2002). Added to this, employee turnover in the SEC is double what is normal for most government agencies. "The cost of not funding the SEC," wrote *Fortune* reporter Clifton Leaf, in a prescient observation, "is more disasters like Enron" (Nocera 2002).

As in the S&L fiasco, few leaders emerged during the crisis to protect citizens because so many played an integral role in the scandal itself. Paralleling the earlier debacle, politicians of both parties were so compromised by contributions from firms urging deregulation that they eliminated or watered down rules designed, at least in part, to prevent corruption. Not many professionals proved ready to put the national interest ahead of greed, ideology, or campaign funds; in fact, too many were themselves implicated in the crisis. Two officials, however—Arthur Levitt and Eliot Spitzer—should be noted. Levitt, SEC chairman during the 1990s, attacked conflicts of interest, struggled to improve accounting practices, and vigorously opposed the 1995 law. But ultimately he was thwarted when it became clear that the Commission's appropriations would be jeopardized if he did not withdraw his objections.

New York's Attorney General at the time, Eliot Spitzer—in the face of considerable political opposition—aggressively investigated Wall Street brokerage houses in what would be the largest case of consumer fraud ever. This was in response to revelations that investors lost millions after being advised to buy stock in Enron (and many other firms) that analysts privately derided as a "POS" (piece of sh*t) to lure companies to become their investment banking clients. In 2003, ten of the country's top brokerages agreed to pay nearly $1.5 billion to resolve the charges. Critics of the settlement (e.g., Huffington 2003) argued that it did not require any admission of guilt or prison sentences, and that the fines, which were tax deductible and/or covered by insurance, were a small fraction of what companies received and investors lost. Spitzer maintained that the entire financial reporting system "will be much stronger . . . and there will be . . . a greater degree of integrity. We need to see how Wall Street implements this deal" (Schlosser 2003). There was speculation that Spitzer may have concluded that attacking some of the most powerful people in the nation might not be prudent for someone interested in higher office. To sum up: while the Enron case produced isolated incidents of leadership, no single individual at the federal level had the resources, skills, or courage to follow through on exposing and correcting the problems that caused so much economic devastation.

The Solution

While high-profile trials and sentencing may be more cathartic and pleasing to the public because of the embarrassment to the accused and the satisfaction of watching criminals being brought to justice, out-of-court settlements, such as those involving the Wall Street brokerage firms, may be preferable for several reasons: the cost savings to both the defense and prosecution, the fact that understaffed prosecutor offices lack the resources to pursue complex securities cases, the difficulty in proving wrongdoing beyond reasonable doubt, and an overall concern about the socioeconomic consequences of guilty verdicts against major corporations. Indeed, highly publicized, "rotten apple" prosecutions, court proceedings, and rare guilty verdicts actually may blunt more effective, systemic change.

A knowledgeable attorney pointed out that the dynamic is one of swift justice but slow reform: "If I were heading the lobbying coalition against [reform], I'd be happy about the human sacrifices as the best way to placate these gods. That's the way it works" (quoted in Labaton 2002a). Thus, the conviction of Enron's accounting firm in 2002 may serve as a warning to auditors tempted to keep clients satisfied, but it may not lead to genuine change (Hilzenrath 2002). Arthur Levitt said, "It is appalling that the clout of the accounting industry may yet keep Congress from adopting meaningful laws" (Labaton 2002b). Among prominent cases, forty-seven executives at seven corporations have been indicted and twenty have pleaded guilty (*New York Times* 2003).

The solutions to the crisis were as obvious as they were likely to be ignored, insofar as past initiatives to improve corporate activities have been thwarted by sham reforms and political donations. As Barbara Roper, director of investor protection at the Consumer Federation of America, opined, "The way this may play out is that you will see a wad of bills proposed. The ones that may have some traction are the ones that don't do much, but allow members [of Congress] to say they did something" (Labaton 2002b).

Applying the Competencies Triangle, it is clear that from a technical perspective accounting rules and disclosure requirements need substantive improvement, as Arthur Andersen's practices were no worse than those of other accounting houses (Apostolou and Thibadoux 2003). Ethically, organizations should foster ethical cultures that complement ethical codes of behavior (Chapter 3) and make sure that standards cannot simply be waived. Companies should be required to go public with any wrongdoing and disgraced executives should be required to return illicit monies, make restitution, and serve time in prison. Finally, leaders must address the root causes of the problem—business deregulation, Wall Street demands for short-term financial results, public oversight eviscerated by political pressure, private campaign financing, and overall failure of professionals to protect the populace.

Indeed, the ease with which organized crime infiltrated unscrupulous brokerage firms (Weiss 2003) illustrates how readily technical expertise, ethical integrity, and competent leadership can be subverted. The Enron crisis made clear that professional norms may be necessary but are insufficient in preventing opportunism, expediency, and easy money from readily trumping fiduciary responsibilities. As eighteenth-century British statesman Edmund Burke famously observed, "All that is necessary for evil to triumph is for good men to do nothing." Without definitive progress in these areas, more examples like Enron were to be expected, as the subprime mortgage crisis a few years later dramatically illustrated.

"Ultimately capitalism will almost certainly survive this onslaught from the capitalists—if only because survival is the most profitable outcome for all concerned" (Eichenwald 2002). Yet built-in corrective policies correct serious violations only after substantial damage occurs. By the time the market recognizes fraud, financial as well as social capital is gone. A more constructive, preventive approach includes the following:

- Establishment of an official commission on white-collar crime to comprehensively address the problem (Barbash 2002)
- Appointment of a federal independent special counsel to investigate wrongdoing
- Redefinition of the terms of state charters that authorize public corporations (Kelly 2001; see also the Program on Corporations, Law, and Democracy Web site at www.poclad.org)

- Initiation of a high-profile "war on fraud," led by the President, to restore citizen trust
- A reconstitution of business schools, which can be silent partners in corporate sleaze, to produce better, more ethically oriented graduates
- Rediscovery of the raison d'être of professionalism—technical, ethical, and leadership competencies

Until these safeguards are put in place, pervasive corporate crime will engender political as well as business scandals, because there is no consistent countervailing power to corporate influence on the policy-making process of the nation. "One of the most important duties of government," wrote William Jennings Bryan more than a hundred years ago, "is to put rings in the noses of hogs." This becomes even more difficult when the "hogs" are not confined to a single company but have been let loose to roam the entire country. This is what happened in the crisis that began in 2008.

The 2008 Financial Meltdown

In mid-2008 a resounding "pop" sent shock waves throughout the United States as the housing bubble that had been rapidly inflating for several years started to burst. (The following account is derived in part from Kuttner 2007 and Muolo & Padilla 2008.) The air in the housing bubble was pumped in through an acceleration of subprime mortgage loans, some of which were originated through predatory lending practices, and the development of a chain of intermediary links between borrowers and the holders of their debt. *Subprime* refers not to the mortgage but to "less-than-perfect" borrowers; people with no or questionable credit histories who are considered to be a high risk and, under normal circumstances, unlikely to secure large loans. Subprime loans usually carry very high interest rates because of the risk of defaults. *Predatory lending* refers to loans made without full disclosure or clear explanations of the loan terms or long-term risks.

Lenders approved millions of subprime loans in the early 2000s (one in every five mortgage loans in 2005 was subprime). In addition, eager brokers negotiated millions of so-called liar loans for individuals with high credit ratings. These loans were secured by a simple statement of income without any documentation to back up the figures. The combination of rising housing prices and anxious buyers created a seemingly endless supply of money to be made throughout the housing industry. The risk to lenders of granting loans to subprime borrowers appeared to be offset both by the increasing house prices and the ability to sell the loans to investment banks or government-sponsored enterprises such as Fannie Mae and Freddie Mac. After years of a booming housing market, the whole process ground to a halt in 2008. As interest rates soared and housing prices declined, hundreds of thousands defaulted on their loans and lost their homes to foreclosure; some estimated that the number would reach 2.5 million. Mortgage banks and investment firms that had taken on the bad loans filed for bankruptcy or were taken over by other firms or the government. The banking industry suffered huge losses and the credit market dried up. The stock market witnessed wild swings as the government sought ways to stem the growing crisis. What turned the American dream of homeownership into a nightmare of foreclosure and financial ruin?

Pawns and Predators

The story begins where the S&L crisis (Chapter 4) left off. With the reregulation of savings and loan institutions, entrepreneurs, investors, brokers, and corporate executives sought new and innovative ways to profitably invest. They found a lucrative niche in the home mortgage market, where mortgage lenders were not bound by the same rules as savings and loans. As financial markets became more complex and financiers discovered ways to carry out intricate speculation in a deregulated marketplace, the mortgage loan process changed dramatically. Gone was the traditional relationship between borrowers seeking loans to buy homes and banks that dispersed loans based on the ability of borrowers to pay them back directly.

In the more complex financial world that developed at the end of the twentieth century, two factors complicated the traditional process by creating a whole series of processes and institutions that intervened between the borrower and the lender. The first was a set of independent mortgage brokers and small mortgage firms that set out to "sell" loans to individuals. The second was a process whereby packages of mortgage loans were sold to investment banks, commercial banks, insurance corporations, and government-sponsored corporations, which in turn created complex financial instruments out of the loans that were then passed on to investors. The home itself became an abstraction: the firms or investors who actually owned it had little idea of what it was really worth.

Mortgage brokers and mortgage lending banks aggressively enticed first-time home buyers with the promise of low-interest, low-payment monthly loans. To disguise the high interest normally charged to subprime borrowers, brokers and lenders offered variable-rate mortgages with very low interest rates for the first year or two that would automatically turn into much higher rates later on, meaning that monthly payments could dramatically increase. Lenders made the loans more appealing by forgoing thorough credit checks and lowering the up-front loan costs by adding them on to later monthly payments. Lenders also targeted existing home owners, who took out equity loans against the value of their homes in order to finance purchases, college tuition, or medical expenses.

Spreading Risk

The whole process was characterized by the middlemen's "risk management": pass risk down (to the borrowers) and up (to big mortgage banks and investors). Borrowers, in turn, passed the risk that they could not pay their mortgages on to mortgage banks and bondholders, who in turn passed the risk that they would be liable for defaulted loans on to investors, the FDIC, and ultimately U.S. taxpayers. MBAs notwithstanding, many entrepreneurs did not understand the risks involved because of the complexity of the mortgage lending system. Some mortgage lenders failed to mention or did not fully explain the risk to borrowers that went along with a subprime mortgage loan—the potential for dramatically higher monthly payments and even the loss of their homes if interest rates rose and housing prices fell. Some borrowers, for their part, either did not understand or did not want to understand the actual terms of the loan, often written in very complicated language in the contract. This was, for many, an unprecedented opportunity to buy the home of their dreams.

Mortgage brokers received commissions for each loan they originated; smaller lending banks collected up-front fees. Both then sold the loans down the chain of institutions that had become part of the mortgage industry since the 1980s, for example, to mortgage wholesalers such as Ameriquest, Countrywide, or Washington Mutual. Wholesalers, in turn, passed on a series of the loans to Wall Street investment firms, such as Merrill Lynch, Bear Stearns, or Citigroup. These firms packaged the loans, "securitized" them into bonds, had the bonds rated, and then sold the bonds to investment funds, such as those held by Deutsche Bank, whose investors purchased them. Fannie Mae and Freddie Mac, run privately but backed by government guarantees and charged with the mission of providing affordable housing to all Americans, also bought packages of subprime mortgage loans. Under pressure from Congress (to support homeownership for low-income groups and minorities) and from investors (to return quick profits on their investments), Fannie Mae and Freddie Mac held almost half of all of the mortgage debt in the United States, valued at more than $5 trillion, at a time when their share prices declined sharply and their capital supplies dwindled (Solomon, Ng, and Craig 2008).

Entrepreneurs and corporate firms got caught up in the whirlwind of activity that targeted a whole group of lower-income people who never would have qualified for mortgage loans when banks had an incentive to make sure that loans could be repaid. A case that stands out is that of Cleveland, Ohio, where brokers carried out an aggressive campaign to entice residents to take out subprime loans. In some poor working-class sections of Cleveland, from 57 percent to 100 percent of home loans made in 2005 were subprime mortgage loans (BBC News 2007).

The Bubble Bursts

In the end, the subprime mortgage business was deeply entwined with the U.S. economy: $800 billion worth of subprime loans were initiated in 2005 and by 2007 subprime mortgage bonds were valued at $1 trillion (BBC News 2007). In 2008 mortgage debt in the United States had reached a high of almost $12 trillion (Bajaj 2008). All of this cash and everything it bought was based on an irrational belief in ever-rising housing prices, sustained low interest rates, and the idea that borrowing today is better than saving for tomorrow. This belief inflated the housing bubble. When the bubble burst it punctured the hopes of hundreds of thousands, perhaps millions, of home owners and compelled the federal government to sponsor the most concerted and costly intervention in the economy since the S&L crisis.

The puncture began when the higher interest rates on variable interest mortgage loans kicked in, as inflation rose and economic growth slowed. Hundreds of thousands of borrowers began to default on their loans. As mortgage and investment banks tried to protect their assets, a wave of foreclosures swept across the country. But lenders suffered the same shock as borrowers who tried to use the equity in their homes as a buffer against financial ruin: housing prices, which had sustained a 20 percent growth rate over several years in some markets, began to decline, at a pace and level not seen for twenty years. In Cleveland neighborhoods where subprime mortgage brokers had made a big push to make loans, one in ten homes were under foreclosure in 2007, and Deutsche Bank Trust, acting in the name of its investors who had purchased the bank's bonds, became the area's largest property owner (BBC News 2007).

These foreclosures, in combination with a tighter money supply and less disposable income, made housing prices tumble. Borrowers could no longer pay the bloated prices sellers were asking, and the presence of unoccupied, unkempt, repossessed properties in thousands of neighborhoods reduced the value of all area homes. In many cases, owners simply walked away from their homes and their responsibilities. Rather than try to sell a property, get less than the cost of their outstanding loan, and cobble together the resources to pay the difference while finding a new place to live, they abandoned their homes, defaulted on their loans, and hoped that it would not be worth the banks' trouble and money to go after them. For those who could or would not walk away, the consequences were devastating. The taped foreclosure notices on their doors, the repossession of their furniture and property, and the humiliation and loss of self respect all took their toll on people dealing with rising gas prices, high medical costs, increasing unemployment, and overall inflation.

When hundreds of thousands of borrowers defaulted on their loans, financial institutions that had taken on mortgage debt lost billions of dollars. The assets of some banks were devalued so quickly that they could not cover their deposit obligations. By the fall of 2007, banks had suffered billions of dollars in losses. During the spring and summer of 2008 the government intervened, taking over mortgage banks and investment firms and subsidizing their sale to other companies, in order to prevent massive losses to clients and investors. The U.S. Treasury stepped in to prevent the total collapse of the Countrywide mortgage wholesaler and the Bear Stearns investment bank, both of which had suffered from debilitating loan defaults. The Treasury organized a fire sale, subsidizing the sale of Countryside to Bank of America and Bear Stearns to JPMorgan Chase at the cost of millions of dollars.

Mortgage banks were in no better shape. IndyMac, one of the largest subprime mortgage lenders in the country, became a victim of its bad loans and was taken over by the FDIC. Over the course of a few months, this scenario was repeated over and over again. The savings and retirement accounts of depositors in these failed banks were covered by FDIC guarantees up to $100,000 but it is estimated that 10,000 depositors at IndyMac had $1 billion worth of uninsured deposits in the bank; depositors in other failed banks suffered similar losses (Paletta 2008b). By mid-2008, Congress decided to take concerted action.

The Government Response I: Housing Rescue

With the help of Treasury Secretary Henry Paulson, Congress passed a sweeping set of measures to reverse the tide of foreclosures and financial institution failures in July 2008. The Housing and Economic Recovery Act contained provisions to help hundreds of thousands of borrowers refinance their loans, but only if lenders were willing to refinance at lower housing values. It set up new regulations for the mortgage industry, including a new regulator for mortgage banks and federal standards for the accreditation of mortgage brokers. It gave the Federal Housing Administration the authority to insure up to $300 billion in refinanced mortgages and the Treasury Department to back up mortgage loans with no upper monetary limit; Congress had to raise the U.S. debt ceiling by $800 billion (to $10.6 trillion) in order to cover these potential obligations.

This massive intervention into the housing industry was labeled the most "sweeping government overhaul of mortgage financing since the New Deal" (Herszenhorn 2008). And yet, in a short two months, it was clear that this "sweeping overhaul" was not enough to turn back the tidal wave of financial devastation instigated by the subprime mortgage crisis. In the autumn of 2008, powerful Wall Street investment firms collapsed virtually overnight, banks that had been stung by bad loans stopped issuing credit, commercial banks hoarded capital to cover their obligations, the stock market swung back and forth like a pendulum, and fear spread throughout the American economy. The trouble on Wall Street soon spread to Main Street as jobs disappeared, savings dwindled, and people saw their dream of home ownership turn into a nightmare of financial devastation. Within a short time, the crisis had accelerated to a point where global actors began to question American preeminence in the world economy and citizens began to question the very foundations upon which their economy is built.

The Fall 2008 Financial Crisis: From Wall Street . . .

The rapidly unfolding crisis stunned Americans and roiled markets worldwide. It began with the failure of one of the oldest and seemingly most rock-solid investment firms on Wall Street: 150-year-old Lehman Brothers Holdings. Caught up in a web of risky mortgage loans and securitized bonds based on the packaging of those loans, Lehman Brothers reached a point of no return in September 2008 when its depreciating assets and rapidly dwindling capital reserves forced it to seek outside funding. In a move that surprised many onlookers, the Treasury Department refused to rescue the investment firm and Lehman filed for bankruptcy. While this came as a shock to Wall Street financiers, some welcomed the approach as a sign that the government would no longer rescue investment firms that took risks well beyond their capacity to suffer the consequences. Just a few days later, this policy was put to the test when the American International Group (AIG), another powerful global firm specializing in investment insurance, suffered a liquidity crisis and saw its credit rating downgraded. This time, fearing the shockwaves that might ripple through the economy, Treasury Secretary Paulson and Federal Reserve Chairman Ben Bernanke organized a government bailout package, whereby AIG received an injection of up to $85 billion in credit in return for an almost 80 percent equity share and control over stock dividends; three weeks later, AIG received another loan of almost $40 billion from the Federal Reserve Bank of New York (Morgenson 2008).

As share prices tumbled and investment funds dried up, big investment banks scrambled to protect themselves, setting off "a . . . drama unseen on Wall Street in modern times" (Solomon, Paletta, Phillips, and Hilsenrath.

2008). When Merrill Lynch, Wachovia Bank, and Washington Mutual Bank threatened to close their doors because of bad loans, investment losses, dwindling assets, and lack of capital, the government stepped in to subsidize their sales to commercial banks, such as Bank of America, Wells Fargo, and JPMorgan Chase. These fire sales, just like those of the previous spring, cost taxpayers billions of dollars.

The biggest dominoes to fall were Fannie Mae and Freddie Mac. Between them, they held $5 trillion of mortgage debt, much of it subprime mortgage loans suffering high rates of default (Paletta 2008a; Hagerty 2008). As their assets dwindled and their stock prices plummeted in light of the failure of other mortgage lenders, Fannie and Freddie were on the brink of collapse. Announcing that these companies were "too big to fail," Paulson and Bernanke offered another rescue package (Goodman 2008b). Under this plan, the government took over control of Fannie and Freddie by placing them under the conservatorship of the new Federal Housing Finance Agency. By assuming responsibility for the liabilities of these two mortgage giants, the government potentially put billions of taxpayer dollars at risk; government ownership of stock offsets takeover costs only when the economy strengthens and sales of that stock can replenish Treasury funds. The government plan was a gamble in a poker game that taxpayers never agreed to play.

As policy makers devised a concerted government strategy to reconstitute the financial sector, American taxpayers responded. Congressional offices were flooded with angry phone calls, letters, and e-mails from constituents, insistent that taxpayer money not be used to bail out greedy Wall Street risk-takers. Citizens wanted financiers to be held accountable for their actions and wondered if indictments were more appropriate than bailouts. They were in no mood for what some called a "No Banker Left Behind" corporate welfare scheme that privatized gains and socialized losses (Achenbach and Surdin 2008). In less than a week, however, Americans discovered that Wall Street and Main Street constitute a single path that cuts straight through the entire economy; soon they would change their tune about the need for government intervention to get the banking industry back on its feet.

... to Main Street

The credit crisis expanded downward and outward from its epicenter on Wall Street. Stung by an accumulation of bad loans, reduced capital, devalued assets, and dried-up investment, banks virtually stopped lending money. They curtailed lending to consumers, to businesses of all sizes, and to other banks. Investors held on to their capital for fear of watching it disappear into the black hole of a highly indebted economy. Credit is the lifeblood of the economic system—the oil that greases the gears of daily economic interactions—so when it disappeared almost overnight nearly every household felt the impact in one way or another.

In the fall of 2008, twelve million U.S. home owners (16 percent of the total) were "under water"—their homes worth less than they owed (Hagerty and Simon 2008: A1). The credit crisis made selling these homes problematic, as potential homeowners found it difficult to secure loans from banks. Construction companies could no longer pay workers or purchase supplies; home building and supply businesses felt the pinch. Furthermore, consumers could not get loans to purchase cars and other items, which negatively affected retailers. Without credit, small businesses could not remodel, expand, or hire workers. Large corporations, which sometimes take out short-term loans from banks to pay employees and other expenses, scrambled to find cash as banks turned them away. Businesses forced to vacate their rental properties caused problems for landlords, who in turn could not make mortgage payments to lenders.

Baby boomers were forced to delay retirement, as the value of their 401(k) pension plans and holdings in the stock and bond markets plunged. Some employees dipped into their 401(k) retirement plans early, paying tax penalties, in order to meet daily expenses. Colleges and universities watched the value of their endowments tumble; many found themselves frozen out of their investment and money market accounts, thereby making it difficult to pay bills. As businesses either cut out or pared down health insurance policies, and as personal savings dwindled, many found health insurance and health care to be a luxury at a time when paying food, utility, and transportation bills was difficult enough. All this led to a spike in unemployment, and a widespread anxiety followed in its wake (Goodman 2008a).

The crisis was viewed as "rapidly wiping out vast amounts of wealth" (Browning and Lobb 2008), and the credit freeze threatened to bring the economy into recession. Perhaps most ominous of all, was the fear that the earthquake in the American economy "signal[ed] a bigger realignment, that [America's] place—our significance—in the world [was] diminishing" (Wurtzel 2008). Facing these domestic and global shocks, Congress and the President were compelled to act; when they did, they created a sweeping rescue plan in which almost no one, including the policy makers who crafted it, expressed much satisfaction.

Government Response II: Financial Institution Rescue

After much agonizing and a failed first attempt, Congress passed the Emergency Economic Stabilization Act of 2008 (EESA) on October 3 and rushed it to the White House that same day for President Bush's signature. The central component was a $700 billion program known as the Troubled Assets Recovery Program, or TARP, which was designed to revitalize credit markets by freeing banks of bad debts. In a sort of reverse auction, financial institutions would bid to sell packages of their bad loans to the government. The U.S. Treasury would hold onto the assets, thus freeing banks and investment firms of debt, allowing them to recapitalize and spur investment, and then sell once the economy rebounded, hopefully at a profit. By that time, the potential cost of the government's various rescue packages had reached $2.25 trillion (Landler and Dash 2008).

Uncertainties surrounding TARP undermined any hope that the earlier Emergency Economic Stabilization Act would unclog credit markets and inject a shot of confidence into a shell-shocked economy in the short term. After the Act was signed into law, the stock market continued its downward spiral and citizens appeared to lose all faith in the economy, the financial system that dominated it, and the politicians who were supposed to have watched over it.

In the ensuing days, Secretary Paulson announced more plans to halt a potentially devastating economic decline. He first advocated direct government loans to industries that could not get bank credit. Then he hinted that the FDIC might guarantee all bank deposits, with no limits, for a specific period of time. To accomplish this, the FDIC committed itself to borrowing up to $1.9 trillion from the Treasury and, ultimately, from taxpayers (Paletta 2008b). None of this calmed anyone's nerves; the hemorrhaging of taxpayer reserves and the government's seeming inability to offer anything except stopgap measures continued to undermine confidence and trust. The stock market continued its decline, seeing wild swings during the course of individual trading days well into October.

Finally, in mid-October 2008, after meeting with world leaders who were worried about their own banking systems, Paulson put forth a recapitalization plan that appeared to restore at least a minimum of confidence in the plan to get the banking system back on its feet. The government injected $250 billion of its $700 billion bailout plan into banks; in return acquiring nonvoting shares—that is, partial ownership—in these banks, including Bank of America, Citigroup, and Morgan Stanley (Solomon and Enrich 2008). Paulson assured those concerned about an unprecedented "nationalization" of the banking system that the government would not assume a controlling interest in the banks. Government shares would be sold, hopefully at a profit to the American taxpayer, once the economy recovered. The day after the Treasury Secretary announced this plan, the stock market continued swinging wildly, but this time in a positive direction: on October 13, 2008, stocks enjoyed their biggest one-day point gain ever (almost one thousand points), only to fall by almost as much two days later.

While the stock market gyrated, people continued their daily struggle to make ends meet. As many citizens tried to cope and observers warned of a realignment in the world economic system, the inevitable focus turned to what was to blame for this greatest upheaval in the economy since the Great Depression and how to prevent it from happening again. One thing is clear: the crisis resulted from an astounding absence throughout the entire financial system of the technical, ethical, and leadership competencies highlighted in this book (Exhibit 5.1).

Government: Problem or Solution?

The most debilitating consequence of the absence of technical, ethical, and leadership competencies in this time of crisis was a sharp decline in trust in the country's leaders and institutions. This lack of trust reinvigorated the fundamental debate that took place at the nation's founding: What is the role of government in American public life (see Exhibit 5.2)?

While most agree that risk and greed fueled the 2008 financial crisis, the larger question of how and why these were allowed to run rampant continues to generate much debate. This debate reflects the fundamental controversy over the very foundations of the U.S. economy and the role of government regulation in keeping it sound and productive. Proponents of deregulation argue that free-market laissez faire policies produce the highest standard of living for the greatest number of people. Regulations, they say, should prevent fraud and corruption but not hamper financial firms and investors from seeking ever more innovative ways of producing and securing wealth. Critics of regulation argue that the 2008 financial crisis was caused by too much misdirected regulation and too little risk management; the former undermined sound financial practices while the latter promoted irresponsible investments (Calomiris 2008). Proponents of regulation counter that the deregulation of the commercial and investment banking system since the 1980s allowed corrupt executives and financiers to engage in high-risk investment and accounting practices for personal gain at the expense of the public purse (Black 2007). They argue that a hands-on regulatory system is necessary both to scupper fraud and to substantively regulate the ways financial institutions do business in order to limit risk and ensure stability.

Both sides blame each other for the subprime fiasco and ensuing financial crisis. Deregulation proponents, for example, point to the Community Reinvestment Act, created in 1977 under the Carter administration, as well as

Exhibit 5.1

Failure of Technical, Ethical, and Leadership
Competencies in the 2008 Financial Crisis

The breakdown of the credit system and the ensuing financial crisis illustrate the disastrous implications of the absence or weakness of these competencies in public life. Below is a partial list of competency problems that fueled the crisis.

Technical

- Legitimate lenders did not foresee the actual risks involved in making both subprime and "liar" loans.
- Some complex financial instruments, such as credit derivatives, were "beyond the ken of regulators—sometimes even beyond the understanding of executives peddling them" (Morgenson 2008).
- Fannie Mae and Freddie Mac used a vast array of mathematical formulas and computer programs to analyze transactions and rate the risk of loans, but they failed to cover the companies' complex subprime mortgage loans and risky transactions (Duhigg 2008).
- More than 80 percent of big institutional investors, according to one poll, believed that their executive boards did not understand the risks embedded in company portfolios, though they are required by law to do so (Rothkopf 2008).
- Some observers pointed out that House and Senate committee members had "nonexistent expertise," were intimidated by the well-versed former Federal Reserve Chairman Alan Greenspan, and lacked the technical savvy necessary to counter him when he proposed deregulatory measures (Goodman 2008c).
- A deputy Treasury Secretary charged with getting commitments from Fannie and Freddie to increase their capital to cover their loans was said to be "unfamiliar with the operations" of these government-sponsored organizations (Duhigg 2008).
- Onlookers were concerned that the Treasury Department "doesn't know much about running a reverse auction" (Smith 2008, A17) and that "nobody knows who is holding the tainted assets, how much they have, and how it affects their balance sheets" (Andrews and Landler 2008, 3).

(continued)

Exhibit 5.1 *(continued)*

Ethical

- Some corporate executives lacked the integrity to follow rules in the absence of enforcement and punishment for breaking them.
- Some in Congress accepted special terms on personal loans from mortgage banks that were supposed to be regulated by Congress and whose executives made political contributions.
- Investment bankers ignored warnings of their own managers and government regulators and gambled away the public purse in the pursuit of short-term profit.
- Aggressive mortgage brokers targeted low-income borrowers without explaining the risks involved in variable-rate loans.
- Some borrowers decided to live beyond their means by knowingly taking out loans for homes and consumer items that they could not afford.
- The economy became one big moral hazard, as individuals and institutions took financial risks for which they could not or would not assume responsibility (Chapter 4).

Leadership

- Wall Street executives failed to resist the temptation to engage in short-term profit-making at the expense of long-term financial stability.
- Government regulators, such as SEC Chairman Christopher Cox, failed to lead their agencies to accomplish their stated missions (Scannell 2008).
- Politicians failed to act in the public interest. One nonpartisan observer claimed: "The bankruptcy exists in our political leadership, not on Wall Street. We need to bail out [Democratic Senate majority leader] Nancy Pelosi and [Republican President] George Bush" (Achenbach and Surdin 2008, 2). Washington politicians had suffered a "leadership breakdown" (Calmes 2008).
- The above indictment was one of the few nonpartisan statements to emerge in the crisis. In a tense election year, partisan attacks on political opponents thwarted the emergence of leaders willing to put politics aside to solve universal problems.
- The failure of leadership undermined the legitimacy of government as a whole, as Americans came to believe that "government did not have the basic competence to do the right thing" (Achenbach and Surdin 2008, 2) and even that government was "contributing to the panic" (Macey 2008).

Exhibit 5.2

In Oversight We Trust

We have the same excesses as other capitalist nations have, because fear and greed are built into capitalism. What distinguishes America is our system's ability to consistently expose, punish, regulate and ultimately reform those excesses—better than any other [country]. How often do you hear about such problems being exposed in Mexico or Argentina, Russia or China? They may have all the hardware of capitalism, but they don't have all the software—namely, an uncorrupted bureaucracy to manage the regulatory agencies, licensing offices, property laws and commercial courts.

Indeed, what foreigners envy us most for is precisely the city that some love to bash: Washington. That is, they envy us for our alphabet soup of regulatory agencies: the SEC, the Federal Reserve, the FAA, the FDA, the FBI, the EPA, the IRS, and INS. Do you know what a luxury it is to be able to start a business or get a license without having to pay off some official? Sure, we have our bad apples, but most of our bureaucrats are pretty decent. In fact, our federal bureaucrats are to capitalism what the New York Police and Fire Departments were to 9/11—the unsung guardians of America's civic religion, the religion that says if you work hard and play by the rules, you'll get rewarded and you won't get ripped off.

Well, count me among those naïve fools with a fundamental belief in the federal government—not because I have no faith in ordinary Americans, but because I have no trust in ordinary Big Oil, ordinary Enron or ordinary Harken Energy to do the right thing without proper oversight. . . . What triggered the 489-point one-day rise in the Dow? It was word that Congress had agreed on a plan to create a new independent oversight board for the accounting industry. Much of America's moral authority to lead the world derives from the decency of our government and its bureaucrats, and the example we set for others. These are not things to be sneered at. They are things to be cherished, strengthened and praised every single day.

Source: Excerpted from Friedman (2002: 13). Copyright © 2002 The New York Times Co. Reprinted with permission.

officials in the Clinton administration during the 1990s. Opponents of this Act argue that it pressured mortgage lenders to loosen their credit requirements and make risky loans to lower-income groups in order to satisfy their political constituencies (*Wall Street Journal* 2008). The Department of Housing and Urban Development (HUD) required Fannie Mae and Freddie Mac to direct their mortgage financing to high-risk, low-income borrowers, they argue, tied the hands of mortgage banks and laid the foundations for massive defaults and the credit crisis. "By pressuring banks to serve poor borrowers," one deregulation proponent claims, " . . . politicians could push for increases in home ownership and urban development without having to commit budgetary dollars," thereby enjoying a "political free lunch" (Roberts 2008). The financial crisis, this group argues, occurred because the free-market system was distorted by politically motivated regulations and "social engineering" rather than sound business practices.

Regulation supporters counter that loans to low-income and minority groups are not the problem, but rather the predatory practices of unregulated individuals and companies that tried to turn those loans into lucrative profits for the financial elite (Black 2007). The combination of an unrelenting laissez faire economic philosophy and a coincidence of interests between the Bush administration and financial elites, they argue, allowed Wall Street to "regulate itself" in the years since 2000 to the detriment of the economy and taxpayers (Vanden Heuvel and Schlosser 2008). Deregulation opponents focus their criticism on the SEC's abandonment of its responsibility to the American public. For example, the SEC is supposed to monitor the risk of investments. A 2004 rule allowed the agency to "rely on firms' own computer models for determining risks, essentially outsourcing the job of monitoring risk to the banks themselves" (Labaton 2008). It was this type of "self-policing" practice, as well as understaffed regulatory agencies and a lack of reinforcement in the regulatory system, critics of deregulation say, that initiated the 2008 financial meltdown.

The two sides agree on one thing: the regulatory system in place is ill-matched to the complex components of the new globalized economy. Former Treasury Secretary Paulson, once a critic of regulation, said that the 2008 credit crisis reflected "a flawed regulatory structure, built for a different model for a different financial system" (Enrich and Paletta 2008). Republicans and Democrats alike in Congress blamed the SEC for failed leadership, lax policies, and the failure to carry out its mission of monitoring firms to prevent irresponsible risk (Scannell 2008, A6). Supporters of laissez faire economic policies admit to having learned a terrible lesson: firms cannot effectively police themselves and the market "does not impose its own self-discipline" (Labaton 2008, A23). Former Federal Reserve Chairman Alan Greenspan expressed "shocked disbelief" that his deregulation policies had failed and admitted his mistakes to angry congressional committee members in October 2008 (Scannell and Reddy 2008, A1).

A New Administration: Early Response

As the economic situation continued to decline throughout the fall and winter of 2008, the November presidential election produced a resounding victory for Barack Obama, the candidate who promised "change we can believe in" and "hope" that Americans could recover their confidence in the economy and opportunities for a better future. Promising an end to Wall Street excesses and the elimination of "politics as usual" in Washington, Obama assumed office with the mandate to creatively use government to re-energize the U.S. economy. Far from viewing government as "the problem," the new President made clear his intention to engage a revitalized government sector that would help stimulate, regulate, cajole, and partner with the private and commercial sectors to solve the financial crisis and establish the foundations for a thriving economy. "Obamanomics," as the President's economic plan came to be called, rejected the concept of "big government" in favor of an "activist government" that strives to become an "acceptable and necessary partner for a stable, market-based economy" (Stevenson 2009). This model, based on an attempt to coordinate the activities of a capitalist market economy with governmental goals of providing a more equitable distribution of wealth and services, was put to the test almost immediately after Obama took the oath of office in January 2009.

By then, the U.S. economy seemed to be in a free fall, as unemployment spiked upward, businesses failed, retail stores abandoned malls in droves, savings dwindled, consumer spending contracted, and government budget shortfalls threatened basic services in cities all across the nation. The crisis, which had a domino effect in countries around the world, sparked "a debate of historical importance" about whether the American model of capitalism as it developed after World War II was still viable as a method of promoting economic growth and providing the best standard of living for the greatest number of people (Stevenson 2009). Critics on the ideological right argued that the crisis could be solved only by allowing a market unfettered by government intervention to apply the necessary correctives to the excesses that led to the problem. Leftist critics countered that an unfettered market was the problem, not the solution, and that only concerted government intervention to provide services, redistribute wealth, and control the financial sector would undo the wrongs that precipitated the crisis. The President, working with Democratic majorities in both houses of Congress, sought a solution based on a balance between the two, with government playing a leading role until markets were sufficiently recovered and regulated.

In the first quarter of 2009, the administration crafted an ambitious agenda to address the short- and long-term problems engendered by the financial debacle. It began with a set of measures to stimulate the economy and establish a broad foundation for an innovative, self-sufficient economic system with a well-educated and healthy workforce. The Obama administration argued that the stopgap measures of late 2008 designed to bail out failing banks or fill particular regulatory gaps had failed to stem the tide of financial disasters or help workers and taxpayers. The President's economic team set out to establish a comprehensive program of government stimulus money combined with an overhaul of education, health care, and energy policies to facilitate short-term economic recovery, stimulate long-term economic growth and sustainable energy production, and provide increased opportunities for a wider swath of the workforce (Abrams 2009). Critics argued that the crisis demanded short-term, precisely-targeted measures directed toward addressing mortgage loan fraud, banking failures, and regulatory gaps and that education, health care, and energy policy changes should be delayed until the economy was back on its feet. But the administration and Democratic majorities in Congress held firm and in February 2009 the stimulus package, or "American Recovery and Reinvestment Act" (ARRA) became law.

The ARRA allocated $787 billion for dozens of programs to stimulate spending, investment, research, and development through tax cuts and funding for state infrastructure projects, education, job training, health care, food and housing assistance, environmental cleanup, unemployment assistance, rural development, sustainable energy, and the implementation of cost-saving technologies in various industries (Hossain, Cox, McGrath, and Weitberg 2009). The enormous sums involved compelled critics to argue that the economic crisis had to be solved by saving money, not spending billions of dollars that would eventually have to come out of taxpayers' pockets. Administration officials countered that only the government, with its access to large reserves of cash, had the capacity to address the problems caused by decades of irresponsible behavior in financial markets and that stimulus funds would jumpstart the economy, as well as undergird its long-term recovery, to the point where government coffers would be refilled without undue burden on taxpayers. And so, three months into the Obama presidency, stimulus funds began flowing, as states received money to proceed on "shovel-ready" infrastructure projects, taxpayers obtained refunds from the "Make Work Pay" tax relief program, and businesses and research firms applied for grants to develop innovative cost-saving technologies and energy sources.

After the ARRA was passed, the problem of the banking and insurance industries remained critical. Timothy Geithner, who replaced Henry Paulson as Treasury Secretary, and Ben Bernanke, who stayed on as Federal Reserve Chairman, devised a plan to compel banks to get rid of all the bad loans on their books, maintain a healthy ratio of assets to liabilities, generate more mortgage and small-business loans, and renounce risky investments and wasteful spending. The task was made even more urgent after the public outcry in early 2009 when some of the very same AIG investment bankers who brought the company—and many of its customers—to the brink of bankruptcy were awarded hefty pay bonuses just weeks after the firm received more government bailout money. Taxpayers, and their congressional representatives, were furious to see public money funneled into pay bonuses for irresponsible bankers.

Geithner and Bernanke decided to retain the TARP program put in place at the end of 2008 but with two changes. First, they devised a more systematic method of deciding which banks would receive government aid in getting rid of their "toxic assets." Second, they created a "public-private partnership" to encourage investors to participate in the process. The Treasury Department conducted "stress tests" of nineteen of the largest U.S. banks to see which would have sufficient capital reserves to remain robust in the event of a continued recession (Solomon & Crittenden 2009). Those banks that failed the test would follow a two-part plan to replenish their assets: first, they would attempt to persuade privately-managed investment funds, encouraged by government guarantees, to buy their bad loans (Bebchuk 2009). If this did not work, either the government would disburse TARP funds, buttressed by an additional $250–$750 billion, to get the bad loans off the bank's books or the government loans would be converted into common stock, thereby increasing the equity of the bank but also giving the government voting rights and a controlling interest in the bank's operations (Andrews 2009).

The plan proved to be fraught with difficulties: the government and, by extension, taxpayers would assume an enormous financial risk both by subsidizing private investment firm involvement in buying bad bank loans and by extending more TARP funds to troubled banks (Guerrera and Luce 2009). Congress, furious at the AIG bonuses and wary of ramping up already historic federal deficit figures, demanded restrictions on banks that received funding, such as limits on executive pay and control over how some of the funding was spent. Alternatively, if the government decided to convert its loans to common equity stock, the resulting control over banking operations would result in the effective nationalization of some banks, which would constitute a controversial sea-change in the role of the government in the banking industry.

Part of the administration's banking plan was targeted toward helping home owners re-finance high interest mortgages and preventing foreclosures. The

"Making Home Affordable" anti-foreclosure plan earmarked $75 billion of bailout money to provide incentives to mortgage lenders to re-negotiate the terms of loans held by troubled borrowers and to subsidize the lowering of interest rates to help qualified borrowers reduce monthly payments (*New York Times* 2009). In an unprecedented move, the government advocated allowing courts to modify mortgages if lenders refused to re-negotiate loan terms with bankrupt homeowners. In early 2009, about 13.6 million homeowners were "under water," with mortgage balances greater than the value of their homes. According to a Web site sponsored by the U.S. Treasury Department and the Department of Housing and Urban Development (http://MakingHomeAffordable.gov), the mortgage program was projected to help 4–5 million home owners refinance their loans and 3–4 million avoid foreclosure. Some argue that the plan did not go far enough to help responsible borrowers who fell behind in mortgage payments because of the economic downturn (Guttentag 2009), while opponents of the plan and the mortgage industry argued that allowing bankruptcy judges to change the terms of mortgage loans would create undue risks and uncertainties for lenders (O'Connor 2009).

The automobile industry was another test case for the extent to which companies proved willing to restructure their operations, re-orient their business practices, and subject themselves to government intervention in order to benefit from the "carrot" of government loans and avoid the "stick" of devastating bankruptcies. Suffering from high debt, low sales, escalating costs, and foreign competition, the U.S. auto industry, one of the pillars of the economy, appeared to be on the brink of insolvency in late 2008. At that time, GM and Chrysler received billions of dollars in federal loans after agreeing to restructure their operations to reduce costs and increase sales (Whorisky 2009). In February 2009, however, the two companies requested an additional $21.6 billion in assistance. The administration responded swiftly and with a stern hand. The President set up an "auto task force" to assess the companies' restructuring plans. Rejecting those plans and arguing that the companies had not gone far enough to reduce costs, the task force gave GM sixty days to streamline its operations by cutting costs, reducing its workforce, and developing internationally competitive, fuel-efficient automobiles (Vlasic and Stolberg 2009).

President Obama pressured GM's chairman to step down in order to provide the company a "clean slate" for moving forward, resulting in "an extraordinary intervention of the federal government into the management of a private company" (Whorisky 2009). Chrysler, which the auto task force decided could not survive on its own, was given thirty days to forge an alliance with the Italian carmaker Fiat (Whorisky and Marr 2009). Responding to fears that the government's strict conditions could lead to a crisis of confidence in U.S. car manufacturers and a drop in sales, the President announced that the government would provide buyers a financial guarantee of GM and Chrysler new vehicle warranties if the companies agreed to the loan conditions. The move was designed to shore up confidence in the ailing industry, but it also potentially added billions more taxpayer dollars to a growing list of promises of government support.

The measures taken by administration officials to address the economic crisis were wide-ranging and addressed fundamental concerns about the ability of markets to regulate themselves and fairly distribute wealth, services, and opportunities across a wide spectrum of the population. Obama and the Democratic majority in Congress argued that the government must spend money in order to help the economy generate money. As the federal deficit moved toward an unprecedented $1 trillion in the first half of 2009, this argument generated fierce opposition on the part of the administration's opponents and some taxpayers, who feared that once the government intervenes in financial, economic, and service markets, it will seek to control those markets and to stay involved in the long term (Reynolds 2009). In rejecting the patchwork approach to specific economic problems as they arise in favor of a fundamental re-orientation of the economy, Obama made the debate take on an added urgency and relevance. The severity of the economic recession and its impact on all citizens compelled government officials to develop pragmatic solutions to a fundamental philosophical problem: what is the optimal role of government in a free market economy and society?

Conclusion

As *New York Times* columnist and 2008 Nobel prize winner Paul Krugman observed, earlier economic crises, such as the S&L fiasco and Enron failure, "should have been seen as omens, as intimations of still worse things to come." Instead, they "had the perverse effect of making both investors and public officials more, not less complacent" (2008) because the scandals, despite considerable damage in the short term, did not undermine the entire economic system in the long term. Demonstrating that capitalism's worst enemies are capitalists, savvy financiers and entrepreneurs learned how to play the regulatory angles to make ill-gotten gains, a game made possible by lax oversight and a lack of communication among regulators (Enrich and Paletta 2008). Stopgap measures failed to solve fundamental problems that allowed the financial sector to take risks that devastated workers, citizens, and the economy as a whole.

President Obama, blaming the weakness of the economy on the "greed and irresponsibility of the part of some," as well as on "our collective failure to make hard choices and prepare the nation for a new age" (2009), promised fundamental changes, based on an activist government, that would establish the foundations for a healthy economy and a new age of opportunities for American workers. In dealing with an inherited crisis, the administration committed itself to the three competencies addressed in this book: technical efficiency through the appointment of officials concerned more with pragmatic solutions to specific problems than with political loyalty, ideological purity, or personal interests; ethical standards imposed by the transparency of government operations; and leadership to move beyond partisan bickering and political interests to create policies that further the common good. As measures were put in place to address fundamental economic problems, there were signs that the economic debacle might produce a necessary corrective to decades of greed, corruption, and irresponsibility. Observers hoped that this crisis of "ethic" proportions might produce a "fiduciary society" in which federal statutes would induce those entrusted with managing other peoples' money "to place front and center the interests of the owners they are duty-bound to serve" (Bogle 2009, A19) and that businesses, not only government, would begin themselves to "speak out against greed" (Miller 2009, 11).

But larger questions remain: How can debilitating industry, corporate, and economy-wide crises be averted by application of the technical, ethical, and leadership competencies analyzed in the previous chapters? What must public servants do in order to avoid "learning exactly the wrong lessons" from earlier mistakes (Black 2002)? What are the right lessons to be learned that will help public servants better serve the common good? The epilogue addresses these questions.

Epilogue

Necessity is the plea for every infringement of human freedom.
It is the argument of tyrants; it is the creed of slaves.
—William Pitt

The Triad of Crises and Competencies

The three crises examined in Chapters 4 and 5—the S&L debacle, the Enron scandal, and the financial meltdown that began in 2008—could all have been averted had the three competencies discussed in this book—technical, ethical, and leadership—been judiciously applied. Failing badly, at the same time and on the same issues, the private and public sectors in all three episodes acted on the belief that markets can do no wrong and government can do no right. When the resulting disasters occurred, the taxpayer was victimized. As markets stabilized, other pressing issues diverted the attention of decision makers, effective corporate governance reform measures died, and business malfeasance went largely unpunished. Common threads, accordingly, connect the S&L, Enron, and financial debacles with respect to the technical, ethical, and leadership competencies explored in these pages.

In terms of the technical competency, proponents of deregulation argued that market participants know best how to apply their skills and they should not be hampered by regulations that stifle creativity and freedom. This may be a good argument in terms of technical skills alone, except that corrupt and greedy entrepreneurs have employed them for their own economic gain to the detriment of others.

Savings and loan financiers used their know-how to game the system; Enron managers and Arthur Andersen accounting firm employees created previously unknown methods to hide debt and conceal the actual value of the company; and subprime mortgage brokers used their talents to deceive borrowers and create wealth for themselves while passing risk, debt, and potential bankruptcy on to investors and government insurers. Regulators have not been able to keep pace with the new and complex technical methods by which speculators and financiers create actual and potential wealth. Many regulations were dismantled at a time when certain complex financial transactions and speculation did not yet exist (Kuttner 2007).

Technical skills that develop unchecked can lead to undesirable outcomes. Professionalism, and certainly the public interest, requires that skills are deployed within the context of a code of behavior that establishes guidelines for their use (Chapter 2), as Adam Smith emphasized. Clearly, executives, financiers, members of Congress, mortgage brokers, bankers, and individuals should engage in ethical behavior. In the case of the S&L and Enron scandals, punishing those who failed to do so was relatively straightforward. In the subprime mortgage calamity, the ethics question is more ambiguous: Can and should individuals be held accountable for decisions made in the context of a culture that places a high value on consumerism and home ownership and of a mortgage industry that sometimes engages in predatory lending? If this conundrum cannot easily be answered, perhaps the pragmatic line is more effective. Regardless of whether or not they *should* make bad decisions, given the opportunity people *will* make bad decisions. The same is true of other economic actors in the home mortgage industry and financial sector as a whole. When money is involved, it is dangerously naïve to rely on the goodwill of business and the false belief that markets are self-regulating.

Mortgage brokers and Wall Street investors ought not encourage risky loans or hide their potential cost, but inevitably some will do this as long as the opportunity presents itself and there are few enforced regulations, restrictions, or retributions that prevent them from doing so. The lessons learned in Chapter 3 can be applied to these private individuals and commercial actors: Individuals should be taught to behave ethically, but there can be no assumption in any given situation that they will behave honestly. In order to make ethical outcomes more likely, personal decisions must be backed up by organizations that encourage an ethical culture and that punish untoward behavior according to established rules. The "organization" relevant to the subprime mortgage crisis is a large part of society, if one includes the millions of private individuals who took out loans and the whole chain of economic actors involved in the process. The only entity that can establish professional standards for the economy as a whole is the federal government—not as a way to determine how people behave, but to ensure that their behavior adheres to certain standards and that their technical knowledge is used in a professional manner.

Without government regulation, technical skills can be, have been, and will continue to be used inappropriately, both in terms of the goals toward which those skills are directed and the unethical behavior that may result. Government needs examiners who are experts in all forms of financial transactions, speculation, and accounting fraud, not to supplant private and commercial actors, but to ensure that their skills are not used for dishonorable ends or to harm the public interest in the pursuit of private gain.

Leadership competency allowed a true leader to emerge during the S&L crisis from the ranks of the bureaucracy to cry wolf as lax standards and complicit congressmen facilitated the corruption. Bill Black had the technical skills, the moral courage, and the leadership abilities to help prevent a complete meltdown of the S&L industry and to take part in its rehabilitation. The Enron and 2008 financial crises produced few such exemplary leaders. Why is this?

In some sense, given the context of a deregulated commercial sector— where financiers and accounting firms had almost free rein to create new methods of producing wealth and hiding debt—Enron was too small and the financial catastrophe too big to produce a leader such as Bill Black. Black was employed first by a government agency responsible for a specific economic sector and then by a private bank charged with examining savings and loans institutions. When he saw the corruption, he could use his position to target a specific group of corrupt financiers. Enron, though a giant corporate conglomerate, was a company whose executives, accountants, and perhaps legal team were involved in a massive series of internal transactions using untested techniques outside the ken of government regulators. Contestation was also unlikely to come from the executive branch of the government. The lobbying relationship between Enron executives and members of the Bush administration, as well as the loyalty expected of government appointees and employees by the executive branch, quashed any possibility that leadership would emerge from either of these ranks. While an Enron staffer had reported suspicious accounting transactions to the authorities, it would have taken someone higher up in the ranks of Enron, Arthur Andersen, or Enron's legal firm to exhibit the leadership abilities necessary to fight company corruption. Only a more highly placed executive could have prevented the firm's ultimate destruction, which was detrimental to innocent employees as well as to the national economy.

Though the financial system has produced upstanding leaders who combine the technical, ethical, and leadership competencies discussed in this book, it would be folly to assume that all, or even most, executives use their skills in ways that advance the public interest. The regulations passed in the wake of the Enron scandal—designed to increase transparency in accounting practices and make executives responsible for their companies' finances—help ensure that corporate skills are used to strengthen the commonwealth, not devise end runs around the law. They allow enough room for honest executives to exercise their technical and leadership skills for the benefit of the company and the economy while enforcing ethical behavior to minimize corruption.

In the 2008 financial disaster, the scope of action was too large for any single bureaucrat or executive leader to prevent or stop a series of complicated transactions—from "risky" loans to complex investments with unknown consequences—that resulted in so much personal tragedy and economic devastation. While individual members of Congress took the lead by trying to provide relief to homeowners and the banking industry, it is nearly impossible for one member of Congress to succeed in preventing or solving such a widespread crisis. The diverse interests, differing opinions, and varied constituencies of House and Senate members impair the ability of Congress to pass legislation fast enough to confront a problem in a timely way. Leadership must come from within the executive branch of the government, such as the President or Treasury Secretary, or from Federal Reserve Chairmen, past and present, who could have applied more stringent monetary policies and regulatory measures to prevent the granting of risky credit from causing so much havoc in the economy. Presidents, for example, can spearhead public campaigns to encourage personal saving as a way to responsibly achieve the goal of home ownership, rather than touting home ownership per se as a complement to the support of business interests. An administration that prioritizes deregulation as a stimulus for Wall Street is unlikely to produce a leader who would have the foresight to prevent such a deeply rooted problem as the subprime mortgage crisis or the ensuing financial debacle. The absence of leadership, as illustrated in Chapter 4, can ruin an organization. This maxim is writ large, and with very severe consequences for individuals, in the S&L fiasco, the Enron collapse, and the 2008 breakdown of the financial system.

Lessons Learned

What lessons can be learned from the three crises in terms of the themes of this book: the use of technical, ethical, and leadership competencies to develop a professional edge in public service? The answer goes back to the Founders of the nation. Although there were many disagreements about the role of government and the balance of power between the federal government and the states, they agreed on one fundamental tenet: American government is *of* the people, *by* the people, and *for* the people. While government is not to play an active role that would inhibit the fundamental freedoms upon which the nation was built, it does play an essential role in ensuring that those freedoms can be as equally enjoyed as possible and that they are not turned into excesses by some. Because the Founders realized that individuals who attain positions of power and the government as a whole may be prone to unethical or tyrannical behavior, they provided for a system of checks and balances based on executive, legislative, and judicial interaction and oversight. The rules and regulations that emerge from this interaction are less likely to result in tyranny, and more likely to be in the public interest, than the informal (and frequently illegal) practices that tolerate deceit, deception, and a disregard of the common good.

Too often in recent decades, the government has been viewed as a detriment to freedom and a drag on innovation and effective service provision. While the Republican Party has traditionally called for less government and views government intervention as inhibiting economic freedoms, the Democratic Party has followed its lead in emphasizing the need to reduce the size of government. One consequence of the approach that big government is the problem has been more than two decades of deregulation, supported by the argument that markets and the people who move them can police themselves. This assumes that the activities of individuals and entities, behaving as rational actors, will result in a common good. The problem with this approach is that sometimes what individuals and entities consider rational acts are not always ethical acts. Economic actors may willfully behave unethically in their own interests or they may perceive themselves to be acting rationally without realizing the long-term cost or harm of their acts, both in terms of ethics and their own best interests.

Both assumptions—that government intervention is inherently bad and that society is comprised of rational actors whose combined actions will result in the common good—go against the tenets upon which the U.S. government is based: that members of government come from the ranks of ordinary Americans (of the people) who participate either directly or indirectly in making policies (by the people) in the public interest (for the people). This formula is designed to prevent tyranny. In order to forestall wide-scale and wide-ranging crises such as the S&L, Enron, and financial debacles, public service must become a source of pride and professionalism, whether it occurs in the ranks of the bureaucracy, the commercial sector, or the nonprofit sphere—and this pride must become part of the national culture. If government service is to be on the leading edge, it cannot be viewed as a bumbling behemoth populated by rubber-stamping bureaucrats interested only in pay and promotions. The fact that government is finding it difficult to replace the wave of retiring workers (Chapter 2) is an indication that many talented Americans turn their sights to the financial, corporate, private legal, academic, or nonprofit sectors rather than to direct government service.

There have been attempts to change the image of government, revitalize its ranks, and encourage innovative practices and excellent service. The reforms made to improve performance in government since the 1990s, the recent emphasis on ethical behavior, and the fostering of leadership in all government agencies as overseen by the Office of Personnel Management (Chapter 4) are steps in this direction. But much more has to be done to provide and preserve a professional edge. Creation of a national public service academy (Ballenstedt 2008a) comparable to the military academies would provide an opportunity to hone that edge in the future.

Conclusion

People with the best technical skills should view government service as a productive, dynamic, challenging, and rewarding arena in which to apply their expertise. The opportunities are endless: computer experts can work in or with the government on developing cyberinformation and cybersecurity; scientists can work on developing ways to enhance national security through biometric techniques and chemical detection; financial experts can be engaged to detect fraud and creatively enhance government regulation of the commercial sector. First and foremost, technical experts must perceive government service as a role that embodies professional satisfaction, service, and status. For public service to be viewed this way by professionals, a reorientation of how government is perceived is crucial.

In terms of ethics, the government must adhere to a code of professional ethics that makes it clear that public servants are held to high standards of performance and trust. Trust in officials is especially crucial in an era when threats to national security compel actions that limit, in some capacity, personal and commercial freedoms. Government agencies are making concerted efforts to enforce ethics codes and to instill an ethical culture throughout the ranks of the government bureaucracy (Chapter 3). There is, however, considerable room for improvement. A steady stream of unethical behavior on the part of members of Congress, the unwarranted and inhumane treatment of prisoners at the Abu Ghraib prison in Iraq, the failure to punish crimes committed against innocent civilians in a war zone that have nothing to do with military actions, and the unwillingness to hold private firms responsible for criminal behavior all weaken the reputation of government service. Exhibit E.1 illustrates how a torture interrogation policy that conflicts with the technical, ethical, and leadership competencies can shame and sully the nation's honor, stature, and self-respect.

In order for the stories of people like Bill Black and the scores of other committed public servants to dominate the headlines, their work must be publicly valued and transgressors brought to justice swiftly so that Americans see that unethical behavior is not tolerated. Transparency in all areas is the key factor in convincing citizens that government service demands superior

Exhibit E.1

Terror and Torture: Detainee Treatment

It is the duty of every patriot to protect his country from its government.
—Thomas Paine

The events of September 11, 2001, presented Americans with stark choices. One of the most controversial was, "Does terrorism sanction the use of torture against detainees in order to prevent terrorist acts?" The elusive nature of contemporary terrorism means that enemies can hatch plots that are difficult to discover until it is too late. The use of the Internet to spread bomb-making techniques, the ability to make powerful explosives out of household ingredients, and the willingness of suicide bombers to kill themselves as well as innocent people may suggest that governments cannot rely on the usual deterrents to prevent terrorism.

Can the U.S. government justify using torture against terrorists? The war on terror began with widespread international support in defense of civilization and has since changed to worldwide condemnation of American actions at the Abu Ghraib prison in Iraq and the Guantánamo detainee camp in Cuba. The facts are undisputed: hundreds of cases of torture and abuse—including suicides and deaths—have been documented by the military, the Federal Bureau of Investigation, human rights groups, and the media (DeYoung 2007; Shane, Johnston, and Risen 2007). While past Administrations sometimes authorized the violation of law and human rights in response to crises, there is no precedent in modern American history for what has occurred since the attacks on the World Trade Center in New York City and the Pentagon.

According to Confucius, the principle problem facing public administrators is how to serve those in power. American military and civilian personnel are expected to reflect the nation's values. Public service, as this book's triangle of competencies has examined, requires technical skill and moral courage in order to lead. The systematic use of torture rests on the belief that it is an effective way to elicit valuable information to prevent future attacks (Smith 2007). There is little available evidence, however, to prove that this assumption is true and a great deal that proves it is not. Military experience and interrogation studies demonstrate that cruel, inhumane, and degrading treatment does not result in reliable information. Indeed, in 2007 the Intelligence Science Board (Smith 2007; *Washington Post* 2007, A14) found that that there is no scientific evidence that brutality produces valid intelligence. Such data explain why the U.S. Army Interrogation Manual

(continued)

Exhibit E.1 *(continued)*

forbids harsh techniques. From a technical viewpoint, it is not an effective method of gathering information and can lead to false confessions. Rather than preventing attacks, the torture of Muslim terrorist suspects not only fans anti-Americanism, but is used as a recruiting tool by Al-Qaeda.

From an ethical perspective, service to the country should adhere to American values and law, as well as international covenants to which the United States is a party: the Geneva Conventions on the treatment of prisoners of war, the United Nations Convention Against Torture, and the United Nations Universal Declaration of Human Rights. Detaining innocent people and brutalizing the guilty are obvious violations. Such behavior implicates public servants in war crimes, endangers captured Americans, compromises national honor, and abandons the rule of law. The American Medical Association's professional standards, for example, specifically prohibit physicians from participating in torture and oblige them to support victims (Kristof 2008). Evidence exists, nonetheless, that doctors have falsified death certificates to cover up homicides, hid evidence of beatings, made a mockery of standards, and revived prisoners so they could be further tortured (see, for example, *New York Times* 2008; Finn 2008).

Confronted with a policy that is technically and ethically deficient, leadership competency can take many forms. At the Department of Defense, high-ranking military officers, the Secretaries of the Army, Navy, and Air Force, and military and civilian attorneys vigorously supported adherence to the Geneva Conventions in the face of intense political pressure (*New York Times* 2005). Some refused to prosecute accused terrorists (in part because of evidence gathered as a result of torture), and others requested transfers, resigned, or retired. When coercive techniques are condoned by top officials, however, those who remain may be intimidated or take a more expedient path. Indeed, a military commission participated in highly politicized tribunal proceedings in 2008 that violated standard American jurisprudence through the use of secret evidence and information obtained by hearsay and brutality (*New York Times* 2008).

The cardinal question for professionals, who must exhibit a high level of moral development (Chapter 3), is an existential one: "Who are we as a nation?" The torture controversy centers not on whether the United States is going to deal with terrorists, but whether it will destroy its democratic principles in doing so. As Senator John McCain pointed out, "It is not about them. It is about us." Torture is technically pointless and ethically

(continued)

Exhibit E.1 *(continued)*

immoral, a policy that compromises and discredits both individuals and countries that aspire to leadership. Disingenuous claims made after 2001 that "this government does not torture," along with the authorization of methods widely regarded here and abroad as torture, constituted evasion, not leadership.

A nation worthy of Jefferson, Washington, and Madison should not only renounce all forms of torture and close Guantánamo prison, but also either establish a policy of reconciliation or appoint a special prosecutor to bring charges against those responsible. "What we need now," writes Anne Applebaum (2009, A15) "is not an endless, politicized circus of a congressional investigation . . . but a carefully targeted legal investigation of the CIA's invisible prisons: who gave orders to use torture, who carried out the orders, what exactly was done, who objected." To reclaim the American heritage of a nation of laws and a people of character, the guilty should be called to account. Not to recognize the technical, ethical, and leadership calamity that this policy has wrought is as disgraceful as the abuses themselves: The real debate is not about what to do in exceptional situations (the "ticking time bomb" scenario, which can short-circuit the need to think rationally about threats), but about the conduct of routine interrogations. Yet the most disturbing aspect of the torture scandals in recent years is the time it took for public outrage to develop against such methods and the slow progress in making certain they never happen again.

levels of ethical behavior for those who commit themselves to working in the name of the common good.

Finally, government needs to attract genuine committed leaders, from the president all the way down to the lowest levels of the bureaucracy. Politicians are often caught between two competing sets of interests: those of specific constituencies and those of the nation. Their challenge is to emphasize the greater good whenever possible, even if it means incurring the wrath of special interest groups. Political appointees are often under pressure to act on the basis of loyalty to the administration; their duty as leaders is to stand up to their bosses when the law demands it or when it is for the public good. Career employees are often at the mercy of elected or appointed officials and feel powerless to counter them. Their charge is that of Bill Black: to know the law and administrative regulations inside-out, have all the technical expertise at their disposal, and exhibit the courage to use the law as a weapon against politicking, conflicts of interest, and any sign of corruption. Currently, the nation is fighting two wars, facing a collapse of its financial system, and experiencing enormous demands in energy, medical, and education policy. People in all sectors—government, commercial, and nonprofit—must express the determination and dedication to serve. In order for this to happen, government business needs to engage the respect of the nation. It will do this by enticing those who have committed themselves to sharpening their professional edge.

References

Abrams, J. 2009. Congress to back deal with big issues, big goals. *Washington Post,* April 18. http://www.washingtonpost.com/wpdyn/content/article/2009/04/18/AR2009041800796.html.

Achenbach, J., and A. Surdin. 2008. For many Americans, fear and distrust run high. *Washington Post,* September 30. http://www.washingtonpost.com/wp-dyn/content/article/2008/09/29/AR2008092903325.html.

Ackman, D. 2002. Enron's lawyers: Eyes wide shut? *Forbes,* January 28. http://www.forbes.com/2002/01/28/0128veenron_print.html.

American City & County. 1998. Landfill closure necessitates privatized waste collection. *American City & County* 113 (9): 14.

American City & County. 2002. Town expands trash collection contract. *American City & County* 117 (1): 15–18.

American Federation of Government Employees (AFGE). 2008. *Privatization of federal services.* http://www.afge.org/Index.cfm?Page=Privatization&File=PrivatizationTalkingPoints2.htm.

American Society for Public Administration. 2000. *Performance measurement: Concepts and techniques.* Washington, DC: ASPA.

American Society for Quality. 2001. Certified quality manager body of knowledge. http://www.qualityamerica.com/QPProducts/2001bok.htm.

Ammons, D. 2002. *Tools for decision making: A practical guide for local government.* Washington, DC: CQ Press.

Anderson, A. 1996. *Ethics and fundraising.* Bloomington: Indiana University Press.

Andrews, E. 2009. U.S. may convert banks' bailouts to equity share. *New York Times,* April 20. http://www.nytimes.com/2009/04/20/business/20bailout.html.

Andrews, E., and M. Landler. 2008. U.S. may take ownership stake in banks. *New York Times,* October 9. http://www.nytimes.com/2008/10/09/business/economy/09econ.html.

Andrisani, P., S. Hakim, and E. Leeds. 2000. *Making government work.* New York: Rowman & Littlefield.

Anonymous. 2002. An aesthetic theory of conflict in administrative ethics. Unpublished manuscript.

Apostolou, B., and G. Thibadoux. 2003. Why integrity matters: Accounting for the accountants. *Public Integrity* 5 (3): 223–238.

Applebaum, A. 2009. Cleanup task for a shining city. *Washington Post,* March 17.

Aulisio, M., R. Arnold, and S. Youngner. 2000. Health care ethics consultation: Nature, goals, and competencies. *Annals of Internal Medicine* 133 (1): 59–69.

Bailey, S. 1965. Relationship between ethics and public service. In *Public administration and democracy: Essays in honor of Paul Appleby,* ed. R. Martin, 282–298. Syracuse, NY: Syracuse University Press.

Bajaj, V. 2008. Housing lenders fear bigger wave of loan defaults. *New York Times,* August 4. http://www.nytimes.com/2008/08/04/business/041end.html.

Ballenstedt, B. 2008a. Outlook for public service academy brightens. *National Journal. com,* November 21. http://lostintransition.nationaljournal.com/2008/11/outlook-for-public-service-aca.php#more.

———. 2008b. Top-notch civil servants lauded at black-tie gala. Government Executive .com, September 17. http://www.govexec.com/story_page.cfm?articleid=40991.

Barbash, F. 2002. It's time to punish corporate sinners. *Washington Post National Weekly Edition,* July 15–21.

BBC (British Broadcasting Corporation). 2007. The downturn in facts and figures. *BBC News Online,* November 21. http://news.bbc.co.uk/2/hi/business/7073131.stm.

Bebchuck, L. 2009. A fix for Geithner's Plan. *Washington Post,* March 31. http://www.washingtonpost.com/wp-dyn/content/article/2009/03/30/AR2009033002607.html.

Becker, E. 1999. Pentagon sets up new center for waging cyberwarfare. *New York Times,* October 8. http://query.nytimes.com/gst/fullpage.html?res=9E0DE6DF1031F93BA35753C1A96F958260.

Belker, L. 1997. *The first-time manager.* New York: AMACOM.

Berman, E. 2006. *Performance and productivity in public and nonprofit organizations.* 2d ed. New York: M.E. Sharpe.

Berman, E., and J. West. 1998. Productivity enhancement efforts in public and nonprofit organizations. *Public Productivity and Management Review* 22 (2): 207–219.

———. 2008. Managing emotional intelligence in U.S. cities. *Public Administration Review* 68 (4): 742–758.

Berman, E., J. Bowman, J. West, and M. Van Wart. 2009. *Human resource management in public service.* Thousand Oaks, CA: Sage.

Berrien County Community Development Department. 2008. City of Benton Harbor: Community Profile, August. http://www.berriencounty.org/econdev/pdfs/benton_harbor_city.pdf?PHPSESSID=af403f66f0c18468c0f8412bbc3e3673.

Bilmes, L., and W. Gould. 2009. *The people factor: strengthening America by investing in public service.* Washington, D.C.: Brookings Institution Press.

Black, W. 2002. Repeating the past. *Newsday,* July 7. http://www.scu.edu/ethics/publications/ethicalperspectives/fraud.html.

———. 2005. *The best way to rob a bank is to own one. How corporate executives and politicians looted the S&L industry.* Austin, TX: University of Texas Press.

———. 2007. (Mis)understanding a banking industry in transition. *Dollars and Sense* 273: 14–27. http://ssrn.com/abstract=1103942.

———. No date. The moral quandaries of a government whistleblower. Markkula Center for Applied Ethics, Santa Clara University. http://www.scu.edu/ethics/publications/submitted/black/whistleblower.html.

Blair, B. 2002. The ultimate management challenge. *Federal Times,* November 25.

Bloom, A. 1988. *The closing of the American mind: How higher education has failed democracy and impoverished the souls of today's students.* New York: Simon and Schuster.

Bogle, J. 2009. A crisis of ethic proportions. *Wall Street Journal.* April 19.

Bok, D. 1986. *Higher learning.* Cambridge, MA: Harvard University Press.

Bolman, L., and T. Deal. 2008. *Reframing organizations.* 4th ed. San Francisco: Jossey-Bass.

Boris, E., and E. Steurle, eds. 2006. *Nonprofits and government.* Washington, DC: Urban Institute Press.

Bowman, J. (1998). *The Lost World* of Public Administration Education: Rediscovering the Meaning of Professionalism, *Journal of Public Administration Education* 4 (1): 27–31.

Bowman, J. 2003. Virtue ethics. *Encyclopedia of Public Administration and Public Policy,* ed. J. Rabin, 1259–1263. New York: Dekker.

Bowman, J., and C. Knox. 2008. Ethics in government. *Public Administration Review* 68 (4): 627–635.

Bowman, J., and J. West. 2006. Ending civil service protections in Florida government. *Review of Public Personnel Administration* 26: 139–157.

———. 2009. To "re-hatch" public employees or not? *Public Administration Review* 69 (1): 52–63.

Bowman, J., and J. West, eds. 2007. *American public service.* New York: Taylor and Francis.

Brookings Institution. 2002. Opportunity lost: The decline of trust and confidence in government after September 11. A Governance Studies Event. http://www.brookings.edu/events/2002/0530governance.aspx.

Bronner, K. 2003. Does government need a Sarbanes-Oxley type reform act? *PA Times* (April): 6–7.

Brook, D., and C. King. 2008. Federal personnel management reform. *Review of Public Personnel Administration* 28: 205–221.

Brousseau, P. 1998. Ethical dilemmas: Right vs. right. In *The ethics edge,* ed. E. Berman, J. West, and S. Bonczek, 35–46. Washington, DC: International City/County Management Association.

Browning, E., and A. Lobb. 2008. Market's 7-day rout leaves U.S. reeling. *Wall Street Journal,* October 10.

Bruce, W. 1996. Codes of ethics and codes of conduct: Perceived contribution to the practice of ethics in local government. *Public Integrity Annual:* 23–30.

Bruno, G. 2008a. The capital interview: General William Lord on cyberspace and the future of warfare. The Council on Foreign Relations Online, April 1. http://www.cfr.org/publication/15899/capital_interview.html.

———. 2008b. The evolution of cyber warfare. Council on Foreign Relations Online *Backgrounder,* February 27. http://www.cfr.org/publication/15577/evolution_of_cyber_warfare.html.

Bryson, J. 1995. *Strategic planning for public and nonprofit organizations: A guide to strengthening and sustaining organizational achievement.* San Francisco: Jossey-Bass.

California Debt and Investment Advisory Commission. 2007. Privatization vs. public-private partnerships: A comparative analysis. CDIAC Issue Brief #07–04. http://www.treasurer.ca.gov/Cdiac/publications/privatization.pdf.

Calmes, J. 2008. In bailout vote, a leadership breakdown. *New York Times,* September 30. http://www.nytimes.com/2008/09/30/business/30assess.html?_r=1&scp=6&sq=Jackie%20Calmes&st=cse&oref=login.

Calomiris, C.W. 2008. Most pundits are wrong about the bubble. *Wall Street Journal,* October 18. http://online.wsj.com/article/SB122428270641246049.html.

Clarke, R. 2008. *Your government failed you: Breaking the cycle of national security disasters.* New York: Ecco.

CNN.com. 2002. Enron employees ride stock to bottom. *CNN.com/Law Center,* January 14. http://archives.cnn.com/2002/LAW/01/14/enron.employees/.

Cohen, S., W. Eimicke, and J. Horan. 2002. Catastrophe and the public service: A case study of the government response to the destruction of the World Trade Center. *Public Administration Review* 62 (special issue): 24–32.

Columbia Accident Investigation Board. 2003. *CAIB Report.* Washington, DC: Government Printing Office.

Combs, G. 2002. Meeting the leadership challenge of a diverse and pluralistic workforce. *Journal of Leadership Studies* 8 (4): 1–16.

Condrey, S., and R. Maranto. 2001. *Radical reform of the civil service.* Lanham, MD: Lexington Books.

Conlow, R., E. Cohen, J. Zayszly, and R. Mapson. 2001. *Excellence in supervision: Essential skills for the news supervisor.* Menlo Park, CA: Crisp Publications.

Cooper, T., and D. Yoder 2002. Public management ethics standards in a transnational world. *Public Integrity* 2 (4): 332–352.

Coplin, W., and C. Dwyer. 2000. *Does your government measure up?* Syracuse, NY: Syracuse University Press.

Council for Excellence in Government. 1998. *Ethical principles for public servants.* Washington, DC: Brookings Institution.

Coursey, D., and D. Norris. 2008. Models of e-Government: Are they correct? *Public Administration Review* 68 (3): 523–536.

Curry, T., and L. Shibut. 2000. The cost of the savings and loan crisis. *FDIC Banking Review:* 26–35. http://www.fdic.gov/bank/analytical/banking/2000dec/brv13n2_2.pdf.

Daley, D., and K. Naff. 1998. Gender differences and managerial competencies. *Review of Public Personnel Management* 18: 41–56.

Davidson, D. 2002. Plugging the Brain Drain. *Federal Times,* November 18.

Davis, Z.S., L.A. Niksch, L.Q. Nowels, V.N. Pregelj, R. Shinn, and R.G. Sutter. 2004. Korea: Procedural and jurisdictional questions regarding possible normalization of relations with North Korea. Congressional Research Service: Report for Congress 94–933 S, November 29. http://digital.library.unt.edu/govdocs/crs/permalink/meta-crs-123: 1.

DelPo, A., and L. Guerin. 2003. *Dealing with problem employees.* 2nd ed. Berkeley, CA: Nolo Press.

Denhardt, R., and J. Denhardt. 2001. Selfless public servants stand apart in heroic response. *Public Administration Times,* September 24.

———. 2007. *The new public service: Serving, not steering.* Expanded ed. Armonk, NY: M.E. Sharpe.

Deutsch, C. 2003. Revolt of the shareholders. *New York Times,* February 23.

DeYoung, K. 2007. Bush approves new CIA methods. *Washington Post,* July 21.

DiNome, J., S. Yaklin, and D. Rosenbloom. 1999. Employee rights: Avoiding legal liability. In *Human resource management in local government: An essential guide,* ed. S. Freyss, 93–132. Washington, DC: International City/County Management Association.

Dionne, E. 2001. Political hacks v. bureaucrats. *Brookings Review* 19 (2): 8–11.

Donahue, J. 2009. *The warping of government work.* Cambridge, MA: Harvard University Press.

Dubnick, M. 1998. Forest service. In *An historical guide to the U.S. government,* ed. G.T. Kurian, 255–260. New York: Oxford University Press.

Duhigg, C. 2008. Pressured to take more risk, Fannie reached a tipping point. *New York Times,* October 5. http://www.nytimes.com/2008/10/05/business/05fannie.html?ref=tod.

Dumke, M. (2008). Can Jack Nicklaus save Benton Harbor? *Chicago Reader,* May 22, 2008. http://www.chicagoreader.com/features/stories/theseparts08/bentonharbor/.

Eichenwald, K. 2002. Could capitalists actually bring down capitalism? *New York Times,* July 30.

Emerson, J. 2003. Lonely at the top? Be a mentor. *Federal Times,* August 4.

Enrich, D., and D. Paletta. 2008. Failed lender played regulatory angles. *Wall Street Journal,* October 3.

enronwatchdog.com. http://www.enronwatchdog.org/topreforms/topreforms8.html.

Facer, R., L. Wadsworth, N. Buckwalter, and K. Johnson. 2008. The role of mentoring in public service career advancement. Paper presented at the 66th Annual Meeting of the Midwest Political Science Association, April 3–6.

Fairholm, G. 1991. *Values leadership: Toward a new philosophy of leadership.* New York: Praeger.

Federal Benchmarking Consortium Team. 1997. Serving the American public: Best practices in customer-driven strategic planning. *FBCT Study Report.* http://govinfo.library.unt.edu/npr/library/papers/benchmrk/customer.html.

Federal Deposit Insurance Corporation (FDIC). 1980. Depository institutions deregulation and monetary control act of 1980. http://www.fdic.gov/regulations/laws/rules/8000–2200.html.

———. 2002. Garn-St Germain depository institutions act of 1982. http://www.fdic.gov/regulations/laws/rules/8000–4100.html.

Fiedler, F., M. Chemers, and L. Mahar. 1976. *Improving leadership effectiveness: The leader match concept.* New York: Wiley.

Finn, P. 2008. Guantanamo prosecutor quits, says evidence was withheld. *Washington Post,* September 25.

Flaherty, M., S. Goo, D. Hilzenrath, and J. Grimaldi. 2003. A troubled history: *Columbia* experienced myriad problems before its doomed flight. *Washington Post National Weekly Edition,* March 23–29.

Frame, D. 2002. *The new project management: Tools for an age of rapid change, corporate reengineering, and other business realities.* 2d ed. New York: Wiley.

Frank, T. 2008. *The wrecking crew.* New York: Metropolitan Books.

Frederickson, H.G. 2003. Clothed in the public interest. *Public Administration Times* (April).

———. 2002. Arthur Andersen, where art thou? *Public Administration Times* (October).

Friedman, T.L. 2002. In oversight we trust. *New York Times,* July 28. http://www.nytimes.com/2002/07/28/opinion/in-oversight-we-trust.html.

Garson, G. 2006. *Public information technology and governance.* Raleigh, NC: Jones and Bartlett.

Gellerman, S. 1986. Why "good" managers make bad ethical choices. *Harvard Business Review* 64 (July–August): 85–90.

Getha-Taylor, H. 2008. Identifying collaborative competencies. *Review of Public Personnel Administration* 28: 103–119.

Gilman, S. 1999. Effective management of ethical systems: Some new frontiers. In *Fighting Corruption,* ed. V. Mavaso and D. Balia, 95–114. Pretoria: University of South Africa Press.

Goodman, P. 2008a. 159,000 jobs lost in September, the worst month in five years. *New York Times,* October 4. http://www.nytimes.com/2008/10/04/business/economy/04jobs.html.

———. 2008b. Too big to fail. *New York Times.* July 20. http://www.nytimes.com/2008/07/20/weekinreview/20goodman.html?_r=1&scp=1&sq=Too%20big%20to%20fail&st=cse.

———. 2008c. Taking hard new look at Greenspan legacy. *New York Times.* October 9. http://www.nytimes.com/2008/10/09/business/economy/09greenspan.html?pagewanted=1.

Gore, A. 1997. Serving the American public: Best practices in performance measurement. *National Performance Review, Benchmarking Study Report.* http://govinfo.library.unt.edu/npr/library/papers/benchmrk/nprbook.html.

Gorman, S. 2009. Electricity grid in U.S. penetrated by spies. *Wall Street Journal,* April 8.

Gorman, S., A. Cole, and Y. Dreazen. 2009. Computer Spies Breach Fight-Jet Project. *Wall Street Journal,* April 21.

Governor's Benton Harbor Task Force. 2003. Benton Harbor. A plan for positive change. Final report of the Governor's Benton Harbor Task Force, October 15. http://www.michigan.gov/documents/BH_final_report_76471_7.pdf.

Guerrara, F., and E. Luce. 2009. Wall St. fears grow over results of stress tests. *Financial Times,* April 18/19.

Guttentag, J. 2009. Rescue net is too small to catch many borrowers. *Washington Post,* April 18. http://www.washingtonpost.com/wp-dyn/content/article/2009/04/10/AR2009041002079.html.

Hagerty, J. 2008. Fannie, Freddie share spotlight in mortgage mess. *Wall Street Journal.* October 16.

Hagerty, J., and R. Simon. 2008. Home loans "under water" grow, pressure the economy. *Wall Street Journal,* Oct. 8.

Harigopal, K. 2006. *Management of organizational changes.* Thousand Oaks, CA: Sage.

Harrington, J. 2006. *Process management excellence.* Chico, CA: Paton Press LLC.

Hart, K. 2008a. Longtime battle lines are recast in Russia and Georgia's cyberwar. *Washington Post,* August 14. http://www.washingtonpost.com/wp-dyn/content/article/2008/08/13/AR2008081303623.html.

———. 2008b. A new breed of hackers tracks online acts of war. *Washington Post,* August 27. http://www.washingtonpost.com/wp-dyn/content/article/2008/08/26/AR2008082603128.html.

Hecks, R. 2006. *Implementing and managing eGovernment.* London: Sage.

Hersey, P., and K. Blanchard. 1969. The life cycle theory of leadership. *Training and Development Journal* 23: 26–34.

Herszenhorn, D. 2008. Approval is near for bill to help U.S. homeowners. *New York Times,* July 25. http://www.nytimes.com/2008/06/25/washington/25housing.html?scp=1&sq=%22Approval%20is%20Near%20for%20Bill%20to%20Help%20U.S.%20homeowners%22&st=cse.

Hilzenrath, D. 2002. Postmortem for a giant. *Washington Post National Weekly Edition,* June 24–30.

Holdstein, W. 2002. An Insider's Advice on Corporate Ethics. *New York Times,* November 24.

Holzer, M., and K. Callahan. 1998. *Government at work: Best practices and model programs.* Thousand Oaks, CA: Sage.

Hosenball, M. 2009. The turf war over cyberwar. *Newsweek*, April 25. http://www.newsweek.com/id/195107.

Hossain, F., A. Cox, J. McGrath, S. Weitberg. 2009. The stimulus plan: how to spend $787 billion. *New York Times*, April 19. http://projects.nytimes.com/44th_president/stimulus?scp=1&sq=%22The%20stimulus%20plan:%20how%20to%20spend%20%24787%20billion%22&st=cse.

HR World. (2007). 30 interview questions you can't ask and 30 sneaky, legal alternatives to get the same info. http://www.hrworld.com/features/30-interview-questions-111507/.

Huffington, A. 2003. *Pigs at the trough: How corporate greed and political corruption are undermining America.* New York: Crown.

Ingraham, P. 2005. Performance. *Public Administration Review* 65 (4): 390–395.

Ingraham, P., and H. Getha-Taylor. 2004. Leadership in the public sector. *Review of Public Personnel Administration* 24: 95–112.

International City/County Management Association (ICMA). 2008. Assessments. http://icma.org/main/bc.asp?bcid=125&hsid=1&ssid1=2521&ssid2=2524.

James, M. 2001. Hactivists plotting over spy plane. ABC News Online, April 13. http://abcnews.go.com/Technology/story?id=97086&page=1.

Jones, J. 2007. Low trust in federal government rivals Watergate era levels. *Gallup News Service.* http://www.gallup.com/poll/28795/Low-Trust-Federal-Government-Rivals-Watergate-Era-Levels.aspx.

Jurkiewicz, C., and R. Brown. 1998. Generational comparisons of public employee motivation. *Review of Public Personnel Administration* 18: 18–37.

Jurkiewicz, C., and K. Nichols. 2002. Ethics education in the MPA curriculum: What difference does it make? *Journal of Public Affairs Education* 8 (2): 103–114.

Kamarck, E. 2007. *The end of government as we know it.* Boulder, CO: Lynne Rienner.

Kaufman, H. 1960. *The forest ranger.* Baltimore: Johns Hopkins University Press.

Kaufman, T. 2003. What feds like and don't like. *Federal Times,* March 31.

Kaye, J., and M. Allison. 1997. *Strategic planning for nonprofit organizations: A practical guide and workbook.* New York: John Wiley and Support Center for Nonprofit Management.

Keene, W. 2003. A sore that needs healing. *Federal Times,* August 12.

Kelly, J. 2002. Andersen has been there before. *Tallahassee Democrat,* January 18.

Kelly, M. 2001. *The divine right of capital.* San Francisco: Berrett-Koehler.

Kettl, D. 2000. *The global public management revolution.* Washington, DC: Brookings Institution.

———. 2002a. Managing indirect government. In *The tools of government: A guide to the new governance,* ed. L. Salamon, 490–510. New York: Oxford University Press.

———. 2002b. *The transformation of governance: Public administration for the twenty-first century.* Baltimore: Johns Hopkins University Press.

Kidder, R. 1994. *Shared values for a troubled world: Conversations with men and women of conscience.* San Francisco: Jossey-Bass.

Klein, N. 2007. *The shock doctrine.* New York: Metropolitan Books.

Klitgaard, R. et al. (2000). *Corrupt cities.* Oakland, CA: Institute for Contemporary Studies.

Kobrak, P. 2002. *Cozy politics: Political parties, campaign finance, and compromised governance*. Boulder, CO: Lynne Rienner.

Kohlberg, L. 1971. From 'is' to 'ought:' How to commit the naturalistic fallacy and get away with it in the study of moral development. In *Cognitive development and epistemology*, ed. Theodore Mischel, 164–65. New York: Elsevier.

———.1981. *The philosophy of moral development and the idea of justice*. New York: Harper and Row.

Kristof, N. 2008. The truth commission. *New York Times,* July 6.

Krugman, P. 2008. Lest we forget. *New York Times,* November 28.

Kung, H. 1998. *A global ethic for global politics and economics*. New York: Oxford University Press.

Kuttner, R. 2007. The bubble economy. *The American Prospect,* September 24. http://www.prospect.org/cs/articles?article=the_bubble_economy.

Labaton, S. 2002a. Bush doctrine: Lock 'em up. *New York Times,* January 16.

———. 2002b. Now who exactly got us into this mess? *New York Times,* February 3.

———. 2002c. Will reform with few teeth be able to bite? *New York Times,* September 2.

———. 2008. Agency's '04 rule let banks pile up new debt and risk. *New York Times,* October 3.

Landler, M., and E. Dash. 2008. Drama behind a banking deal. *New York Times,* October 15. http://query.nytimes.com/gst/fullpage.html?res=9401EEDF1F39F9 36A25753C1A96E9C8B63&scp=17&sq=%22Landler&st=nyt.

Lee, C. 2003. The workers are getting restless. *Washington Post National Weekly Edition,* March 31–April 6.

Lee, M. 2003. Noncredit certificates in nonprofit management: An exploratory study. Milwaukee: University of Wisconsin-Milwaukee (Department of Governmental Affairs). Unpublished paper.

Leicht, K., and M. Fennell. 2001. *Professional work: A sociological approach*. Malden, MA: Blackwell.

Lewis, C. 1998. Strategies and tactics for managerial decision making. In *The ethics edge,* ed. E. Berman, J. West, and S. Bonczek, 123–29. Washington, DC: International City/County Management Association.

Liff, S. 2007. *Managing government employees*. New York: AMACOM.

Light, P. 1999. *The new public service*. Washington, DC: Brookings Institution.

———. 2002. *Government's greatest achievements*. Washington, DC: Brookings.

———. 2003. Fact sheet on the true size of government. The Center for Public Service, The Brookings Institution. http://www.brookings.edu/articles/2003/0905politics_light.aspx.

———. 2004. Fact sheet on the continued thickening of government. The Brookings Institution. http://www.brookings.edu/papers/2004/0723governance_light.aspx.

———. 2006. The tides of reform revisited. *Public Administration Review* 66 (1): 6–19.

———. 2008. *A government ill-executed*. Cambridge, MA: Harvard University Press.

Linden, R. 1995. *Seamless government: A practical guide to re-engineering in the public sector*. San Francisco: Jossey-Bass.

Lynn, D. 2001. Succession management strategies in public sector organizations. *Review of Public Personnel Administration* 21: 114–132.

Macey, J. 2008. The government is contributing to the panic. *Wall Street Journal,* October 11. http://online.wsj.com/article/SB122367942018324645.html.

Magala, S. 2005. *Cross-cultural competence.* New York: Routledge.

Mallaby, S. 2002. A worm at the core of capitalism. *Washington Post National Weekly Edition,* June 17–23.

Mareschal, P. 1998. Insights from the Federal Mediation and Conciliation Service. *Review of Public Personnel Administration* 18: 55–67.

Markoff, J. 1999. Blown to bits: Cyberwarfare breaks the rules of military engagement. *New York Times,* October 17. http://query.nytimes.com/gst/fullpage.html?res=9C04E6DC1E30F934A25753C1A96F958260&scp=1&sq=%27Cyberwarfare%20breaks%20the%20rules%200f%20military%20engagement%22&st=cse.

Marston, C. 2007. *Motivating the "What's in it for me?" workforce.* New Jersey: John Wiley & Sons.

Matthews, J. 2003. *The lawsuit survival guide: A client's companion to litigation.* Berkeley, CA: Nolo Press.

McClelland, D. 1973. Testing for competence rather than for 'intelligence.' *American Psychologist* 28 (1): 1–14.

McConnell, J. Michael. 2008. Annual threat assessment of the Director of National Intelligence for the Senate Select Committee on Intelligence. Unclassified Statement for the Record, February 5. http://nefafoundation.org/miscellaneous/FeaturedDocs/SSCI_Mcconnellfeb08.pdf.

McFadden, R. 2003. A revolutionary program troubled from the start. *New York Times,* February 2.

Mead, M. 2001. *New lives for old: Cultural transformation—Manus.* New York: Harper-Collins.

Melzer, E.J. (2008). Benton Harbor park controversy draws national attention; City Commission faces hard choice. *Michigan Messenger,* June 9. http://michiganmessenger.com/?s=Benton+Harbor+Park+Controversy+Draws+National+Attention%3B+City+Commission+Faces+Hard+Choice.

Menzel, D. 1997. Teaching ethics and values in public administration: Are we making a difference? *Public Administration Review* 57: 224–30.

———. 2009. *Ethics moments in local government: Cases and controversies.* New York: Taylor & Francis.

Menzel, D., and C. Carson. 1997. Empirical research on public administration ethics: A review and assessment. *Public Integrity* 1 (3): 239–264.

Michigan Technological University. (2009). Affirmative Programs Office. MTU hiring guide. www.admin.mtu.edu/hro/forms/whatyoucanandcantasklongversionmay05.pdf.

Miller, Matt. 2009. Business needs to speak out against greed. *Financial Times,* April 21.

Miller, Michael. 2002. Enron's ethics code reads like fiction. *Business First of Columbus,* April 1. http://columbus.bizjournals.com/columbus/stories/2002/04/01/editoria13.html.

Mills, E. 2008. Radio Free Europe DDOS attack latest by hacktivists. *Cnetnews.com,* May 1. http://news.cnet.com/8301–10784_3–9933746–7.html?tag=mncol.

Mintz, J. 2003. Ridge's rise to Homeland Security. *Washington Post National Weekly Edition,* March 10–16.

Morgan, D., R. Green, C. Shinn, and K. Robinson. 2008. *Foundations of public service.* Armonk, NY: M.E. Sharpe.

Morgenson, G. 2008. Behind insurer's crisis, blind eye to a web of risk. *New York Times,* September 28. http://www.nytimes.com/2008/09/28/business/28melt. html?th=&emc꞊

Mosher, F. 1982. *Democracy and the public service.* New York: Oxford University Press.

Moysich, A. 1997. The Savings and Loan crisis and its relationship to banking. In *History of the eighties—Lessons for the future,* vol. I, ed. FDIC Division of Research and Statistics. http://www.fdic.gov/bank/historical/history/167_188.pdf.

Muolo, P., and M. Padilla. 2008. *Chain of blame: How Wall Street caused the mortgage and credit crisis.* Hoboken, NJ: Wiley Publishers.

National Commission on the Public Service. 2003. *Urgent business for America: Revitalizing the federal government for the 21st century.* Washington, DC: Brookings Institution.

National Mentoring Partnership. (2008). Checklist for mentoring programs. http://www.ed.gov/pubs/YesYouCan/sect3-checklist.html.

Nelson, S. 2004. The state of the federal civil service today. *Review of Public Personnel Administration* 24: 202–215.

New York Times. 2003. Corporate scandals: A user's guide. *New York Times Week in Review,* May 21.

New York Times. 2005. The prison puzzle. *New York Times,* November 3.

New York Times. 2008. Guilty as ordered. *New York Times,* August 7.

New York Times. 2009. Mr. Obama's foreclosure plan. *New York Times,* February 19.

Nocera, J. 2002. System failure: Corporate America has lost its way. *Fortune,* June 24.

Northouse, P. 2003. *Leadership: Theory and practice.* 3rd ed. Thousand Oaks, CA: Sage.

Obama, B. 2009. Inaugural address, transcript. *New York Times,* January 20.

O'Connor, S. 2009. Opposition and bankers scent blood on Obama mortgage bill. *Financial Times,* April 21.

O'Neill, R., and Christopher, G. 2002. Wildfire protection: A lesson in management. *Federal Times,* October 7.

Organization of Economic Cooperation and Development. 2006. Glossary of statistical terms. http://stats.oecd.org/glossary/detail.asp?ID=7111.

Osborne, D., and P. Plastrik. 1998. *Banishing bureaucracy: The five strategies for reinventing government.* New York: Penguin Putnam.

Pack, J. 1989. Privatization and cost reduction. *Policy Sciences* 22 (1): 1–25.

Paine, L. 1994. Managing for organizational integrity. *Harvard Business Review* 72 (2): 106–117.

Paletta, D. 2008a. Treasury to outline Fan-Fred plan. *Wall Street Journal,* September 7. http://online.wsj.com/article/SB122073255846107191.html.

———. 2008b. U.S. weighs removing deposit insurance limits. *Wall Street Journal,* October 10.

Partnership for Public Service. 2008. Our strategy for change. http://www.ourpublicservice.org/OPS/about/.

Partnership for Public Service. 2009. Service to America medals. http://servicetoamericamedals.org/SAM/.

Pear, R. 2005. Homeland Security Department loses labor rules fight. *New York Times,* August 14. http://www.nytimes.com/2005/08/14/national/nationalspecia13/14secure.html.

Perry, J., J. Brudney, D. Coursey, and L. Littlepage. 2008. What drives morally committed citizens? *Public Administration Review* 68 (3): 445–458.

Petersen, M. 1998. Keating convictions in collapse of an S&L thrown out again. *New York Times,* February 6. http://query.nytimes.com/gst/fullpage.html?res =9D01E4DE123DF935A35751C0A96E958260&scp=11&sq=Keating%20 released&st=cse.

Pfiffner, J., and D. Brook. 2000. *The future of merit: Twenty years after the Civil Service Reform Act.* Baltimore: Johns Hopkins University Press.

Pincus, W. 2008. Cybersecurity will take a big bite of the budget. *Washington Post,* July 21.

Radin, B. 2007. Qualified to learn the job: Donna Shalala. *Public Administration Review* 67 (3): 504–510.

Rainey, H. 1997. The "how much is due process" debate. In *Handbook of Public Law and Administration,* ed. P. Cooper, 237–53. New York: Marcel Dekker.

Rest, J., and D. Narvez. 1994. *Moral development in the professions.* Hillsdale, NJ: Erlbaum.

Reuters. 1996. *Burn forests to save them, says U.S. Forest Service.* July 30, record number 0D6FE92370B8ACA.

Reynolds, G. 2009. Tax day becomes protest day. *Wall Street Journal,* April 15, A15.

Riccucci, N. 1995. *Unsung heroes: Federal execucrats making a difference.* Washington, DC: Georgetown University Press.

Robbins, M., O. Simonsen, and B. Feldman. 2008. Citizens and resource allocation. *Public Administration Review* 68 (3): 564–575.

Roberts, R. 2008. How government stoked the mania. *Wall Street Journal,* October 3.

Rocheleau, B. 2007. Whither e-Government? *Public Administration Review* 67 (3): 584–588.

Rothkopf, D. 2008. 9/11 was big. This is bigger. *Washington Post,* October 5. http://www.washingtonpost.com/wp-dyn/content/article/2008/10/03/ AR2008100301969.html.

Salamon, L. 2002. The new governance and the tools of public Action: An introduction. In *The tools of government: A guide to the new governance,* ed. L. Salamon, 1–47. New York: Oxford University Press.

Sang-Hun, C. 2008. North Korea destroys tower at nuclear site. *New York Times,* June 28. http://www.nytimes.com/2008/06/28/world/asia/28korea.html?_r =1&scp=6&sq=North%20Korea%20plutonium%20nuclear%20reactor&st=cse &oref=slogin.

Sanger, D., J. Markoff, and T. Shanker. 2009. U.S. steps up effort on digital defenses. *New York Times,* April 28. http://www.nytimes.com/2009/04/28/us/28cyber.html.

Scannell, K., 2008. SEC faulted for missing red flags at Bear. *Wall Street Journal,* September 27.

Scannel, K., and S. Reddy. 2008. Greenspan admits errors to hostile House panel. *Wall Street Journal,* October 24.

Schatz, P.E., T.J. Bush-Zurn, C. Ceresa, and K.C. Freeman. 2003. California's professional mentoring program. *Journal of the American Dietetic Association* 103 (1): 73–76.

Schleicher, A. 2003. North Korean nukes. PBS News Hour Extra, posted January 8. Available at http://www.pbs.org/newshour/extra/features/jan-june03/nkorea.html.

Schlosser, J. 2003. Spitzer speaks. *Fortune,* May 27.

Schwartz, J. 2007. Bit wars: When computers attack. *New York Times,* June 24. http://query.nytimes.com/gst/fullpage.html?res=9400E7DB1E3FF937A15755C0A9619C8B63&sec=&spon=&&scp=2&sq=when%20computers%20attack&st=cse.

Shalala, D. 1998. Are large public organizations manageable? *Public Administration Review* 58 (4): 284–289.

Shane, S., D. Johnston, and J. Risen. 2007. Secret U.S. endorsement of severe interrogations. *New York Times,* October 4.

Sherwood, F. 2000. Research needs on the public service. In *Public service: Callings, commitments, and contributions,* ed. M. Holzer, 356–70. Boulder, CO: Westview Press.

Smith, J. 2007. A war under law. *Washington Post,* February 22.

Smith, V. 2008. There's no easy way out of the bubble. *Wall Street Journal,* October 9.

Snell, R. 1993. *Developing skills for ethical management.* London: Chapman and Hill.

Solomon, D. 2008. Bailout's next phase: Consumers. *Wall Street Journal,* November 13.

Solomon, D., and M. Crittenden. 2009. Which banks are stressed? Not? *Wall Street Journal,* April 15.

Solomon, D., and D. Enrich. 2008. Devil is in bailout's details. *Wall Street Journal,* October 15.

Solomon, D., S. Ng, and S. Craig. 2008. Rising cost of debt stokes fears on Freddie's prospects. *Wall Street Journal.* August 20.

Solomon, D., D. Paletta, M. Phillips, and J. Hilsenrath. 2008. U.S. to buy stakes in nation's largest banks. *Wall Street Journal,* October 14.

Stenberg, C., and S. Lipman. 2007. *Managing local government services.* Washington, DC: International City/County Management Association.

Stevenson, R. 2009. Obamanomics: Redefining capitalism after the fall. *New York Times,* April 19. http://www.nytimes.com/2009/04/19/weekinreview/19stevenson.html?partner=rss&emc=rss.

Stogdill, R. 1948. Personal factors associated with leadership: A survey of the literature. *Journal of Psychology* 25: 35–71.

Svara, J. 1997. The ethical triangle. *Public Integrity Annual* 2: 33–41.

———. 2007. *The ethics primer for public administrators in government and nonprofit organizations.* Sudbury, MA: Jones and Bartlett.

Terry, L. 1995. *Leadership of public bureaucracies: The administrator as conservator.* Thousand Oaks, CA: Sage.

Thompson, D. 1998. Paradoxes of government ethics. In *The ethics edge,* ed. E. Berman, J. West, and S. Bonczek, 47–60. Washington, DC: International City/County Management Association.

Thompson, J. 2001. The civil service under Clinton. *Review of Public Personnel Administration* 21 (2): 87–113.

———. 2007. Federal labor management reforms under Bush. *Review of Public Personnel Administration* 27: 105–124.

———. 2008. Personnel demonstration projects and human resource management innovation. *Review of Public Personnel Administration* 28: 240–262.

Tolbert, C., K. Mossberger, and R. McNeal. 2008. Institutions, policy innovations, and e-Government in the American states. *Public Administration Review* 68 (3): 549–563.

Tonon, J. 2008. The cost of speaking truth to power: How professionalism facilitates credible communication. *Journal of Public Administration Research and Theory* 18 (2): 275–295.

Trevino, L., G. Weaver, D. Gibson, and B. Toffler. 1999. Managing ethical and legal compliance: What works and what hurts. *California Management Review* 40 (2): 131–51.

Trottier, T., M. van Wart, and X. Wang. 2008. Examining the nature and significance of leadership in government organizations. *Public Administration Review* 68 (2): 319–333.

Underhill, J., and R. Oman. 2007. A critical review of the sweeping federal civil service changes. *Review of Public Personnel Administration* 27 (4): 401–420.

United Nations, General Assembly. 1948. United Nations Universal Declaration on Human Rights, www.un.org/Overview/rights.

Ury, W. 1991. *Getting past no: Negotiating your way from confrontation to cooperation.* Rev. ed. New York: Bantam Books.

U.S. Air Force. 2008. United States Air Force mission. http://www.airforce.com/learn-about/our-mission/.

U.S. Air War College. (2009). *Air Force Policy Directive 36–34.* http://www.au.af.mil/au/awc/awcgate/awc-prof.htm.

U.S. Department of Agriculture. 2006. Wildland fire and fuels research and development strategic plan: Meeting the needs of the present, anticipating the needs of the future. http://www.fs.fed.us/research/pdf/2006–10–20-wildland-book.pdf#xml=http://www.fs.fed.us/cgi-bin/texis/searchallsites/search.allsites/xml.txt?query=strategic+plan&db=allsites&id=47c3255a0.

U.S. Department of Transportation (U.S. DOT). 2009. Departmental Office of Human Resource Management. *DOT mentoring handbook.* www.au.af.mil/au/awc/awcgate/mentor/mentorhb.htm.

U.S. Forest Service. 2009. About Forest Service research and development. http://www.fs.fed.us/research/.

U.S. House of Representatives. 2001. Subcommittee on Forests and Forest Health of the Committee on Resources. *National fire plan implementation.* March 8, Serial No. 107–103.

U.S. Office of Management and Budget. (2009). Office of e-Government and information technology. www.whitehouse.gov/omb/egov/.

U.S. Office of Personnel Management (U.S. OPM). 2008a. Analysis of federal employee retirement data. http://www.feddesk.com/freehandbooks/060508–1.pdf.

———. 2008b. Facts and figures: Plum Book. http://www.opm.gov/ses/facts_and_figures/plumbook.asp.

———. 2008c. The leadership journey: Competency-based learning. http://www.leadership.opm.gov/AboutUs/LeadershipJourney/index.aspx.

———. 2008d. Senior executive service survey results. http://www.opm.gov/ses/SES_survey_results_complete.pdf.

———. 2008e. Welcome to the senior executive survey. http://www.opm.gov/ses.

U.S. PIRG. No date. EnronWatchdog.org. "Close the 'anything goes' accounting loopholes and regulate all transactions." http://www.enronwatchdog.org/topreforms/topreforms8.html.

U.S. Senate Committee on Homeland Security and Government Affairs. 2008. *Offline and off-budget: The dismal state of information technology planning in the federal government.* Subcommittee on Federal Financial Management, Government Infor-

mation, Federal Services, and International Security. Hearing, July 31. http://hsgac.
senate.gov/public/index.cfm?Fuseaction=Hearings.Detail&HearingID=abd51710-
f9b3–42cd-8457-ce958096933f.

Van Wart, M. 1998. *Changing public sector values.* New York: Garland.

———. 2003. Public sector leadership theory. *Public Administration Review* 63 (2):
214–228.

Van Wart, M., D. Rahm, and S. Sanders. 2000. Economic development and public
enterprise: The case of rural Iowa's telecommunications utilities. *Economic Development Quarterly* 14 (2): 131–145.

Vanden Heuvel, K., and E. Schlosser. 2008. America needs a new New Deal. *Wall Street
Journal,* September 27. http://online.wsj.com/article/SB122246953790280655.
html.

Varnak, P. 2008. Supervisory/managerial responsibilities and merit system principles.
Fedsmith.com, Sept. 12. http://www.fedsmith.com/article/1710.

Ventriss, C., and S. Barney. 2003. The making of a whistleblower and the impact of
ethical autonomy: James F. Alderson. *Public Integrity* 5 (4): 355–368.

Virtanen, T. 2000. Changing competencies of public managers. *International Journal
of Public Sector Management* 13 (4): 333–341.

Vlasic, B., and S. Stolberg. 2009. U.S. expected to give more money to automakers. *New York Times.* March 27. http://www.nytimes.com/2009/03/28/business/
economy/28auto.html?_r=1&scp=1&sq=%22U.S.%20expected%20to%20
give%20more%20money%20to%20automakers%22&st=cse.

Volcker, P. 2003. *The National Commission on Public Service.* Washington, DC:
Brookings Institution.

Wall Street Journal. 2008 Re-seeding the housing mess. *Wall Street Journal,* September
27. http://online.wsj.com/article/SB122247015469280723.html.

Walters, J. 2002. *Life after civil service reform.* Washington DC: Pricewaterhouse
Coopers Human Capital Series. http://www.businessofgovernment.org/pdfs/
Walters_report.pdf.

Wartick, S., and D. Wood. 1998. *International business and society.* Malden, MA:
Blackwell.

Washington Post. 2002. Watching the watchers. *Washington Post National Weekly
Edition,* May 27–June 2.

Washington Post. 2007. A return to abuse. *Washington Post,* July 25.

Weber, M. 1991. Politics as a vocation. In *From Max Weber: Essays in sociology,* ed.
H. Garth and C. Mills, 77–112. New York: Routledge.

Wee, H. 2002. Corporate ethics: Right makes might. *Business Week,* April 11. http://
www.businessweek.com/bwdaily/dnflash/apr2002/nf20020411_6350.htm.

Weir, M. 2004. New civilian personnel system brings sweeping changes. *Air Force
Link,* October 27. http://www.af.mil/news/story.asp?id=123009030.

Weiss, G. 2003. *Born to steal: When the mafia hit Wall Street.* New York: Warner
Books.

West, D. 2005. *Digital government.* Princeton, NJ: Princeton University Press.

West, J. 2009. Ethics and human resource management. in *Public Personnel Administration: Problems and Prospects,* ed. S Hays, R. Kearney and J. Coggburn. Upper
Saddle River, NJ: Prentice Hall.

West, J., and E. Berman. 2001. From traditional to virtual HR: Is the transition
occurring in local government? *Review of Public Personnel Administration* 21
(1): 38–64.

———. 2004. Ethics training in U.S. cities: Content, pedagogy, and impact. *Public Integrity* 6(3): 189–206.

———. 2006. *The ethics edge.* Washington, D.C.: International City/County Management Association.

White, L., and L. Lam. 2000 A proposed infrastructural model of the establishment of organizational ethics systems. *Journal of Business Ethics* 28: 35–42.

Whoriskey, P. 2009. GM chief to resign at White House's behest. *Washington Post,* March 30. http://www.washingtonpost.com/wp-dyn/content/article/2009/03/29/AR2009032900708.html.

Whoriskey, P., and K. Marr. 2009. Obama is stern with automakers. *Washington Post,* March 31. http://www.washingtonpost.com/wp-dyn/content/article/2009/03/30/AR2009033001239.html.

Windt, P., P. Appleby, M. Battin, L. Francis, and B. Landesman, eds. 1989. Ethical issues in the professions. In *Selected codes of professional ethics: Model rules of professional conduct,* 555–566. Englewood Cliffs, NJ: Prentice Hall.

Wise, C. 1996. Understanding your liability as a public administrator. In *Handbook of Public Administration,* ed. J. Perry, 713–734. San Francisco: Jossey-Bass.

Wurtzel, E. 2008. The world will miss our heyday. *Wall Street Journal,* October 11. http://online.wsj.com/article/SB122367984585224675.html.

Yukl, G. 1998. *Leadership in organizations.* 4th ed. Englewood Cliffs, NJ: Prentice-Hall.

About the Authors

James S. Bowman is professor of public administration at the Askew School of Public Administration and Policy, Florida State University. His primary area is human resource management. He is author of more than 100 journal articles and book chapters as well as editor of six anthologies. Bowman co-authored (with Evan Berman, Jonathan West, and Montgomery Van Wart) *Human Resource Management: Paradoxes, Processes and Problems,* Third Edition (Sage 2010). He also co-edited *American Public Service: Radical Reform and the Merit System* with Jonathan West (Taylor & Francis 2007). He is editor-in-chief of *Public Integrity,* a journal sponsored by the American Society for Public Administration and four other professional associations. A past National Association of Schools of Public Affairs and Administration Fellow as well as a Kellogg Foundation Fellow, he has experience in the military, civil service, and business.

Jonathan P. West is professor of political science and Director of the MPA program at the University of Miami. His research interests include human resource management, productivity, local government, and ethics. Professor West has published eight books and more than 100 articles and book chapters. His most recent books are *American Public Service: Radical Reform and the Merit System,* co-edited with James Bowman (Taylor & Francis 2007) and *The Ethics Edge* with Evan Berman (ICMA 2006). His other recent co-authored book (with Evan Berman, James Bowman, and Montgomery Van Wart) is *Human Resource Management: Paradoxes, Processes and Problems,* Third Edition (Sage, 2010). He is the managing editor of *Public Integrity* and has taught at the University of Houston and University of Arizona. He has also served as a management analyst in the U.S. Surgeon General's Office, Department of the Army, Washington, D.C.

Marcia A. Beck is the author of *Russia's Liberal Project: State-Society Relations in the Transition from Communism* (Penn State Press, 2000) and a co-author of *People, Power, and Politics,* Third Edition (Littlefield Adams,

1993). She has also published articles in *Comparative Politics, The Review of Politics, Russian Review, Demokratizatsiya,* and in edited collections. Dr. Beck has taught in the Government Departments of the University of Notre Dame and Bowdoin College, where she was a tenured faculty member until 2003. She has been a National Fellow at the Hoover Institution at Stanford University and received a National Endowment for the Humanities grant to pursue archival research in Russia. She is the recipient of an award for excellence in teaching at Bowdoin College and a teaching commendation at Notre Dame.

Index